P9-DWU-819

DEATH OF A REBEL

DEATH OF
A REBEL

Marc Eliot

ANCHOR BOOKS
Anchor Press/Doubleday   Garden City, New York
1979

The Anchor Books edition is the first publication of *Death of a Rebel*.

Anchor Books edition: 1979

Library of Congress Cataloging in Publication Data

Eliot, Marc.
    Death of a rebel.

    Discography
    Includes index.
    1. Ochs, Phil. 2. Singers—United States—Biography.
I. Title.
ML420.O29E4   784.4′92′4 [B]   77-25586
ISBN: 0-385-13610-2
Library of Congress Catalog Card Number 77-25586

The author gratefully acknowledges the following for permission to reprint:

ALMO MUSIC CORP. for "Bach, Beethoven, Mozart and Me," by Phil Ochs, copyright © 1971 by Barricade Music, Inc.; "The Ballad of Billie Sol Estes," by Phil Ochs, copyright © 1978 by Barricade Music, Inc.; "The Ballad of Davey Moore," by Phil Ochs, copyright © 1978 by Barricade Music, Inc.; "The Ballad of John Henry Faulk," by Phil Ochs, copyright © 1978 by Barricade Music, Inc.; "The Ballad of John Train," by Phil Ochs, copyright © 1978 by Barricade Music, Inc.; "The Ballad of William Worthy," by Phil Ochs, copyright © 1978 by Barricade Music, Inc.; "Boy in Ohio," by Phil Ochs, copyright © 1971 by Barricade Music, Inc.; "Bracero," by Phil Ochs, copyright © 1978 by Barricade Music, Inc.; "Cannons of Christianity," by Phil Ochs, copyright © 1978 by Barricade Music, Inc.; "Changes," by Phil Ochs, copyright © 1978 by Barricade Music, Inc.; "Che," by Phil Ochs, copyright © 1978 by Barricade Music, Inc.; "Chords of Fame," by Phil Ochs, copyright © 1971 by Barricade Music, Inc.; "Cops of the World," by Phil Ochs, copyright © 1978 by Barricade Music, Inc.; "Crucifixion," by Phil

For Lenard and
the children of the sixties

INTRODUCTION

It was my third visit to the Warner Brothers Movie Studios in Burbank where Larry Marks had his office. He'd come a long way from his days as a record producer, from the house in Connecticut and the endless cross-country shuttles, seeming always to be coming from, or going to, another recording session.

I'd interviewed Marks twice before. At the end of our previous meeting, I suggested we listen together to the three Phil Ochs albums he'd produced. He thought it was a good idea, but he didn't know where his copies were.

"I'll bring mine."

As at the previous two meetings, Marks was friendly and warm when he greeted me. His phone started ringing every few minutes. Excusing himself each time, he answered every call. He had a screening to go to in forty-five minutes. I still had lots of questions to ask.

He sighed and reached for "Pleasures of the Harbor." As the first moments from the title cut filled the room, Marks's head turned slowly. He took his phone off the hook. His eyes closed, his left hand began to conduct the strings as he leaned back in his chair. "I'd forgotten how beautiful this album is. . . ." He began to reminisce about Phil, each cut reminding him of another story, until, as it came time for him to go to the screening, he forced himself back to the present. I thanked him for his time. "It was my pleasure," he said, adding softly, "Good luck."

I decided to write this book the day after Phil Ochs killed himself. I began to map out a journey, a time-trip through Phil's life. I wanted to talk to anyone who knew him at all, and everyone who knew him well. I began with the family, spending an afternoon in the country with Sonny, Phil's sister. I flew to Los Angeles and spent a week with Michael Ochs, his brother, staying at his house, talking through the nights and days, my tape recorder running constantly. Together we pored over the archives he'd kept of Phil's career. We found old pictures, forgotten letters; we listened to acetates of Phil singing songs he'd never released. As the days passed, the gaps in Michael's memory began to fill in. We made a list of people I should see. I started making arrangements.

I went back and forth across the country six times during the year and a half I researched Phil's life. I began to act like Phil; when seeing Andy Wickham I dressed a little bit sloppier than usual. We went out for cheap Chinese food and talked about women and sex. I lived with Alice and Meegan for a week in Mill Valley; going out for McDonald's, watching color television, getting high. I took lessons so I could play Phil's songs on the guitar. I wanted to feel what it was like to move my fingers through his music.

And I thought about death a lot. As I wrote, the names of the dead kept appearing: James Dean, Buddy Holly, Howard Hughes, Jim Morrison, Sal Mineo, Elvis Presley. Presley died as I was writing about Phil's gold-suit concert. I kept wanting to reach for the phone, to call Phil for the ultimate comment on Presley, the Ochsian touch needed to put us all into proper mourning.

Now, it's over for me, as it begins for you. I've taken an extraordinary journey these eighteen months, the result of which is this book. Yet I would toss the manuscript into the fire tonight and never think of it again for the chance to turn my head once more and see Phil on a stage, his Gibson slung over his shoulder, his head bobbing and weaving; to hear the opening lines of his newest song, and that beautiful voice stretching a single note over an octave and a half.

Adiós, my friend.

Marc Eliot
New York City
February 1978

To sing you must first open your mouth. You must have a pair of lungs, and a little knowledge of music. It is not necessary to have an accordion, or a guitar. The essential thing is to want to sing. This then is a song. I am singing.

Henry Miller, *Tropic of Cancer*

Have we left our ladies for the lyrics
of a song
That I'm not singing, that I'm not singing
Tell me I'm not singing.

Phil Ochs, "The Scorpion Departs but Never Returns"

DEATH OF A REBEL

Prologue

They start lining up along West Third Street at seven o'clock. By seven-fifteen they are beyond McDonald's, nearing the corner. Inside, Train sits at one end of the bar drinking orange juice with rum. The phone rings constantly. He picks up the receiver and tells them to come down for the second show, midnight, they just might be able to get in. Mike Porco shakes his head from side to side as he rinses a beer mug in the gray smarmy dishwater. With him behind the bar is Barry, Mike's best bartender, a sexy, titty chick with a thin gold chain wrapped around her shiny naked belly. She hates Train. She makes him ask two, maybe three times for another drink.

Rose is at the service end, setting up the cherries. Ice spills over the tin bucket. It is going to be like the old days. Lots of music, lots of drinking.

Waiting for Train by the stage are two men; grisly, tee-shirted. Their function is to supply Train with orange juice and rum every four minutes. The drinks are important. The ice numbs Train's throat; the alcohol makes it easier for him to hit the high notes.

Eight o'clock. Showtime. The house is packed. The waitresses are having trouble getting to the service station. Porco is every-where—replacing stock, taking tickets, seating people, cracking seals on scotch quarts and squeezing cork-bottomed tips into their necks. Every few minutes Porco squints toward the stage to see who's on. Phil Ochs has promised to fill the evening with his friends. Porco wonders if all those who have sung so far are really, in fact, Phil's friends, or just a bunch of singers trying to score a set.

Another hour crawls by before Train reaches the stage. So fat, with his stomach starting around his chest and underbellying beneath his dungaree zipper. His face a dead man's. Strands of greasy, colorless hair drooping through the scarecrow hat on his head, his eyes arrogantly unfocused.

Train's mission now is to introduce young Sammy Walker, a singer he's discovered. Walker, young and shy, comes to the mike, strums a few notes, then slips into song. The audience greets him warmly. Encouraged, Walker introduces Phil Ochs and Sis Cunningham to help with "Song for Patty." By now, Train is piss drunk.

With drink in hand, he begins to speak. His words come in spurts, haunted by the familiar stutter. "Okay . . . now . . . now we have a song here about Patty Hearst . . . now . . . now I for one . . . I'm not a fan of Patty Hearst myself . . . I don't know who she is . . . she could be a revolutionary like Sammy thinks she is . . . she could be a triple agent like the girl who killed Che Guevara . . . her name was Tanya . . . Che Guevara was killed by some cunt who turned him in to the CIA and KGB . . . who found him in Bolivia and . . . and killed him, because of . . . because of her. They killed her immediately, but it took awhile to kill him . . . uhh . . . Patty Hearst was called Tanya . . . it's like a CIA code word . . ." His runny eyes are darting everywhere. The audience is silent.

". . . She's probably a double agent . . . Bob . . . Bobby Dylan tried to write a song about Patty Hearst but he failed . . . I was too afraid of who she might be, so I wouldn't dare write a song about Patty Hearst without taking a stand . . . he said, look we'll meet at the holocaust valley, hell . . . you know . . . hell . . . the burning place where they burn people . . ." Sis Cunningham steps to the mike and says, smilingly, "It comes out in the song." The audience laughs with relief. Train becomes defensive. "Yeah, but they don't understand, if you know about Steve Forrest and the SWAT team, they kill people like fly swatters, like flies . . . that's what they did in Vietnam . . . they put people into a room like this and swat . . . you can laugh nervously now, but that's what they did . . . men, women, and children . . . they didn't give a shit . . ."

Most of the young people in the crowd have never seen Phil

Ochs perform, and know him only from his records. Some are surprised, most confused. Train launches into a tirade about William
Colby.

"The guy in charge of the program was Colby, the head of the
CIA. I put out a contract on Colby for a hundred thousand dollars. I told Colby he's got a half year to get out or he's dead. They
can kill me but he's dead. He's a dead man now . . . William
Colby is dead . . . unless he quits, commits suicide, gets a con-
venient disease, or resigns. All right? Hard to believe but true . . .
all right . . . in the meantime you will now hear the best song
written in the seventies about Patty Hearst, a girl I don't particularly like . . . but for some reason he likes her . . . so we'll hear
the song." Walker sings.

Several orange juice and rums later, a chair is placed on the
tiny stage and Train, carrying his guitar like a .45 magnum, eases
himself into the saddle. He hitches his feet to the rail of the stool.
"Now, as you might have heard, I've gone through a minor change
of life. You might have known me as Phil Ochs. You're now seeing the last show of Phil Ochs." He rolls up his right sleeve, as if
he were a doctor about to perform surgery, or a drugger about to
shoot up. "Tonight at eight and midnight. As of tomorrow morning, my name is officially changed. John Train. John Train is John
Wayne, John Ford. I'm known as Howard Hughes, Jr., I'm known
as the outlaw. I live outside the law. I've no respect for the law.
I've got no respect for any human being alive in this room. I'd kill
you all as soon as look at you, believe me I will. I've got a hammer . . . where's my hammer . . ." Train gets off the stool and
reaches behind for his hammer, a large claw with black rubber
grip. He holds it up and warns, "I don't trust nobody. I don't trust
any woman. I consider all women . . . well, I won't use the word.
You know what I think they are." He tries to put the hammer
under his belt, as if it were a pistol. He sucks in, but the hammer
won't slide. He tries again, and someone yells from the audience,
"What's the matter, hemorrhoids?" Train tries to focus through
the spots, but finally gives up and dismisses the crack with an almost wistful, "No, no hemorrhoids." He puts the hammer behind
him. Then he strums an E bass, a chord, and has another drink.

"Starting tomorrow, I'm the bartender at my own bar. I own
eighty per cent of my own bar and it's called 'Che.' After Che

*Guevara." Smattering of applause. "Better known in some circles
as Ernesto Guevara, an Argentine doctor who gave up his life for
you assholes . . . you're all middle-class enough to afford the five
dollars I charged for this show, but it's the last time you'll ever see
me . . . next time I see you I'll see you dead, or with a gun . . .
we're taking over the country as of tomorrow. All right? That's it
. . . I've taken a contract on William Colby. The head of the
CIA. He's dead in six months unless he quits. This is it . . . life
and death . . . you can laugh nervously . . . anybody comes up
to me tomorrow and says, 'Are you Phil Ochs?,' you get the hammer in the old temple, you're dead . . . all right? You get a broken arm, a broken leg, that's it . . . but tonight you get the last of
Phil Ochs . . . but even Phil Ochs doesn't want to be Phil Ochs
any more." His head rolls to one side, his hands strum a G chord
in the familiar tra-la, tra-la-la, tra-la of Dylan's "Mr. Tambourine
Man."*

*"Now, I know the most beautiful woman in the audience to-
night wouldn't be reading* Penthouse *magazine, she'd be reading . . ." TWANGG. His right hand slipped off the top of the neck
and dragged down the strings. ". . . that awful cunt paper* Ms.,
*run by that CIA agent . . . what's her name . . . Steinem, CIA
Steinem. I called Gloria Steinem last week . . . I said, 'Gloria,
how about you and me, babes? . . . we already have National
Secretary Week where every secretary gets to play the role of executive . . . every executive gets to play the role of secretary, just
for the sake of argument for all you feminists, re: counterrevolutionary pig-cunts, Tanyas that kill Ches . . .'" He becomes
Steinem. "'Gee, Phil, that's too strong for us. That's too strong for*
Ms. *magazine, to demand that.'"*

"I said, 'Fuck you, Gloria . . . you're full of shit . . .'"

*The noise from the bar increases. Train breaks from his story
and shouts, "Hey, hold it down . . . I'm trying to make a serious
statement here." From somewhere in the back, "It's not very
serious!"*

"It's very *serious!"*

"It's not very serious!!"

*"Who are you? Come up on stage, pal, Mr. Serious, Mr. Not
Very Serious, come up on stage right now!" No reply. "Hey, idiot,
come up on stage right now!" Still nothing. The faces of the young*

girls down front twist with confusion, their eyes are pasted to the arrogant hulk on stage. "Chickenshit . . . I'll sing, asshole . . ."

When he does finally start to sing, it is not Phil Ochs music, but Johnny Cash songs, a medley of the country/western balladeer's best tunes. Train, with what is left of Ochs's voice, rasps a low register, and air-tones the highs, vainly searching for a way to make the throat work again. It hasn't been the same since the accident in Africa. The spiraling sensuality is lost forever.

Train introduces what he calls the last Phil Ochs song. "Here's a song about Sonny Liston . . .":

> Well, I don't know how Sonny Liston died
> Maybe he killed himself, maybe he even tried
> Or maybe the boys weren't satisfied
> I don't know, I'm sorry I just don't know
>
> Sonny, Sonny, Sonny, why'd you have to take a dive
> If you don't then you won't be alive . . .

From "Sonny" he segues into the last song of the first set, "There but for Fortune." Knotty bulges show from beneath the skin of his thick and wrinkled neck. The song over, he staggers off the stage and heads for the bathroom, where he holds himself up in front of the washbasin, his eyes shut tightly, his piss running down the side of his pants.

The hat comes off for the second show, the eyes are a bit clearer, the voice shyly sweeter. For openers, he croons a Sinatra, bringing a chuckle from the midnight crowd: ". . . and now the end is near . . ." Train's final curtain.

"Good to see you, Phil," someone shouts. Train responds with "Sonny Liston," followed by the Johnny Cash set. His vocal chords are iced and slippery. The high notes, still out of reach, are easier to fake.

Midway through Cash's "There You Go" (you're gonna break another heart, you're gonna tell another lie . . .), he calls for another drink. When nothing comes from the bar, he angrily throws his guitar down and walks off the stage.

A drink is quickly passed over the heads of the crowd. When it reaches Train, he holds it up triumphantly, to cheers.

Minutes drag on while Train tries to retune his guitar. Its neck has split. Out of the confusion of the tuning, Train bursts into song.

> *Found him by the stage last night*
> *He was breathin' his last breath,*
> *A bottle of gin and a cigarette*
> *Were all that he had left . . .*
> *I can see that you make the music*
> *'Cause you carry your guitar,*
> *But God help the troubadour*
> *Who tries to be a star . . .*

Train travels through old folk songs, Irish ballads, Western tunes, "Whisperin' Pines" . . . "Bachelor Till I Die" . . . "Sea of Heartbreak" . . . "Eight More Miles to Louisville" . . . "Maybe Tomorrow." Back to the roots, back to the days at the military academy when a young Phil Ochs first became addicted to the flinty sound of country/western. It is as if Ochs's life were flashing before Train's eyes.

"As you know, this is my final performance. You'll never see me again. I formed a company called Barricade, Ltd. If you watch Channel D—D for death—you'll see one of the first Barricade movies, Coup d'État in America. *It shows the fifteen guys who killed J.F.K. I know no one's particularly interested . . . I called up the New York* Times *and said, 'Hey, you're full of shit . . . all the news that's fit to print except who killed John Kennedy, is that the story?' 'Hey man, we've been investigating since . . .' 'Fuck you, man, watch television, it's on the air, names, dates, faces . . . uh, Frank Sturgis shot John Kennedy, with his pal E. Howard Hunt and thirteen Cuban assholes. In case you're interested. I'm sure you're not . . .'"*

For his final song of the evening, he chooses "Crucifixion." It is the last song he will ever perform for pay.

It is over at 3:15 in the morning. Train lifts the guitar slowly over his head. He whispers, "Adiós," into the mike. While the crowd cheers and stands, he walks past the bar and out the door. Down by MacDougal, over to Houston, on past Wooster, until he drops asleep in a filthy alley between two buildings somewhere in Soho.

He would give himself another eight months of life, and then off it. Before the end, Train would career through Ochs's last days, getting arrested, threatening friends, beating up men and women. Finally, on a cold, shadowless morning in January 1976, John Train, the highest of highs, evaporated, and what was left of Phil Ochs tried to retrieve the lease on his soul.

The last months were the loneliest. He was convinced that as John Train he'd gone too far. With quiet determination, on Friday, April 9, he hanged himself to death.

I

I'm just a city boy
Born and grown
That's all I've ever known.
Where the lights would greet the dawn
There's a factory for a farm
Sure the city has its charm
When you're a city boy.

Phil Ochs, "Boy in Ohio"

Jacob Ochs was born on St. Nicholas Avenue in New York City, delivered at home by his uncle. Although the date was August ninth, his birthday was officially noted as the eleventh, because Dr. Clemenko, invigorated with the business of birthing, forgot to fill out the birth certificate. It hadn't been too many years earlier when the good doctor, in order to escape conscription in Poland, had dressed up in women's clothing, even as a Russian sergeant beat impatiently at the door. Vodka for the soldier, pats on the back, latches secretly opened, ladders placed and withdrawn, to a refugee ship, and bound at last for the new country.

The family settled in New York City, their trades and habits intact from Central Europe. They baked bread, set type, sewed hats. Everyone lived under one roof, a railroad flat on Manhattan's East Side. It was a lower-class enclave filled with the aroma of snapped soup greens and boiled chicken; kreplach, cold whitefish, and bagels on the breakfast table; brown and gray portraits of dead relatives, stiffly posed and unsmiling on the bureau.

Jacob's mother sewed for a dollar a day. They shared one room of the apartment with a miller, who paid her and didn't mind if she worked in the next room, while the children (four of them, including Jacob) fought for her attentions. She quit when she discovered he wasn't really paying her to make hats, but to see to it her family had enough money. She found work in a sweatshop, six dollars a week for sixteen hours of work a day in an airless tomb along with sixty others.

When Jacob was nine years old the family moved to Far Rockaway. The youngster was able to find work almost immediately, building bungalows. His father found a vacant shop and filled it with an inventory acquired by auction. At one point he owned a thousand unmatched shoes. It was a life, and on weekends Jacob and his father would fish in the bay, or go crabbing on the Sound. The construction work helped young Jacob's muscles to harden. Soon he began to dream of travel. One day, without telling anyone his plans, he signed with a local promoter and set out for the South, doing pick-up fights, punching his way across America. When money ran out he returned home, bruised a little but older and stronger.

With his family's encouragement, he applied to and was accepted at the University of Virginia, the first step on his way to becoming a doctor. The initials M.D. were the highest "thank you" to his parents that a refugee's child could give. He would serve all of his people well, the Jews and the Americans.

Only the promised land said, Thanks but no thanks. After university, Jacob discovered medical schools were heavily quota'd, and so, after all, he went to Europe, to study medicine at the University of Edinburgh.

Gertrude Phin lived in a fancy gray stone house at the tip of Edinburgh, where the spice tonic of the Scottish air embraced the blue-black waters. She was slight, erect, and precise. Her pretty steel eyes were round, small circles on a larger round face, soft except for the two star-shaped dimples tightly clinging to the ends of her lips.

Her younger brother, Harry, was a medical student at the nearby university. One day he brought a handsome American to the house with him to share a warm home-cooked meal. By now, Jacob easily mixed dreams and reality into an entertaining stew of conversation. His stories and jokes charmed Mr. and Mrs. Phin and their daughter. Soon, Mr. Phin would offer Jacob a bowl of the finest tobacco he kept in the house, the choicest blend from his shop in Edinburgh.

Jacob and Gertrude would sit by the Scottish mountainside, and the stories would come. He would tell her about his own home in New York, a beautiful house, a string of bungalows, servants, automobiles. When the proposal of marriage came, as her parents hoped it would, everyone was excited and happy. Jacob was an excellent choice for their daughter—Jewish, soon to be a doctor, and from the United States. As they prepared for the large wedding, Gertrude dreamed of the life that awaited her on the other side of the Atlantic. She knew the family would grow quickly. Already their first child was on the way.

Jacob finished his studies with little trouble, and did a year's interning in York, England. Sonia, their little blond baby, seemed a blessing from God on their marriage. At last, they packed their belongings and boarded a ship for America.

The pictures in Gertrude's mind's eye were slashed with confusion. Where was the house? Surely this wasn't what Jack had been describing when he talked of "home." And where were the servants?

Almost immediately Jacob was drafted into the Army and assigned to a CCC camp in Columbus, New Mexico. Everyone was talking war, and as 1940 came to a close, Jacob, Gertrude, and Sonia shifted south to Tex-Mex country, to prepare for this new adventure, and another. Gertrude was expecting again.

Philip David Ochs was born six days before Christmas, 1940. He was named after Gertrude's grandfather, following the Jewish tradition of naming the newborn after a dead relative. Gertrude chose the hospital in El Paso to deliver because there wasn't one she considered acceptable in New Mexico, where Jack was stationed.

For the next two years, Jack was moved to San Antonio, then to Austin. In 1943, Gertrude gave birth to another little boy, Michael. It seemed she was building her own little army.

After two more years of training, Jack was sent overseas as a combat medic, where he was in the front lines at the Battle of the Bulge.

It was more than he had ever dreamed. The fierce armies ever pushing; medics running out to scoop the ashes and still sizzling flesh. It would stay with him forever. And it would change him. Long after this war was over, another battle would rage; a battle within his brain.

With Jack away, Gertrude and the children returned to live in New York with his parents. Fanny Ochs, Jack's mother, was the unquestioned matriarch. Her husband rarely spoke, preferring to sit by the radio in the evenings listening to the news of the war. In the mornings he would come for breakfast asking for fried eggs. Fanny would tell him to scramble them. He'd shrug his shoulders and snap the shells against a cup. The next day he would suggest scrambled, and she would tell him fried. Gertrude didn't understand this house.

Fanny was proud of her kosher cooking. Chickens seemed still to bristle from their fresh plucking as they were dumped whole into large pots of boiling water. One evening Gertrude lifted a lid and saw the button eyes of the dead chicken staring up at her as the water boiled into yellow, fatty soup.

One day in 1945 Jacob came marching home. Before he was able even to think about starting a medical practice, he was gone again. This time the battlefield was on Long Island, the diagnosis whispered. Disturbed. The war. Medical discharge. Manic-depressive. The hospital drugged him into a controllable stupor, even resorted to shock treatment to maintain a semblance of the doctor's sanity.

In 1947, Jacob came home again. He was calmer and talked again about starting his practice. Far Rockaway seemed the perfect place; lots of families moving in, they'd need a doctor.

Young Philip Ochs was a dreamer. His head was filled with soldiers, cowboys and Indians, cops and robbers, the movies. He was seven, Michael five. Gertrude frowned upon the thought of baby-sitters. Instead, she gave the boys money to go to the movies. With

three theaters in Far Rockaway, each showing double features and
changing the programs every Wednesday and Sunday, Philip and
Michael could see five or six films a week. They would spend all
day Saturday in the movies, until the matron chased them out
when it was time for her to go home. *King Kong, Mighty Joe
Young, Frankenstein.* Best of all were the Westerns and the king
of the cowboys, John Wayne. He was the biggest, the toughest, the
fairest. He handled things the way a cowboy had to, with his fists.
He was tough, yet around women he'd always remove his hat, turn
away, look down, and mumble. His pals were always the same:
Ward Bond, Ben Johnson, Harry Carey. They helped the stage-
coaches get through rough Indian territory to settle the frontier.
They cleaned up little towns from two-gunned, black-suited bad
guys. They drove cattle from Texas to Kansas so the pioneers
could feed their families. They were self-appointed, divine.

Their worshipers included the two little boys from Far Rockaway who watched, transported, at the flickering dream-wall. Philip
was with the cowboys when they opened their sleeping bags, put a
few sticks together under the desert moon, and brewed a strong
pot of nutty coffee. To be a cowboy, that was the life . . .

"Philip." No answer.

"Philip." Still nothing. Miss Jocelyn wrinkled her upper lip as
she called the youngster's name. He was staring out the window
again. Sonia, bless her, pretty Sonia was such a fine student, one
of P.S. 39's brighter little girls. But this Philip. He never paid attention. He always seemed to be away, somewhere out that window. Miss Jocelyn: one of the elderly teachers who commanded
their charges to face front, fold their hands, and learn. Never mind
imagination, this was school. The severe teacher shortage worked
to the advantage of the disciplinarian approach that the women
with corn-colored hair used to indoctrinate their students. They
wore purple tent dresses with twisted roses scattered on them,
and they picked their noses with their thumb on the inside, as if it
were okay to do it that way. Internationalism wasn't taught; the
word "communism" was forbidden. Air raid drills were as common as the two o'clock milk break. History was a subject about
dead people, and ideas came only from the shiny pages of thick
and official texts.

Philip preferred the stories of Hollywood to the lessons of Miss Jocelyn. When he stared out the window, his imagination flourished while his teacher scolded him for "not listening," being "lost in thought."

"Philip."

Finally, Miss Jocelyn brought Sonia into the classroom.

"PHILIP OCHS," she screamed, louder than she wanted to.

"Huh?"

"Now, tell your mother about this, Sonia. Tell her he's this way all the time."

Gertrude wasn't surprised. He was the same at home. Always daydreaming. It was time, perhaps, to take the kids home for a while, to the hills of Scotland, to her family. Away from movies, away from Far Rockaway. Away from everything.

The trip was long and difficult. The ship was covered with snow. One day, Gertrude and the three children were on the chilly deck, which was covered with a pancake of ice. Philip was staring again, lost in thought, when suddenly his legs went high in the air and his bottom slid speedily along the ice. Gertrude watched, petrified, as her boy headed toward the edge. She covered her mouth with her hands as he slipped away. Suddenly, he reached out and grabbed a volleyball net the crew had left by the rail. She ran to him. He looked up at her, silent and frightened. She held him tightly, rocking him gently to the pitch of the ocean.

The children attended school four of the six months they spent in Scotland. Every day Philip left his books on the streetcar. Every evening Gertrude took him to the local lost-and-found to pick them up. Exasperated, she put his books into an old music case she found in her parents' house, a big black suitcase that used to hold her music lessons when she was a child. The next day he left that on the streetcar. Hopeless, thought Gertrude. Just hopeless. That boy is in another world.

If she sent him to the store, she had to write down exactly what she wanted. He would lose the list, the money, and never even get there. He'd wander off to sit in the warm, green mountains.

The only activity he seemed to enjoy, besides daydreaming, was teasing his little brother. Michael was the perfect target, for he was a smiling, trusting little boy who suspected nothing and was forever the dupe. Philip was always making deals with him. He would lend a nickel if he could get back a dime. He would trade one comic book for two. He would tell a secret for a piece of candy. The secret: don't give away your candy for a secret. He made deals with Sonia. If she wanted to borrow a dollar—and Philip always seemed to have a bank—it would cost her a dollar and a quarter. When confronted, Philip would stare vacantly, his tongue pushing between his teeth, his clipped brown wispy hair nowhere near his large, floppy ears, his big nose stuck on his small face like the wrong piece on a Mr. Potatohead.

If he weren't with Michael and Sonia, he'd be going to the movies and, with his Brownie Hawkeye, snapping photos of the marquees to add to his collection. It was good to know that the Duke was here, so far from home.

Finally they returned to Far Rockaway and Jack. He was lethargic, slumping, barely able to talk. The children liked him, but didn't know him. It was as if he were a guest in the house. For Philip, John Wayne was only in the movies.

The two brothers shared a large bedroom in the house by the beach. One time, Philip was going through the dark toy closet trying to find something. He lit a match to see better. The tiny flame caught the bottom of a piece of clothing. Philip calmly walked to the kitchen, got a pot, filled it with water, and returned. By now the fire was out of control. He walked next door and told the woman who answered the door that his house was on fire. Only after she questioned him about specifics did she believe him and finally call the fire department. He stood outside to watch as the fire trucks raced up Empire Avenue.

Afterward, smoke smell filled the house. The fire chief warned Philip about the dangers of playing with matches. The boy said nothing. Whenever he was afraid or upset, the words wouldn't come out right, piling up in his mouth, causing him to stutter, a habit that stayed with him the rest of his life. When the fire chief left, Gertrude held Philip closely, smoothing his hair with her palms, telling him everything was all right, everything was fine. He looked at her silently. She pulled him closer and hugged him for a long time.

By 1951, Jacob's practice was finished in Far Rockaway. The frequent lapses and hospitalizations made it impossible for him to continue. The only places he could find work were TB hospitals, the lowest job a doctor could have. As Philip was about to enter the fifth grade, the Ochs family moved upstate to Perrysburg.

Perrysburg, population 250, near Gowanda, forty miles south of Buffalo, known for having the largest glue factory in the country.

The family settled into an apartment above the J. N. Adams Memorial Hospital, where they could hear the nervous whinny of the horses about to die.

Gertrude, while listening to the "Make Believe Ballroom" on the radio, decided the boys needed hobbies. Sonia had already begun piano lessons. Perhaps the boys could learn to play instruments. Philip already had a hobby: the movies. Besides going to see them, he collected movie magazines and took snapshots of marquees. He could tell you every star's name, even the character actors. Guy Kibbee, Elisha Cook, Jr. He loved Elisha Cook, Jr.! Always getting killed, believing that hard, tough blonde really loved him, when all the time she'd set him up. Or Peter Lorre. He was great! John Ireland, Edward Everett Horton, Audie Murphy, he knew them all, every picture, every role.

Gertrude sat the boys down and told them they would have to take up musical instruments. This was bad news for Philip. He hated music. He was always coming out of his room asking Gertrude to turn off the radio. The boys were instructed to choose an instrument and join the school band. Philip chose trumpet, Michael saxophone. Philip returned from school the next day and told his mother he couldn't take lessons because the band didn't need any more trumpet players. Gertrude told him to choose another instrument. He went back asking for the saxophone. Same story. Finally, Gertrude told him to ask for any instrument that wasn't taken, and he came home to report that he was going to learn to play the clarinet.

A week later, Gertrude received a telephone call from Mr. Navaro, the band teacher, requesting that she buy Philip a clarinet. Gertrude insisted it was too soon, the boy was only studying it because she was forcing him. If he kept at it though, she might consider it.

Before long Philip's talents became obvious to Gertrude. She purchased a French Oblet clarinet for him, the finest available. Philip was a very good player, perhaps exceptional, Mr. Navaro seemed to feel. Every day after school Philip would rush to his room and practice. Over and over he would play a piece until he'd mastered it. At the end of five months, he was performing more difficult solos than those played by students who had been with the band for years.

Michael could hit a few notes well, but his playing was only average. What made it seem worse was how good Philip sounded on the clarinet. Michael finally gave his saxophone to Philip, who picked it up even faster than he had the clarinet.

Philip was taken before the Fredonia State Teacher's College for a rating. He received an "A" on the clarinet, unusual for someone who had been playing less than a year. He was rated "excellent, displaying a very warm tone quality, mature interpretive abilities." Gertrude was advised that if he kept playing, he would be an exceptional player.

Jacob in the living room, in his easy chair, reading the paper. He looks up, toward Philip's room. Gertrude in the kitchen, preparing dinner. She glances over her shoulder toward the music. Sonia doing her homework, Michael playing with his toy soldiers. The music comes from the second-floor bedroom. It lingers. There is life in the little house above the hospital for the dying.

II

Creek was runnin' down the road
And the Buckeye sun was ashinin'
I rode my bike down Alum Creek Drive
When I was a boy in Ohio.

Phil Ochs, "Boy in Ohio"

The move to Perrysburg brought many changes. After living by the Far Rockaway beach, Gertrude was forced to adjust to the severe winter cold, the endless snowstorms, the muddy summer rains of upstate New York. Philip and Michael were swept along, one place as good as another. Only Sonny, as Sonia liked to call herself, seemed to enjoy living in Perrysburg. She loved the natural country life, the smell of fertilizer after a spring rain, the feel of thick, creamy mud coming up around her naked toes.

Gertrude received a small inheritance from her father's estate, and decided the money should be used to improve the children's education. Sonia was shipped to a Swiss finishing school directly upon graduation from high school. While being trained abroad, loathing the life of the proper young lady she was forced to lead, she received word from Gertrude that the family was moving to Columbus, Ohio. The TB hospital in Perrysburg was being converted to a treatment center for mentally retarded children. Jack had no choice but to search for another job, another TB institution, this one in Ohio.

Sonny was outraged. Now there would be no home for her to come back to. If she were to come back at all.

By now, Philip was the best clarinet player in the school. When Mr. Navaro learned that the Ochs family was moving away in January, he called Gertrude again. He asked if he could keep Philip in his own home for the last six months of the school term.

Impossible. Gertrude would not allow Philip's education to continue at the little country school. She did promise Mr. Navaro she would look for a suitable music teacher for Philip once they arrived in Ohio.

The Benjamin Franklin Hospital was located in the southeast section of Columbus. The family lived in an apartment on hospital property. Across from the sprawling grounds was an old-age home; on the other side, railroad tracks. An elderly patient, about to die, would be shipped to the TB hospital, keeping the mortality statistics attractively lean at the home. Around the corner was the cemetery. Jack had no difficulty fitting into the daily routines. They varied little from hospital to hospital.

Gertrude went to the nearby Capital University Conservatory of Music to secure the services of a young music teacher. Once a week Philip would take a private lesson at home. Almost immediately, the teacher realized Philip's musical talent was special. So special he brought Philip to audition for the college orchestra. He was accepted even though he was only fifteen years old.

This pleased Gertrude. She'd been angered by the fact that the boys had to go to a small country school because they were located one block outside of the city school limits. The tiny Marion Franklin school was, in her opinion, not suitable. She smiled with satisfaction when he would leave the house with his clarinet case in hand, on his way to practice. She wished she could share this pleasure with Jack.

Unfortunately, Jack was busy with his own practice. And his own problems, like that heated bitch of a head nurse who wasn't allowing the student nurses to play ping-pong in the residence. How dare she deprive these hard-working, dedicated young ladies a bit of harmless recreation? Jack egged the girls on, telling them they had a perfect right to play ping-pong if they wanted to. Ping-pong was a right, not a privilege!

At home, his speeches turned to rantings, his arguments to tirades. One moment he would be sitting quietly, alone in a chair.

The next, he'd be shouting about the injustices of hospital life. Over the years, Gertrude had come to recognize the pattern. It didn't really matter what the cause was, as long as there was a cause for Jack to rally to, each time his rage greater than before. Gertrude would fly at him, weary and familiar with the process, helpless to stop it. Even in front of the children, she would shout, trying somehow to keep him in check. His arms would flail, he would knock things over. He would take the two boys and throw them in the car. He would floor the gas pedal, sixty, seventy, seventy-five, leaving Gertrude behind to worry whether they would return alive.

It was inevitable. Jack needed to "rest" again for a while. They'd all been there before.

Soon after his sixteenth birthday, Philip was leading soloist at the Conservatory. He appeared in the Second Summer Music Clinic Festival concert. He was featured in Sammartini's "Symphony in D Major," Bach's "Prelude and Fugue, in D Minor," and "Turkey in the Straw," a local favorite.

On the way home from practice one day, Philip was recognized by one of the boys from school. Philip had no friends, and never bothered to spend time after school playing ball or talking with the guys. As he passed a couple of them on the street, one called out, "Hey, Jew-boy." Philip didn't realize they meant him, or that "Jew-boy" was intended as an insult. There hadn't been much religion at home; "being Jewish" meant nothing to any of the children, other than getting off from school for the Jewish holidays.

Dave Sweazy ran up to the kid with the clarinet case in his hand. He punched Philip in the mouth, and a moment later they were going at it. The fight was broken up by the others when Philip pinned Sweazy down and started punching him back. They shook hands and went home. Philip had passed the test.

The next day Philip brought Dave over to the house. Sweazy was a filthy kid. His hair was long, stringy, dirty. His clothes were ripped and smelly. He wore no shoes. Philip asked Gertrude if Dave could join them for dinner. "Of course," Gertrude replied. She felt sorry for the youngster, and wondered about his parents. When she served dinner, Dave seemed embarrassed, not knowing how to hold his silverware; how to sit at a table with other people.

Dave became Philip's first, closest, and only friend. Gradually, Dave began to improve his appearance, trying to dress the way Philip did, with clean shirts, ties, combed hair, shined shoes.

They became inseparable. Gertrude was amazed at the changes in Dave. He would call Philip on the telephone, and if Gertrude answered, he would ask her how she was. He and Philip would spend long hours together, alone, either upstairs in the attic, or walking along the streets of Columbus. Philip asked Dave one day if he could photograph him, and they spent a weekend taking pictures. Philip put one of Dave's pictures into his private photo album, the one filled with his snapshots of movie marquees and TV shows he'd taken directly off the television screen.

They went to the movies every moment they could get away— Philip from the orchestra and practice, Dave from the guys on the corner.

Philip's favorite stars were Marlon Brando and James Dean. Brando with his black motorcycle jacket and scar over his left eye, like Philip's. James Dean with his red zipper jacket and DA haircut, the pretty wet eyes and cupid lips. After *On the Waterfront,* Philip dreamed about boxing in a ring for the championship. After *Rebel Without a Cause,* he wanted to wear a red jacket and comb his hair back. After *Duel in the Sun,* he began to practice quickdraw. Dave Sweazy had real pistols, and one day, while practicing in the woods, Philip shot himself just below the knee. The story made the local papers, and Gertrude figured it was time her boys were sent to schools where they wouldn't shoot themselves playing cowboys and Indians.

She told the boys they would be attending Columbus Academy in the fall. Michael was no problem, but Philip insisted he didn't want to go there; they had no orchestra. Gertrude told him he should choose a school, any school, and it would be all right with her. He announced his choice. Military school. He'd seen an ad in the New York *Times Magazine* of boys dressed in fancy uniforms, with a marching band behind them. Staunton Academy, Virginia. He showed his mother the ad, and she agreed, as she'd said she would. He was enrolled in the fall class of 1956. He would be away from home for the first time, away from the hospitals and the cemeteries, away from Dave Sweazy, away from the silver shadow of his father.

Barracks life was exciting. Uniforms, orders of the day, the
tough competitive line—in the classroom, on the field, in the band.
He was one of the boys playing soldier, smoking two packs a day,
drinking 3.2 beer in the canteen and going to the Catholic church
to steal change from the collection plate. At night, Philip and a
group of students would use one of the empty rooms in the dorm
as a place to lift weights. On weekends they'd go downtown to the
movies. Afterward, they'd come back to the dorm and listen to
country music on the radio. During the week, Philip would study
in his room while listening on his own radio to country music.
Johnny Cash, Hank Williams, and Faron Young filled the long
hours with songs of heroes, prison, women, and booze.

Johnny Cash could tell a story in a few bars the way a book
could in a few hours. . . . Faron Young, his sweet high voice diving into notes, was a sound Philip would remember, a sound he
would later try to imitate. Impossibly high on the scale, sweet,
musical sugar. . . . The Everly Brothers . . . Gene Vincent . . .
Buddy Holly . . . And always The King. Elvis, the truck driver
who made good with his hips. The boy who loved his mother,
went to church, and kicked ass.

Playing in the school marching band wasn't as much fun as
Philip had thought it would be. For one thing, he had no solos. For
another, the conductor was more concerned with how the band
marched than how it played. Philip loved Sousa's marches. He
could hear them in his head the way they were supposed to sound,
not the way the band tried to play them.

He continued to listen to country songs, keeping his radio on all
the time. Every once in a while he would write down a line from a
song, if he really liked it.

Philip gradually began to write little stories of his own. One,
"White Milk to Red Wine," won second prize, ten dollars, in a
short-story writing contest at the Academy:

> I had never been so worried in all my life. When I got out of
> bed that morning a cold sweat came over me. I knew I had to
> fight him sooner or later, and today was it. He had bullied me so
> often, and now I had finally reached my breaking point. If a per-
> son is stronger than others, he doesn't have the right to pick on
> people smaller and weaker than him.

He insulted me in front of my friends. I had to make a stand. In a moment of anger, I challenged him to a fight the next day after lunch. When he accepted, he threw back his head and laughed cruelly.

I went to school the following day feeling like David when he went to meet Goliath. Unfortunately, I had no slingshot to cover me. My morning classes seemed to pass too quickly and the lunch I ate had no taste. When I walked towards the meeting place, I knew how a condemned man feels as he walks the last mile. All of a sudden a hand gripped my shoulder. I spun around and there he stood. The only difference was that the triumphant look was gone from his face. He stammered nervously and said that he didn't mean to pick on me, and that he didn't want to fight.

With a sigh of relief I agreed, and we walked back to the school to spend another routine kindergarten afternoon.

Here, in his first attempt at writing, was a story about courage, and the desire to stand up for "people smaller and weaker." Philip David Ochs, David against Goliath. "White Milk to Red Wine" was published in the school literary magazine which was edited by Michael P. Goldwater, son of the future senator from Arizona.

Summers, the Ochses would return to Far Rockaway to visit Jack's family. There Philip decided to break the news to Gertrude. He was giving up the clarinet. She pleaded with him not to, he'd worked at it so hard, he played so well. She hired a student from Juilliard to come to the house and give Philip lessons. Reluctantly, he agreed to continue. However, after ten sessions, Philip started to complain about his lip, how it was hurting. There was nothing Gertrude could do. The clarinet was over, and she knew it. The concertos and preludes were gone, replaced by a constant humming, which would burst into a sudden la-la-la, then recede into an easy hum once again.

All summer the boys argued about music. Michael insisted the "colored" music they played in Ohio was the greatest. Every night Alan Freed played Frankie Lymon, The Clovers, Lee Andrews, The Drifters on his "Moondog" show. Philip told Michael about the country and western music he'd heard in Virginia. "That stuff's for hicks," Michael told Philip. "Except for Elvis." They both agreed about The King. He was above everyone else, and always would be.

Sonny was gone now. She'd married a soldier that spring, against her mother's wishes. In the fall, she and her new husband, Rick Tanzman, paid a visit to Philip at Staunton. They went on a fried-chicken picnic. Philip looked away as he ate, staring into space, saying little. He wondered why they'd come. He'd hardly known Sonny before she went to Switzerland, and had seen little of her since. She told him she was never going back to the house in Ohio. Philip listened, but was thinking about other things. Graduation was coming up, and "Mr. Universe," as he was called by his buddies at the Academy, was looking ahead to college. Weightlifting had helped him to shed his baby fat. His hair was long on top, greased back with Dixie Peach, like Elvis'. Only one thing still bothered him, still held him back. That nose. It made his face seem a mile long.

He graduated with lots of ribbons, and played in the Corporal Band one last time. In the yearbook he appeared in full military dress. Across the top of the page where his picture appeared was the headline, "DON'T LET DEFEAT CAUSE SORROW . . . ," completed on the next page, "THINK OF THE VICTORIES OF OLD."

A few weeks before classes started at Ohio State, Philip went to his mother and told her he wanted to have his nose fixed. It was important.

"All right, if that's what you want." Gertrude made the arrangements. A few days later, Philip entered the hospital.

After the surgery, Gertrude was allowed in to visit. What she saw surprised her. Not the bandages around his head, not the black eyes. Something else. Lying on the bed, surrounded by several pretty giggling nurses, Philip was laughing through the pain and the gauze.

"How do you feel, Philip?" she asked.

"It doesn't hurt, Ma. You know why?"

"No, why?"

He told her. "Because I'm going to be a star."

III

Oh I am just a student, sir
And I only want to learn
But it's hard to see through the risin' smoke
Of the books that you like to burn.
So I'd like to make a promise
And I'd like to make a vow
That when I've got something to say, sir
I'm gonna say it now.

Phil Ochs, "I'm Going to Say It Now"

He arrived at Ohio State University wearing a red jacket like the one James Dean wore in *Rebel Without a Cause*. Philip was used to dormitory life after his military school days. It didn't matter much what his room was like as long as he could play the radio all hours of the day and night, tuned to country music or Alan Freed's rock and roll.

It was 1958; Elvis was starring in *Loving You*. Philip went to see it over and over until he knew every song by heart. To Philip, Elvis was like The Duke: no matter who he was supposed to be on screen, the character became another version of Elvis, singing tough, the dungaree jacket curled around his neck like Presley's lips around a lyric.

Classes ended the first week in January. Philip was putting a few things together to take back home to Cleveland, where Jack and Gertrude had recently moved from Columbus, when Hank Williams was interrupted on the radio by a news bulletin. Fidel Castro had marched into Havana and taken control of Cuba. A revolution was in progress a blink away from Miami Beach. Almost immediately, a new hero entered Philip's pantheon. He couldn't wait to get the newspaper's extra edition. There on the front page was a picture of Fidel, his curly hair and swarthy skin, his watery eyes and fat cigar. He looked like a revolutionary, or, as Hollywood might have called him, a "soldier of fortune." In the background was the cool Dr. Che Guevara, tough and silent, his face aimed one way, his eyes another.

Castro and Guevara were instant media heroes in the United States. Their pictures were everywhere. The press treated the invasion of Havana as if John Wayne had taken Dodge City from a gang of bandits. Castro appealed to the fantasies of the romantics, and with good reason. During the forties he'd been a Hollywood extra, appearing in numerous American films, trying to make a name for himself in the Desi Arnaz tradition of Latin-American stars: dumb but sexy. He'd learned a lot about image while at MGM; he would never be seen in public out of costume, the beard, the cigar, the fatigues, the women. He was a star. A shining knight come to slay the dragon. His army greens clung sexily to his broad shoulders, his collar rose up to meet his beard.

Philip's support of Castro's government went beyond politics. He was enthralled by the Cuban leader, and he wasn't alone. CBS News stationed reporters on Havana rooftops to report Fidel's march of triumph through the streets. Jack Paar had Castro on "The Tonight Show" as a guest.

By the time Philip reached Cleveland Heights, his mind was made up. After dinner, he sat with Gertrude in the living room and told her he was dropping out of college. He stared out the large bay window, watching the fluorescent snow fall from the smoky sky. He was lonely at school. He had no friends. He wasn't learning anything. It wasn't fun.

College wasn't supposed to be fun, Gertrude told him. Unless he received his degree it would be difficult to get a good job, she added.

They discussed it for hours. Finally, Gertrude asked him what he planned to do.

"Go down South. Travel. Maybe get a job as a singer."

Gertrude threw up her hands. "You don't know how to sing,

Philip. You have no experience." She could see it was no use. "All right, go wherever you want. But I won't support you."

He turned to her. "I'm wasting my time and your money at school. I don't see the point."

The next day, wearing his red jacket, he left.

He arrived in Miami a few days later and was promptly arrested for vagrancy. He was sentenced to fifteen days in the county jail. As he would recall years later, "The time in jail was great. It was the best schooling I ever had. Everybody sat around singing Hank Williams. I talked to a lot of alcoholics and bank robbers, all kinds of weird people." The sheriff took a liking to Philip and became concerned about his being in the same cell with the older prisoners. There was something about the youngster that didn't seem criminal. He made up chores for the boy to do around the jailhouse to help pass the time. Every day Philip was to wash the sheriff's car, which he did with the Motorola turned on, playing Lefty Frizell, Les Paul and Mary Ford, Faron Young, and Buddy Holly.

When he was released he went to a few clubs to apply for a job as a singer, but there was little interest in the straggling youth with the dirty chinos and faded red jacket. With no money and no place to stay, Philip began living on the beach. At night he shared Italian bread with the seagulls. When the moon rose in the sky he would try to see to the shore of Cuba, which he was sure was just beyond the horizon.

As the days passed, he took whatever work he could find. He washed dishes for a few days. He sold shoes to old ladies in a store on Lincoln Avenue. The money wasn't enough to buy a decent meal. He started to ache for food. His gums turned red from pyorrhea. His skin became pasty, his stuttering more severe. Finally, he called Cleveland collect and asked for enough money to buy a bus ticket to come home.

As he stepped off the Greyhound in Cleveland, he collapsed into Michael's waiting arms.

Philip was ready to return to Ohio State that fall. He left Cleveland a week early to set up an apartment off campus. He met his roommate the first day, and then proceeded to hang pictures of

Elvis everywhere—large color shots from concerts, and stills from *Love Me Tender* and *Loving You*. On his small phonograph he stacked Elvis records along with Faron Young and Buddy Holly. The records played all the time. His roommate let it be known he was shopping for a quieter place to live. When Philip found out, he just shrugged his shoulders and turned the volume up.

It was the wall of Elvis pictures which first caught the eye of the student from the floor below as he passed Philip's room one day on his way to a study group. "Heartbreak Hotel" was on the phonograph. Jim Glover walked into Philip's room to get a closer look.

"Where'd you get the pictures, man?"

"I collect them," Philip said, without looking up from the magazine he was reading, while he sat on his bed.

"Do you have any pictures of Woody Guthrie?"

"Never heard of him."

Jim asked Philip if he'd ever heard of The Weavers. He said no. Or Pete Seeger. Not him either. Jim took him down to his room. He wanted to play some of his own records. A couple of 78s later, Philip told Jim he was looking for a new roommate. The next day he helped Jim move his stuff upstairs.

Jim was Philip's first and only friend at Ohio State. They were together constantly, even signing up for the same classes. Jim's parents lived not far from Philip's house in Cleveland Heights. They were warm, friendly working-class people, happy when Jim brought friends home. Whenever Philip came by there was plenty of food to eat, and lots of time to eat it. Dinners were carefully prepared—salads, thick homemade soups, broiled chops, baked casseroles, warm pie with scoops of ice cream dripping down the sides. Dining was something the family looked forward to, a time to gather, to talk, and to relax.

Mr. Glover often sat at the head of his table, leading the boys and Mrs. Glover in fascinating and entertaining conversation which always led, sooner or later, to politics. Mr. Glover was a Marxist, as he put it, and was delighted with Philip's and Jim's shared enthusiasm for Fidel Castro.

Philip's contribution to dinnertime discussions always centered on the movies, his favorite subject. Mr. Glover would listen patiently to the plots of films, especially the ones starring John Wayne. Philip knew nothing about Wayne's politics. He just assumed Wayne was a Democrat. Like his father. Like everyone's father. Mr. Glover told the boys about HUAC, and Philip asked him what the word meant, he'd never heard of it. Mr. Glover explained that the initials stood for the House Un-American Activities Committee. He told the boys that HUAC was the government's tacit admission that it had, indeed, more than a passing interest in the entertainment world. HUAC's biggest mistake, he added, had been its war on Hollywood. It was a victory for the Left because the attack had eventually resulted in a recognition of the legitimacy of Hollywood's liberal faction of actors, screenwriters, and directors. Sometimes Mr. Glover would talk about McCarthyism, how it was rampant during the early fifties, how the pendulum seemed, at last, to be swinging the other way.

Philip loved Mr. Glover. He wanted to learn everything he could from him about politics. Most of all, he wanted Jim's father to like him, the way he'd wanted his own father to like him. The problem had always been that Jack was never around long enough to spend much time with the kids. These days, if he wasn't working at the TB hospital all day and into the night, he was a patient himself. Since Philip spent most of his time now at Ohio State, he hardly ever saw his father anymore. They were strangers.

Jim and Philip spent long hours, late into the night, staying up and talking politics in their apartment at school. Philip read every book on politics he could find. Marx, Engels, Mao Tse-tung; these he got from Jim. He also read Jefferson, Adams, Tom Paine, *The Federalist Papers,* Abraham Lincoln. He read histories, the history of Cuba, learning how it had come under U.S. influence during the Spanish-American War. He brought a hundred questions back to Mr. Glover, who explained to Philip the exploitation of the Cuban workers by such organizations as United Fruit, which would enter a foreign country to exploit its resources for profit, leaving the nationals behind, in poverty. As Philip's ideas about the government and its policies began to develop and change, he wanted to know more, all there was. With Jim he became interested in American folk music of the thirties and forties, the Dustbowl ballads, the union organizing songs. Jim, an excellent guitarist and banjo player, would sing the songs of Woody Guthrie and Pete Seeger for Philip. Their records were played over and over. Sometimes the boys would spend an afternoon sitting on the grass behind the house where they were rooming, forgetting everything they had to do while they harmonized a Weavers tune or a Guthrie ballad.

It wasn't long before they began to apply their political feelings to their everyday existence at Ohio State. They began to question the university rules and regulations. ROTC was mandatory for all male students. Philip, Staunton Military School graduate, and Jim decided to devote their full time to having the military presence on campus removed from the academic environment. They cut their classes for the cause. Boycotts, marches, rallies. Philip would plan the events, recruit sympathetic students. Jim would sing at the rallies.

Meanwhile, a young senator from Massachusetts was making a horse race out of the presidential elections. Hubert Humphrey, the apparent favorite of the Democratic Party, was defeated in the primaries by the youthful, confident John F. Kennedy. During the first week of the fall term, Philip calmly announced to Jim that J.F.K. would defeat Nixon in November. It didn't matter that Kennedy was Catholic, that Nixon had been Vice-President for eight years. Kennedy would win. He was so sure, he bet fifty dollars on Kennedy against Jim's Kay guitar. Jim figured there was no way Nixon could lose.

Philip asked Jim to teach him how to play his new guitar. A month later he was playing songs, and soon after that writing them. At first they were no more than two-chord melodies, but, as with the clarinet, he was able to bring a style of playing to the instrument, so that even the simplest tunes became distinctive. He would hold the neck of the guitar higher than its body and strum briskly, adding an extra strum every fourth time, a bonus jangle to the quarter-time rhythms he played. Next he began to add lines to the melodies, a rhyme here, a stanza there. Jim would lay pretty harmonies around Philip's melodies. If Philip sang high, Jim would come underneath. If Philip took the melody line, Jim would come above, always able to compensate so their voices blended in key. They began to work out routines—original Philip Ochs tunes along with lots of Kingston Trio hits. Once in a while they did a few Pete Seegers, and an occasional Faron Young. Philip's voice was clear, distinctly rhythmic. His speech pattern had an ever-so-slight Scottish lilt, which undoubtedly influenced his melodies.

That fall, Philip chose journalism as his major. He began hanging around the offices of *The Lantern,* the Ohio State student newspaper, and soon was being assigned to cover stories on a regular basis. Sometime before Christmas, he decided to move into Steeb Hall, where most of the journalism majors and the entire staff of *The Lantern* roomed. Jim helped him pack his things.

He attended all the meetings of the journalism fraternity, and believed he had a good chance to become Editor-in-Chief in his senior year, a position that traditionally went to the student with the best grades. He was applying himself now to his studies, staying up late into the night, with his radio on, hitting the books. His grades were consistently high, something he pursued matter-of-factly; it was necessary for attaining the position he wanted.

At Steeb, a new house constitution was being formulated outlining the rules and regulations for the day-to-day maintenance and operation of the dormitory. It was clear to Philip that the upperclassmen had worked out the document to give themselves total control of the dorm, leaving the menial, non-decision-making chores to the freshmen and sophomores. At a floor meeting Philip called, he read a statement of his views to the other students, urging them to reject the document being proposed by the seniors. He warned them not to be complacent, to sit back and accept whatever the seniors said, just because they'd said it. He managed to get them excited, and the original hall constitution was defeated by ballot.

To the senior staff members of *The Lantern,* this incident marked Philip as a troublemaker, so they decided to remove him from all political assignments. The official reason given was that his views were too "controversial," particularly his continuing admiration for Fidel Castro. Philip argued his position, citing freedom of speech as his justification for declaring Castro a hero in print. However, the decision to remove Philip from political stories remained in effect.

All right then, he would start his own newspaper. *The Word* would contain the political truth that *The Lantern* was so obviously afraid of. He would stay up through the night typing, duplicating, stapling, folding. In the daytime, he continued to work on

The Lantern. He also began writing letters to the Editor of the Cleveland *Plain Dealer,* attacking the editorials the paper ran. When turmoil in Indonesia threatened to erupt into war, the *Plain Dealer* attacked Sukarno as an imperialist. The next day a letter from Philip Ochs appeared:

> . . . You state that President Sukarno now has designs on Dutch New Guinea. In case you don't know it by now, every country that is partially or wholly colonized has designs on their rightful territories, and Russia is backing them all without reservations. It will be incredibly difficult to fight against this invincible movement and maintain the delicate balance we have now in the Cold War.
>
> You mention that the Dutch "cannot in honor yield to open threats." However . . . Imperialism is dying! Colonialism is dying! These are the cries of the world today, and we can no longer remain deaf to them. If Nehru has erred in his means, he should be criticized; but since his end was historically and morally justified, there is no excuse for the torrent of abuse heaped upon him by the Western powers.
>
> To attack a dying institution is pardonable by historical standards; to attack a growing giant recklessly without realizing its significance could prove to be political suicide.
>
> Philip Ochs
4182 East Road
South Euclid 21
(Ohio State U. Student)

It was a double assault upon *The Lantern.* His own paper, *The Word,* was purely political; and his letters were being published by the largest newspaper in Cleveland. *The Lantern* continued to assign him to nonpolitical stories, usually concert reviews.

He was writing all the time now, and even began writing letters to the Editor of *The Lantern.* The letters were published in the "Letters to the Editor" section. His musical reviews would run alongside. Now he had more space than anyone else on the paper. Philip's defense of Fidel Castro appeared opposite his review of Andrés Segovia:

> Our papers are quick to preach how terrible the Castro dictatorship is, but how often do they criticize Salazar, Franco, or Chiang Kai-shek?

Had we attacked Cuba . . . Russia's screaming of "Yankee Imperialism" would have a strong ring of truth throughout the world.

Philip Ochs

In "Allegro" by H. Vieuxtemps he displayed his remarkable technique, a technique distinguished by the artist's awareness of the music in each individual note, in spite of the marvelous speed . . . he made it impossible to believe that these piano pieces could have been written for anything but guitar.

By Phil Ochs

Philip Ochs, political commentator. Phil Ochs, musical critic. It was the first time he acknowledged the fact that both politics and music were important, if separate, aspects of his developing talents. He found it necessary to demonstrate the split interest, or at least what he felt at the time to be a split interest, by giving himself two names: Philip and Phil. Once Phil Ochs appeared in print, though, Philip Ochs, the shy, daydreaming boy who grew up in various cities, who fantasized about cowboys and Indians, who lived in his dreams, gave way to Phil Ochs, the easy, funny, guitar-playing entertainer who lived out his dreams. The king was dead. Long Live The King. The King was going to be Editor of *The Lantern*. That would be the ultimate conquest. No more crew-cut dormitory bullshit. Viva Fidel!

Jim and Phil called themselves "The Sundowners" after the movie starring Robert Mitchum. Phil also referred to the group as "The Singing Socialists," although the name never quite caught on.

They'd been playing together, mostly for themselves, in Phil's basement on weekends, when, on a clear day in April, the "Bay of Pigs" invasion of Cuba by the CIA spit into the face of The New Frontier. That night Jim and Phil talked about the invasion, arguing its implications. The next morning Phil put his guitar over his shoulder and played his newest piece, his first real song, for Jim:

> *A thousand went to take the island*
> *Chances strong as broken twigs*
> *A thousand stayed there on the island*
> *Met their fate at the Bay of Pigs.*

Why were they wearing my country's clothes
Why were they spending my country's gold
Who were my friends and who were my foes
The headlines were lying, why wasn't I told?

They were told when they arrived
They'd be helped by Castro's men
Those who survived, they found out
The CIA was wrong again . . .

"What do you think?"

Every day Phil would read the newspapers, and by evening he would have a new song. He and Jim would sing them at parties, or just find a spot on the campus where they could sit and play their guitars, practicing. Students always managed to find them and request the songs they wanted to hear. One of the early favorites was "Billie Sol." Whereas "Bay of Pigs" had been full of open rage, "Billie Sol" was satiric; more attractive, therefore more effective. The lyrics always broke the kids up as they sat and listened:

And now I'd like to say
That crime sure doesn't pay
But if you want to make some money on the sly
Well you can always rent
The U.S. Government
It's the best one that money can buy.

Stand tall, Billie Sol
We don't know you at all
Take down those pictures from the wall.
Well, we don't want to handle
An agriculture scandal
We have got to face elections in the fall.

He wrote a song and sent it to radio station WERE, the outlet for the Cleveland Indians. He wanted the baseball team to adapt his song as their theme. He received this letter back from the station:

Dear Phil:
I want to thank you for sending me your song and the tape with it. Your song shows a lot of originality and much fine spirit. It

Gertrude Phin Ochs
(*Courtesy of the*
Phil Ochs estate)

Officer Jack Ochs
(*Courtesy of the*
Phil Ochs estate)

Philip at nine months of age
(*Courtesy of the Phil Ochs estate*)

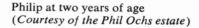

Philip at two years of age
(*Courtesy of the Phil Ochs estate*)

Philip, Sonia, Michael, 1944
(*Courtesy of the Phil Ochs estate*)

Dr. Ochs after the war
(*Courtesy of the Phil Ochs estate*)

Sonia, Michael, and Philip
aboard ship on the way to
Scotland (*Courtesy of the
Phil Ochs estate*)

Gertrude and children, 1949 (*Courtesy of the Phil Ochs estate*)

Michael, Jet (the family dog), and Philip (*Courtesy of the Phil Ochs estate*)

Philip (age 12), 1953
(*Courtesy of the Phil Ochs estate*)

Grade ___7___   Order of Appearance _____

JUDGE'S COMMENT SHEET
FOR GRADE AND JR. HIGH SCHOOL EVENTS

Vocal and Instrumental Solo

Name ___Philip Ochs___

Address _____

School ___Marion-Franklin___ City ___Marion twp.___ County ___Franklin___

Selection ___Adagio and Tarantella-___ Instrument or Voice ___clarinet___

Use A B C D or E in Square to indicate the quality of performance
Please make comments constructive.

		ADDITIONAL COMMENTS
TONE	Ⓐ+	Excellent Playing.
INTONATION	Ⓐ	A very rich & warm tone quality.
INTERPRETATION	Ⓐ+	
POSTURE	Ⓐ	Intonation very accurate.
BREATH SUPPORT	Ⓐ	
PHRASING	Ⓐ	Interpretation superior.
ARTICULATION (Diction)	Ⓐ	Phrasing and control of dynamics
RHYTHM CORRECTNESS	Ⓐ	very mature.
VOWELS AND CONSONANTS (omit in instrumental event)	Ⓐ	A few very high tones not
EMBOUCHURE (omit in vocal event)	Ⓑ	well controlled.
GENERAL EFFECT;	Ⓐ	You have exceptional musical
MAJOR STRONG POINTS;		feeling and the ability to
MAJOR WEAK POINTS;		transfer it on your instrument
SUGGESTIONS FOR IMPROVEMENTS;		is abundant.

Just keep up the good work. You
can be an exceptional player

RATING ___I___
(I II III IV or V)

Judges Signature _____

OMEA Jr. High and Elem. form No. 1

(Courtesy of the Phil Ochs estate)

Playing in the school band

The high-school yearbook photo
of "Mr. Universe"

Dave Sweazy (*Photo by Phil Ochs*)

The only known photograph of "The Sundowners" (*Courtesy of the Phil Ochs estate*)

Phil at Faragher's, 1961 (*Courtesy of the Phil Ochs estate*)

Faron Young, an early influence on the "Phil Ochs sound" (*Courtesy of Mercury Records*)

might make a fine specialty number. I would suggest that you send this tape directly to the ball club.
Best of luck to you.

Keep listening,
Jimmy Dudley

Phil would write the songs, Jim would do the arrangements. The Sundowners performed original Phil Ochs songs, Pete Seeger tunes, and a couple of Kingston Trio hits. They practiced in the basement of Phil's house every day that summer. Mrs. Chang, a neighbor whose husband worked at the hospital with Jack, called to tell Gertrude that the two young lawyers living in the house across the street were opening a coffeehouse in Cleveland and were looking for performers. When she hung up the phone, Gertrude went to the basement to tell The Sundowners they had their first professional audition.

They arrived at La Cave early in the afternoon. After doing half of one song they were hired. Twenty-five dollars. Between them. Weekends. If they made it through the first weekend, they could come back the next.

That night, Phil went over all the material they had. He decided it wasn't enough and started to go through old records, looking for some new songs. Jim waved his hand and told Phil not to worry. They would get by. No, they wouldn't, Phil insisted. What if they got an encore? He handed Jim a new song and told him to learn it by the next morning.

Phil woke early, dressed, had a glass of milk and ran over to Jim's house. He opened the door, glided past Mr. Glover and flew up the stairs. He found his partner still sleeping. He shook him awake and asked if he'd learned the song. No, Jim mumbled, he hadn't even looked at it. Phil turned his back and stomped out, vowing never to talk to Jim again.

As opening night approached, Jim tried to cool things between them. He went downtown and bought two black cowboy shirts for The Sundowners to wear. They'd be slick as the night. Phil refused the shirt, refused to show for the show. He'd meant what he said. Jim went to La Cave himself and was fired, along with Phil, *in absentia.* The career of The Sundowners was over.

A week later, Jim called to say goodbye. He was quitting school and heading for New York. Would Phil like to come along? No. Good luck. Click.

Phil was more determined than ever. He went around to all the clubs in Cleveland. Finally, one place decided to give him a chance, to see what he could do.

Faragher's was a new coffeehouse in Cleveland Heights, run by Danny Dalton, of the original "Dalton Boys." When Phil asked him for a job, Danny said he couldn't afford to pay him anything, but he would allow him to sing for free. If he worked out the first week, he could come back the second.

Phil rehearsed at home for days. The day before he was to start, he stayed up for twenty-four hours, falling asleep on the floor of his bedroom, too tired to crawl to bed and under the covers.

He was asked back. Danny told him there still wasn't enough money to pay him. Phil shrugged his shoulders and continued to show up every night. The audiences loved his songs, particularly the one about the AMA:

> *Hooray for the AMA*
> *And for us doctors let's have higher pay*
> *If you can't afford my bill*
> *Don't you tell me that you're ill*
> *Because that's the free enterprise way!*

It didn't matter that his voice often cracked. It didn't bother anybody that the songs all seemed to sound the same. There was something about the boy with the brown hair pushed back to a Presley pomp, the way he rocked slowly from side to side when he sang, curling his lip as he tossed his head.

And who ever heard of singing a song about a Texas millionaire accused of price-fixing?

Gertrude asked if he was making any money. He said no. It didn't matter, though, they would pay him when they could. He loved what he was doing, and didn't mind singing for nothing. "Which is what you're doing it for, Philip."

He grinned.

Crisis time at Faragher's "Rising Moon Room." The electricity turned off. Drinks served by candlelight, acts singing very loudly. Danny Dalton needed a lot of money, and soon. In a last, desperate attempt, he called the producers of the Mike Douglas Show, then an afternoon local talk show originating from Cleveland, and asked to speak with Tom Smothers. The Smothers Brothers were in town to appear on the Douglas TV'er. Danny and Tom were friends from the old days in San Francisco. Danny explained the situation, and the Smothers Brothers agreed to play his club on the weekend, as a favor.

Saturday night Faragher's was jammed for the first time. Extra tables had to be set up, standing room was sold out. Danny wanted to frame the fire department summons he received for exceeding the legal number of occupants in the "Rising Moon Room." He appeared the next day before the judge, who found Danny guilty and sentenced him to give a private concert in his chambers. Everything was "Mayberry RFD" until Phil sang "Billie Sol." The judge listened, unsmiling, his fingers at his lips. He immediately had the chambers cleared. Danny made sure no other laws were violated that summer.

With the money from the Smothers Brothers shows, Danny was able to get the lights turned back on, the phone bill paid, and back salary checks issued to his crew. He gave Phil a twenty-five-dollar bonus and a fifty-dollar-a-week salary.

The Smothers Brothers weekend proved to Danny that the only way to keep Faragher's going was to bring in name acts. For the remaining seven weeks of the summer season he brought folk-circuit headliners to Cleveland Heights—among them Judy Henske, The Stu Ramsey Trio, The Greenbriar Boys, The New Wine Folk Singers. Every night, Phil would open the show by doing two songs and introducing the featured performers. He would then take a seat at the side of the stage, put his glasses on, and study how the singers set up a song and built a rapport with the audience.

All the performers liked Phil. They'd pat him on the back, say "good show" instead of "goodnight," and wish him luck when they moved on, telling him to "stick with it" and "keep singing." Bob Gibson, the Chicago-based folk singer, came to play a week in July, and took a special interest in Phil. He listened closely to the youngster's songs, and, after the opening-night early show, offered to buy Phil a drink.

Gibson's career had begun in controversy. He'd been a member at one time of American Youth for Democracy, an organization sympathetic to the anti-Franco forces during the Spanish Civil War. Eventually, HUAC began an investigation into members of that organization. Gibson was questioned about his political affiliations. Although he was not cited for contempt, as Pete Seeger was later on, Gibson's career was efficiently damaged. He was denied appearances on the radio and television networks. His recordings received no air-play. Gibson earned his living playing small clubs, traveling the circuit, singing mostly nonpolitical material.

He'd seen it all during his years battling to survive. When he heard Phil do "Billie Sol," it was almost like watching a replay of his own younger days. "It was his innocence," recalled Gibson years later. "It made the song even more powerful, working against what he was saying. You know, he was a nice kid, wholesome."

Over a beer, Gibson told Phil he really liked his songs. "Be careful, though. When you do political material, it doesn't always matter if the song is really good or not. If the audience agrees with you, they'll love it. You can become impressed with yourself easily, and fall into a groove lasting as long as there's an issue to sing about." Phil said nothing. "Of course, the other side of it is that you make enemies. Those who don't agree with you might want to silence you, so no one else can hear what you have to say." Gibson sighed, leaned back on the two rear legs of his chair and began getting easier. He picked up his guitar and played a lick for Phil. Gibson was full of melodies. Not three-chord folkie strums, but sophisticated, jazzy syncopations. When he finished he smiled at Phil, who got up and left without saying a word.

"Mr. Gibson, can I see you a minute?" The second show had ended. The chairs were stacked on the tables, the floor had already been swept. Gibson was tired and wanted to get to his hotel, but he didn't want to refuse the boy.

"Sure. Let's have a drink." They sat at the edge of the stage.

"Five minutes to closing, Phil," Danny called out, playing his own melody on the cash register. Phil reached for his guitar. He played the Gibson tune, the one he'd heard a few hours earlier, during the lecture. He'd written some words for it, called it "One More Parade":

> *Hup, two, three, four*
> *Marching down the street*
> *To the rolling of the guns*
> *And the trampling of the feet*
> *While the general salutes*
> *While the widows stand and weep*
> *Here comes the Big Parade*
> *Don't be afraid*
> *Price is paid*
> *So start the parade.*

He'd caught a lyric all right. His words expressed a sense of ordered irrationality. He was a writer, Gibson thought to himself. So start the parade.

He approaches the mike, strumming his guitar. He wears pre-cuffed chinos, cowboy boots, a black garrison belt with a brass buckle, a freshly ironed white shirt. His hair is thick and pushed back like Elvis', pulled down around the temples to simulate the sideburns his tender skin can't grow. He never looks directly at the audience. His voice is high-pitched, suede. His sentences don't end, they fade. "Hi, I'm Phil Ochs . . . I'd like to do a medley of my smash flops . . ." His voice cracks; it doesn't matter. His guitar is out of tune; they don't notice. He finishes his set; they applaud. He gives; they take. He is the performer. His life begins in spotlight and ends in memory. He is the minstrel of their souls.

He was a celebrity on campus that fall, invited to lots of parties and always asked to sing. He dated for the first time. Girls asked him to take them for a drink, or a slice of pizza. He was extremely shy around them. There was one he really liked, a toothy blond beauty from Indiana. She lost interest when he insisted that she go around with him all the time, even to sit silently nearby while he wrote. They split up over how to spend a Friday night. She wanted to go to a party; he wanted to go to the movies.

He never spoke to her again.

He was sure he was the next Editor-in-Chief of *The Lantern*.
He was pulling straight "A's" now, and continued to demonstrate
his abilities as a journalist. He was assigned to cover a Roger
Williams concert for the school paper. After interviewing the popular musician, he wrote a lengthy profile, which began:

WILLIAMS RISKED HIS HANDS AS PARTNER FOR JOHANSSON
by Phil Ochs

> One of Ingemar Johansson's sparring partners during the
> Patterson fight series was an amateur pugilist named Roger Wil-
> liams, whose hands have made him the best-selling instrumentalist
> of all time . . .
> When asked about the danger to his uninsured hands, Williams
> shrugs, and with his ever-present grin he says, "Hands were made
> to use in many ways, so why limit them?"

Even as the Williams piece appeared in *The Lantern, The Word*
was headlining a story about Fidel Castro, proclaiming him "perhaps the greatest figure the Western Hemisphere has produced in
the last century."

Phil picked up a regular weekend gig playing at Larry's, a small
club in Cleveland Heights near Faragher's. At Thanksgiving, Jim
came home to visit his parents and called the other "Sundowner."
Phil was glad to hear from him, the summer blowout no longer an
issue. They hung around campus all afternoon, Phil telling Jim
about Faragher's, Jim telling Phil about New York. Phil invited
Jim to sing with him at Larry's that night. "What should I wear?"
Jim asked, and they both laughed.

Jim remembered all the arrangements. They each did a solo,
and then their version of "Oh, Mary, Don't You Weep." The applause made Jim laugh. Phil, unsmiling, nodded slowly to the audience.

The editorial board passed over Phil and chose someone else to
run *The Lantern*. He was told his political views were "too controversial." If he were in charge, college funds might be withheld,
the paper might have to stop publishing.

Those bastards! That night, Phil went to a meeting of the journalism fraternity. He listened to the same people who'd punished him because of his views canting about the importance of the First Amendment. He left the meeting and went to his room to pack. He left his door open as he walked along the hall, down the back steps to the street and home. Didn't matter, he had only one more term to go for his degree. Didn't matter, he was going to New York. He was sure Jim would put him up for a couple of nights until "The Sundowners" were rolling. Gertrude pleaded with him to return to school. "Not this time, Ma. Not this time. I'll call you when I get to New York."

He was on the next bus heading East.

IV

When the troubles of the world
Rest upon your weary shoulder,
When the wind that blows upon your face
Is blowin' colder,
And every hour's tellin' you
You're growin' older,
No you can't get stoned enough
Phil Ochs, "You Can't Get Stoned Enough"

1962. Anyone with a pocketful of tunes, a guitar, and the guts to get up on stage was singing folk music, and Greenwich Village was the place they came to do it. The world seemed to revolve around Bleecker and MacDougal, just south of Washington Square Park, where Ginsberg, Orlovsky, and Corso had proclaimed an end to prosaic existence, the beginning of the poetic life.

The young people doing Kingston Trio songs knew little, if anything, about the political controversies which had evolved during the thirties, forties, and fifties, when folk songs were defined as "music as a weapon." The songs of Guthrie, Seeger, and The Almanac Singers were components of a political movement aimed at organizing and strengthening the workers and, by extension, the Left.

Hardly anyone just starting out was aware of the seemingly never-ending Congressional investigations, the in-battles between Oscar Brand and Irwin Silber, the controversial People's Song Inc., and the People's Artists Inc.

The leotard women with high, toneless voices, singing their humorless songs of deathy sadness, the untidy boys with wool sweaters and three-chord songs who gravitated to the Village weren't folk singers at all. They really wanted to be pop stars. Most, like Phil, had their musical roots in country and western or rock and roll. The new "folk music" was unappealing and monotonous, yet somehow it began to attract the record-buying public. By 1962, every major record label was coming regularly to the Village coffeehouses to search for new acts. Folk music, politically inappropriate only a few years earlier, was fast becoming the hottest form of music in the country, and all because 1959 had been such a lousy year for rock and roll.

Elvis had been shorn by Uncle Sam. Buddy Holly, Richie Valens, and the Big Bopper took a dive and came up dead. Alan Freed and Dick Clark were brought before the House Legislative Oversight Subcommittee investigating illegal activities in broadcasting. "Payola" was lumped with the quiz show pay-offs by the press. Rock and roll itself was on trial, accused of being as corrupt as Charles Van Doren.

The fifties, still a bit dizzy from its McCarthy postwar paranoia, offered an interesting political construct. What the HUAC investigations and blacklisting proved was that the American Government responded to sociological rather than political pressure. Juvenile delinquency was the result of the teenage idolization of three heroes—Marlon Brando as "The Wild One," James Dean as the "Rebel Without a Cause," and Elvis Presley as Elvis Presley. Brando, handed an Oscar for *On the Waterfront,* began swimming in the mainstream. James Dean was erased while driving his Porsche, and Presley was drafted. Black leather jackets, Impalas, pompadours, and rock and roll remained. The "silent" generation was screaming to a two-beat.

Rock and roll gave the fifties the 45-rpm "single," a modern version of sheet music. The seven-inch disc with the godzilla hole in the middle became a staple of the "majors," the few labels that handled most of the industry's product. The American Society of Composers, Authors and Publishers (ASCAP), a guild operation, was responsible for tracking royalty payments, air-play, sheet music sales, and cover recordings. During the forties, ASCAP battled radio stations over the issue of payment for air-play to the writer as well as the performer of recorded music. ASCAP insisted that every time a record was played on the radio the writer and performer were entitled to collect royalties, since the music was used to attract advertising revenue. The radio stations were afraid the royalty policy would eat up their profits. Their only alternative was to play records not controlled by ASCAP. A maverick organization was formed. Heavily supported by the radio stations, Broadcast Music Incorporated (BMI) began signing artists not already in ASCAP's camp. BMI paid its royalties faster, and signed many short-term artists, whereas ASCAP was more interested in long-term agreements. Available were mostly small, independent labels, which at the time recorded mostly "Negro music," previously ignored by the majors, and never played on general (i.e. white) radio. BMI, representing less powerful labels, recognized that it was better to negotiate for smaller royalties if it meant gaining access for its artists to the airwaves previously unavailable to them. Rhythm and blues, a major form of "Negro music," had only been played on stations catering to "colored" listeners.

Even into the fifties, only two black recording artists received broad radio air-play—Nat "King" Cole early in the decade, Johnny Mathis later on. Both of these artists sang Anglo ballads, with no trace of the hard rhythm and blues sound. Other performers, like Harry Belafonte, affected "nativity." Belafonte was responsible for introducing calypso, a benign form of island music which enjoyed a brief popularity: "Day-O," "Jamaica Farewell," "Matilda."

Rock and roll was BMI's creation, born out of the growing assimilation of BMI product into general radio programing. Southern rhythm and blues became popular through the music of Chuck Berry, Bo Diddley, Fats Domino, Clyde McPhatter, and others. When Alan Freed, a Cleveland disc jockey, began playing "colored" music on his "Moondog" show, the response was electric. White teenagers who'd only heard the Crew-Cuts (ASCAP) version of "Sh-Boom" were suddenly offered the original, superior Chords (BMI) version. La Verne Baker's "Tweedlee Dee" sold competitively with Georgia Gibbs's cover version. Groups sprang up with names reflecting ethnic ghetto values: The El Dorados,

The Medallions, The Imperials, "bird" names like The Crows and The Penguins, derivative acknowledgments to the music of Charlie Parker.

Frankie Lymon and The Teenagers wore white turtleneck sweaters. They looked like any other teenagers—they could be going to school down the block. The strong undercurrent in the lyrics of their hits disturbed white parents, as it thrilled their kids:

> *Come on, take me by the hand*
> *Tell me I'm your lover man*
> *You for me, me for you*
> *We'll have fun, yes we will*
> *Ooh, ooo, ooo, ooo*
> *I love you baby*
> *And I want you to be my girl.*

Groups like The Students and The Five Satins were becoming more popular than The Four Lads and The Ames Brothers. BMI artists who were able to survive on their tiny candy-store labels were becoming rich. ASCAP artists and, by extension, Tin Pan Alley, that strip of buildings on Broadway where every office had a piano, where songs were sold like dresses on Seventh Avenue, were being financially undercut. By recognizing the social outrage that "Negro music" was producing among the white middle class, established recording-industry executives were able to effectively lobby Congress to begin investigations into "payola," resulting in what would be a political solution to a sociological problem. The paranoia of the fifties struck again as a justification for governmental suppression within the entertainment industry. The payola investigations were different from the earlier HUAC investigations. The "Hollywood Ten" were martyrs; Alan Freed was a criminal.

Governmental action was strong, fierce, and extremely popular. Rumors spread that Alan Freed was really Jewish (he was half-Jewish) and, worse, a nigger (he was white). If Brando, Dean, and Presley turned teenagers on to juvenile delinquency, national exposure of "Negro music" suggested total integration, and not just of middle-class music, but middle-class life. Something had to be done.

Freed was convicted in 1960 of receiving bribes to play certain records. This was an incredibly naive interpretation of the business of radio, where a sponsor can just as easily and legally keep any controversial song or performer off the air by simply canceling advertising, exactly the way Nat King Cole was handled on network TV. His highly rated show was canceled for lack of a major commercial sponsor. Alan Freed was off radio, and his TV show, "The Big Beat," had a new host, Richard Hayes, a white singer from the New Jersey dinner-club circuit, very un-rock and roll.

The careers of the "Negro" rock stars were finished. Stations removed their records from air-play, fearing reprisals. Where there's dark smoke, there must be payola. Frankie Lymon and The Teenagers grew up. Lymon died broke at the age of twenty-seven from a hot shot in a Harlem bathroom. Little Anthony and The Imperials became a Vegas lounge act singing show music. The originators of "New York Doo-wop" went on to careers as garage mechanics, waiters, or junkies. Chuck Berry got five to twenty for statutory rape.

It was over. By the end of 1960, there were no major active black acts left in rock and roll. The natural, artistic progression of rock music had been aborted. Interestingly, Dick Clark survived the investigations and was absolved, even though his involvements seemed much more sophisticated than Freed's had been. Clark had financial interests in record companies which recorded the likes of Frankie Avalon, Dion and The Belmonts, Fabian, and Annette, all regular guests on his TV shows. But Clark was white, urban, clean-cut, and so was the music he played. Frankie Avalon sang about "Venus," and the mothers and fathers of white America sighed in relief.

A trio of white college kids with short hair, guitars, and banjos came along, filling the desperate need for new product in the industry. The Kingston Trio released "Tom Dooley" and became an overnight sensation. They were white, did mostly ASCAP-controlled material, and recorded for Capitol Records, one of the majors. They were so celebrated they played on college campuses, something no other popular recording artists had ever done before.

With the aid of the American Government and its structured annihilation of black rock and roll, the "folk-boom," as *Time* magazine called it in 1962, had arrived. Folk music was at the head of the industry, its records at the top of the charts—even though it had no established stars and, seemingly, nowhere to go.

William Gerde was eighty-two years old when he decided to sell the family restaurant. He offered good food, warm cream ale, a place Greenwich Village families could come to for a traditional Sunday European dinner. Mercer at Third belonged to William Gerde.

Mike Porco, a diminutive Italian cook from the Bronx, was looking to buy a place of his own after working for many years in other people's restaurants. "Gerde's" seemed the perfect choice. In the spring of 1957, Mike Porco bought the restaurant, promising to continue the tradition of good, wholesome family dining. By 1959 Mike was doing so well he was thinking of adding a second dining room.

The first warm breeze of spring brought the announcement by the City of New York that a nine-square-block area of Greenwich Village, from Third Street to Houston, from Mercer to La Guardia, had been condemned. It was seen as no less than peacetime ethnocide by the Italian and German residents, and spelled financial ruin for the neighborhood merchants. The store owners formed a group and obtained legal counsel. After a long, bitter, and confusing fight in the city's courts, it looked as though the people had won their battle. The condemnation order was thrown out. Relative calm was restored in the community, only to be shattered once again six months later. The city machinery moved quietly, political oil keeping the parts from squeaking. New York obtained a higher-court reversal—the condemnation order became law.

Curiously, it was later discovered, the city paid seven dollars a square foot for the condemned property and sold it at fifteen dollars per to New York University. By then, it was too late to stop the derricks that bit into the generations of Greenwich Village homes and destroyed the century-old neighborhood. The families were relocated, dissipated throughout the five boroughs. For Mike Porco, it meant the end of Gerde's clientele.

He reopened on the perimeter of the war zone, hoping to survive with the business of those families relocated still close enough to bring the family in for that home-cooked meal. He moved to Fourth Street, where today The Bottom Line stands, and borrowed eighty thousand dollars to renovate the new location, attempting to recreate the ambiance of the old Gerde's. Soon, he was letting much of his help go.

One afternoon as the aroma of sour cabbage hung lazy in the paneled rooms of Gerde's, Porco flashed. The place needed livening up, something to attract new customers. Some musicians, maybe a combo. He hired a jazz piano and guitar. Unfortunately, the musicians didn't produce enough revenue to offset their extra expense. In desperation, he hired a trio for Saturday night. Still nothing.

He stood behind the dark oak bar rubbing a cloth in a slow spiral, wiping away rings that weren't there, staring into the face of failure. He hardly bothered to look up as the two young men came in.

They ordered a couple of brews. Mike drew them off the tap, put them in front of the two, and a hand came across. Mike shook it slowly.

"Hi, Mike. I'm Izzy Young. This is Tom Prendergast. We're proprietors of The Folk Center."

Their names meant nothing to Porco. Izzy smiled and asked if Mike would be interested in having folk music at Gerde's. Porco shrugged his shoulders. Izzy asked if Mike had a cabaret license. "Sure, I got a license. Otherwise, how'm I gonna have the piano player here on the weekend? To tell you the truth, I never heard of folk music."

"Ever hear of Pete Seeger?" asked Izzy.

"Yeah."

"Well, Pete Seeger is a folk singer. Ever hear of Burl Ives?"

"Look," Mike said, as he waved the two men closer, even though they were alone in the room. "I'll tell you something. The combo I got, I don't like the crowd it brings in. The cops are all the time lookin' for, you know, marijuana. Everyone is smoking. I thought it was a special tobacco. The cops warned me I could lose my license . . ."

Izzy and Tom reassured Mike that folk music appealed to college kids. With NYU so close, Mike should be able to pay his rent for a year on the sale of beer alone. Izzy suggested that Mike keep the bar and let the gate belong to the musicians.

Porco agreed to give it a shot. He didn't know who these two men were, but it didn't matter very much at this point. He'd try anything to save Gerde's. He'd even change the name of the place to "The Fifth Peg," a name Izzy suggested. For the next five weeks he booked only folk acts. At first, there was a slight surge in business, but the partnership proved to be a brief one when Izzy and Tom asked Mike for a larger piece of the action. Not being able to come to terms, they decided to pull out. Mike changed the name of the club back to Gerde's. Izzy asked Mike not to continue booking folk acts. Porco resisted, telling Izzy, "I'm sorry, but this is my club, and nobody can tell me what type of entertainment to book. You got the right to do whatever you want. So do I."

Mike kept folk acts at Gerde's. Monday was "talent nite." The other clubs were traditionally dark and Gerde's was the only place to hear live music. After a few weeks the uptown journalists started drifting in, seeking a story for the Tuesday editions. Bob Shelton, a music critic for the New York *Times,* became friendly with Porco. They'd sit at the bar, comparing notes on performers, talking about who was booked into what club. Shelton introduced Mike to Paul Rothchild, a Village regular friendly with all the folk singers. It was Rothchild who suggested to Porco that "talent nite" didn't really describe Mondays at Gerde's. He suggested calling it "Hootenanny."

"How do you spell it?" Mike asked, as he took a fat pencil with no eraser and wrote on the back of a paper bag. The next day he called the newspapers to place ads for the following Monday's HOOTENANNY AT GERDE'S FOLK CITY.

Few people showed up. Weeks went by with the club barely making enough to survive. Gradually, though, the word spread about Mondays. One night, fifteen people showed up; the next week, fifty. Soon there were hundreds, then five hundred at a time. Beer fifty cents a bottle, admission free. Mike put two emcees to work: Brother John Sellers and Gil Turner. Their job was to send the crowds back to the bar for more beer between acts.

Other club owners, including Fred Weintraub from The Bitter End and Clarence Hood from The Gaslight, came to Mike and asked how he'd feel if they started hoots on other week nights. Porco remained consistent with what he'd told Izzy Young and Tom Prendergast. They all owned clubs: they could do what they wanted. Mike assured them any club that did business in the Village was good for everybody. Soon, every club in the Village had a hoot. By the end of 1962, hootenannies were a national phenomenon, conveniently dovetailing with The Kingston Trio's elliptical string of "folk" hits.

Early '61. Porco is tapping a keg in the basement. He hears a burst of applause, then cheers. He goes upstairs to see who. Nods to himself as he heads for the bar, the customers five and six deep. Takes his book out, puts a mark next to "Dylan." He gets a paying gig. Next comes Peter Yarrow. He sings two songs, asks the audience if they mind his bringing up two friends. The Folk City microphone is umbilical. "Let's have a round of applause for Peter, Paul and Mary."

Jean Ray moved to New York from California in 1960 because she wanted to be a Broadway actress. She enrolled at the American Academy of Dramatic Arts on Twenty-third Street, where Sanford Meisner taught. To pay for her schooling she looked for waitress work in Greenwich Village, where all the coffeehouses were. She made the rounds. The Cafe Rafeo's manager told her he didn't need any more waitresses, but there was a spot open for a singer. She jumped on it and got an audition which led to a pass-the-hat. She sang a little Baez and some Pete Seeger at the request of the management, but mostly did Ella Fitzgerald and Joni James.

A short time later, a tall, lanky fellow from Ohio walked into the club carrying his banjo, looking for a gig. He was hired because he could sing any song Pete Seeger had ever written. A week after he started, they became "Jim and Jean." For Jim, she was the perfect resolution of "The Sundowners." Jean's voice was strong, flexible. Jim could dive under her high notes and swim around her mid-range like he'd done with Phil. They developed an intense following at the little club just off Sixth Avenue on Third Street.

Neither of them noticed him at the bar sipping a glass of house white, unsmiling, watching them as they did a familiar version of "Oh, Mary, Don't You Weep." Phil Ochs had arrived in New York.

When their set was finished, Jim and Jean went to the bar for a drink. Jim threw his arms around Phil, telling him how happy he was to see him. Jean waited patiently for Jim to introduce his friend. Finally, she introduced herself.

Jean had an apartment on Thompson Street which Jim had moved into with her. It was small for one person, crowded for two. When Jim found out Phil had no place to stay, he insisted there was enough room for everybody in the apartment. Jean thought it would be for a day or two, not for the several weeks it became. Jim and Phil became inseparable again, as they'd been at Ohio State. Jean was threatened by Phil's presence. It had taken weeks for Jim to kiss her the first time; now they were never alone. Phil became, in a sense, her rival. She feared she was going to lose Jim. She didn't know how to deal with Jim's idolization of his friend. Wasn't he this? Wasn't he that? Didn't he this? She wanted Jim to tell Phil "The Sundowners" were over, it was now "Jim and Jean." Jim told Phil fifty times before he heard. They cared, even liked each other, but there were jealousies. Two of the three went on stage; two of the three hung out till dawn drinking coffee and wine, discussing politics.

Jim saw himself as a proletarian singer, a voice in a collective crowd of workers. Phil talked about stardom. The effects on each other were positive, Jim becoming more aware of the stage, Phil even more interested in politics. To Jean, both seemed extreme. She simply liked the way a song sounded. One day, while Jim was out, she asked Phil what he thought of her singing. He shrugged his shoulders, looked away from her eyes and told her she was too show-biz-baby. Music had to be relevant. "That's when I came legitimately to folk music," recalled Jean years later. "Just to hold my place in the duet. Young people in the sixties who had any touch on the pulse of folk music couldn't be satisfied with going and doing all the external movements of selling a song like pop singers do, with hand movements and all. It became taboo to do that. You were just to stand up straight and deliver your message. No frills. No fancy phony stuff."

Phil wrote songs for Jim and Jean, which they incorporated into their act. Phil would come to Rafeo's at night and watch them perform, while he sipped white wine at his table and made notes.

At Thompson Street, newspapers piled up, laundry wove around the floors, empty beer cans and cereal boxes decorated the kitchen table. Roaches were everywhere. The boys sat, oblivious to the mess, fantasizing about their careers. For Jean it was becoming intolerable. She was reduced to being the house mother while her fear of losing Jim to Phil grew stronger. Something had to be done.

Jean went to acting school with Alice Skinner, a young girl from a wealthy Philadelphia background also intent upon having a Broadway career. Jean got Alice a job as a waitress at Rafeo's, and one night she introduced her to Phil, hoping they would hit it off. Phil, still very shy around women, ignored Alice, who would wait on his table evenings at the club.

Jim started writing notes to Phil during shows, using Alice as the messenger. She would drop a note off at Phil's table and pick up his note to Jim on the return trip.

From Jim to Phil:

> Upon the authority of the United States Senate, you are hereby summoned to appear before the House Un-American Activities Committee for questioning concerning your Communistic activities in the field of folk song. Sincerely,
>
> > John Hancock
> > Tom Paine
> > John Birch

From Phil to Jim:

> In reply to your correspondence of 14 August '62 I now reply.
> I am not now nor (triple negative) have I ever been a folk singer.
> It's not true that my songs are Communistic.
> As proof I offer my newest song—
> > Roses are red
> > Violets are blue
> > What can I say
> > Workers of the world Unite!

Just because it was written to the tune of "Moscow Nights" doesn't prove anything, comrade. New song:

Two astronauts on their way
Repeat above line
Repeat line above above line
They went together
They must be gay
—Stay real

Neno Funk (AR*)
*Astronaut Reject

Alice was attracted to Phil. He was very funny, always cracking jokes when he was with Jim and Jean. He was around every night, and even started saying hello to her, once in a while taking her for a drink after she got off work.

Jean heard that an apartment below hers on Thompson Street was available and made sure Alice got it. Jean wanted Alice to take Phil off her hands. If Phil stayed in her apartment any longer, she told Alice, it would mean the end of "Jim and Jean." She loved Jim, she wanted to marry him, and Phil, although a great guy, was screwing everything up. Alice solemnly promised she would do anything she could to help. Sure, it would be all right for Phil to stay with her.

Dear Jim and Jean,
   Thank you a lot for letting me stay here and mess up your house. See ya soon.

P. Ochs

For Phil, courtship was unfathomable. For Alice, eighteen, Philadelphia blueblood and Irish Catholic, coming to Phil was out of the question. So she slept in her bed, and Phil took the sofa. He would make an attempt to be with her, she would politely resist. He would throw his red jacket on, go for long walks, come back and lock himself in the bathroom. After an hour, Alice would bang on the door and ask him what he was doing in there.

"Writing songs."

Now that Phil was with her, Jean saw less of Alice than before. It was Jim and Jean again, and nothing was going to interfere this time.

Alice became friendly with another waitress at Rafeo's, Betsy Dotson. Betsy, like Alice and Jean, had come to New York, but not to pursue the life of an actress. Going to work for her was partying, a great social life. Waiting on tables was like having people over for drinks, only with tips. Between filling the salt and pepper shakers and cleaning the ketchup bottle caps, Alice reported to Betsy on her sexual progress with Phil. Which was still nothing. Betsy shook her head, a wrinkled lip on her face. She had little use for Phil, didn't understand what Alice saw in him. He was a slob, unkempt, uncool, tense. She would criticize him, put him down in front of Alice. "For Christ's sake, tuck your shirt in. Your belly button's hanging out." He'd never get angry with her. Instead, he would grin, and while making a feeble attempt to tuck in a shirttail somewhere, he would shoot back a lyric, and ask Betsy what she thought of it. Betsy knew a lot of musicians. To ask an opinion of a woman was a big thing, and although she hated to admit it, she was happy that Phil asked for hers. At the same time, she wondered why he would make himself so vulnerable. "What do you think, huh? What do you think?" If the response were positive, he would question it, push until it became negative. Then, of course, he would love defending his material.

Betsy told Alice the only way she was ever going to get any results with Phil was to take matters into her own hands. The next day, Phil, as usual, was sitting at the kitchen table turning out songs like shopping lists. Alice sighed, took him by the hand, led him into her bedroom, and brought him home for the first time.

Gertrude was happy the family was coming back to Far Rockaway that summer. With Sonny gone, Phil living in New York, Michael away at school, and Jack at the hospital, Cleveland was a very lonely place. Now, with Michael and Phil nearby, it would be better. Michael had heard all about Phil's days in the Village and was eager to meet the folk singers.

When Phil and Alice heard Gertrude was coming to New York, they tried to get their apartment into some kind of shape. The place reeked of cat urine. The bathtub was in the kitchen. Phil bought a shower hookup. He brought it back to the apartment and laid it out in front of the tub, where it remained until the day they moved.

When Gertrude and Michael arrived, Phil took the subway out to Far Rockaway to see them. The first thing Gertrude asked when she saw him was why he hadn't yet gotten rid of that red jacket. She took Phil back to the Village to buy him some new clothes. They went to Paul Sargeant's on Fourth Street, the only store Phil knew that didn't sell used clothes. Neither of them had any idea what to buy. Gertrude picked out a few shirts and a couple of pairs of jeans, and then insisted Phil buy a sport jacket. Without looking or caring, Phil picked one off the rack, a tweed three-button jacket with a belt in the back. He tried it on and asked Gertrude how he looked. She threw up her hands: she had no idea. There were a couple of young men down the aisle picking out clothes. She walked over to them and asked if she could disturb them for just a moment.

"Do you think that jacket looks good on my son?" They said it looked all right. She bought it.

Later that day, Phil introduced Gertrude to Alice. He never really spelled it out, but Gertrude knew they were living together. She had to hold back her disbelief when she waded through what seemed a century of the New York *Times* on the floor to get to the faded sofa in the "living room," as it was called by Alice. Gertrude refused anything to drink. As the evening approached, Phil asked his mother if she'd like to see him perform. Of course she would. He took Gertrude to the corner of Bleecker and Mac-Dougal, where he opened his guitar case and sang. Gertrude dropped coins into the case whenever a crowd built up. At the end of the night, Phil put the coins in his pocket and jangled back to the apartment. Gertrude offered to cash in the coins for paper. Over the kitchen table Phil carefully counted out his money and slid it toward Gertrude. He wants to be an entertainer, Gertrude thought to herself.

In July, Phil got into his first Folk City Hootenanny. Porco had been getting fifty to sixty acts showing for the hoots. He'd devised a system of having each act draw a numbered card from a bag. Usually the first twenty numbers got to perform. Higher draws could stick it out if they wanted, but most didn't bother to hang around. Phil had been trying for a couple of weeks and drawing high. Now he was number three. He got up on the stage, strumming, getting quickly into his songs. The room hushed as people began listening to his words. Porco made a little mark next to Phil's name in the big book.

Also in the audience was Jerry White, a friend of Mike's. White was the program director of WNJR of New Jersey, and had the only regular folk music show heard in New York City. White was involved with the Palisades Amusement Park Sunday Band-shell Concerts hosted by Hal Jackson. Jerry caught Phil as he came off the stage and asked if he'd be interested in playing Palisades the next Sunday. No pay but good exposure. Phil was stunned, and accepted the offer. That weekend Mike Porco, at Jerry White's invitation, drove out to Palisades to see Phil sing, mostly Faron Young, a little Johnny Cash. After the show, Mike drove Jerry White, Phil, and Mrs. Porco back to Long Island for a Sunday dinner. Phil sat silently in the back of the big Buick while Mike and Jerry talked about the show. The first time Phil spoke since that afternoon was when Mike asked if he would like to open for John Hammond sometime during the winter. Phil broke into a grin and shook Mike's hand, thanking him over and over for giving him his first paying job. Mike drove him back to the Village, where Phil promptly went to The Gaslight to celebrate by getting drunk on cheap wine. He called Alice. There was no answer. Phil didn't like that. It was Alice's job to sit by the phone in case he got offers for work. Where was she?

"Across the street in the Cafe Wha, having a drink with David Cohen," Betsy said, putting a bottle of beer to her lips. This is the end of my life, thought Phil. Staggering now, he got up and stumbled his way out the door. "Alice," he cried at the top of his lungs, "Alice, I love you . . ." He wound up in the gutter, on his knees, his arms stretched toward the sky, wailing her name over and over, convinced he would never have her again.

Alice was having a drink with David Cohen, telling him about Phil. Cohen, an unemployed actor, was toying with the idea of singing to pay the rent. He'd never heard of Phil, but was very much into Dylan, and was telling Alice all about him when they both heard her name being screamed by Phil outside the club. She excused herself, telling Cohen she thought Phil was calling her.

Several months later, Porco made good his promise. On Friday night, March 15, 1963, Phil Ochs opened for John Hammond at Gerde's Folk City. For the occasion, Phil announced to the opening-night audience he'd written a new song. "The Power and the

Glory," taken from the title of a Graham Greene novel he'd seen while browsing through a Village bookstore. As soon as he saw it, he knew it would be a great title for a song. He acknowledged the melodic influence of his friend and mentor Bob Gibson, who was in the audience.

> *C'mon and take a walk with me through this green and*
> *growin' land,*
> *Walk through the meadows and the mountains and the sand,*
> *Walk through the valleys and the rivers and the plains,*
> *Walk through the sun and walk through the rain*
>   *Here's a land full of power and glory*
>   *Beauty that words cannot recall*
>   *Oh her power shall rest on the strength of her freedom,*
>   *Her glory shall rest on us all.*
> *Yet she's only as rich as the poorest of the poor,*
> *Only as free as a padlocked prison door,*
> *Only as strong as our love for this land,*
> *Only as tall as we stand . . .*

The Guthriesque celebration of the land brought the Folk City crowd to its feet, hollering and stomping its approval. Phil backed away from the mike, turned sideways, looked down and strummed under the thunder.

The emcee at Phil's debut was Gil Turner. He invited Phil to come to the next meeting of *Broadside* magazine. Pete Seeger had first suggested the idea for a new magazine after he'd returned from touring England late in 1961. While there, he'd been surprised at the proliferation of political folk music, at the number of songs being written demanding an end to atom bombs, political corruption, and governmental oppression of the people. Seeger had been through a lot during the forties and fifties, including a conviction on conspiracy charges that nearly resulted in a jail sentence before the decision was reversed. The Seeger case had received little coverage in the media, overshadowed by Hollywood's troubles with HUAC. The only publication which covered Seeger's trial in depth was Irwin Silber's *Sing Out*. Silber, an avowed Communist, had covered the proceedings somewhat hysterically. Later, it was felt by many that he'd added greatly to the fracturing of the Left, especially after he'd printed an attack against Oscar Brand, another HUAC subject, for his refusal to comment upon the Com-

mittee's tactics. HUAC had wanted Brand to testify, and he'd refused. Silber then wanted Brand to attack HUAC in *Sing Out,* and
again Brand refused, stating that Silber was acting as a left-wing
HUAC. Brand didn't want to be forced to say anything he didn't
want to say. As a result, Silber suggested in *Sing Out* that Brand
was sympathetic to the actions of HUAC, that perhaps he'd secretly testified.

Seeger and others were dissatisfied with Silber's magazine. Many
times they had talked about forming their own publication. Finally, Seeger approached Sis Cunningham, one of the original Almanac Singers, and her husband, Gordon Friesen, about the possibility of starting a new magazine, one that would be devoted to the
"new music," topical songs like those Seeger had heard in England.

The first issue of *Broadside* was mimeographed in Sis's apartment in February 1962. It stated: *"Broadside* may never publish a
song that could be called a 'folk song.' But many of our best folk
songs were topical songs at their inception . . ." *Broadside* No. 1
carried "Talking John Birch Blues," the first publication anywhere
of a Bob Dylan song. *Broadside* No. 2 debuted the writing team of
Pete Seeger (music) and Dr. Alex Comfort (lyrics) collaborating
on a song entitled "One Man's Hands," a song about political revolution. This was years before Dr. Comfort would write about another revolution—this time sexual—in his best-selling *Joy of Sex*
volumes.

For Phil, who would join the magazine for its thirteenth issue,
September 1962, with the publication of "Billie Sol," *Broadside*
was a perfect extension of *The Word.* He became a regular con-
tributor, and eventually an editor. It was while working at the
magazine that Phil and Bob Dylan first got to know each other.

Phil was writing songs all the time. Many of them appeared in
the pages of *Broadside.* Phil would choose a subject, usually from
an article he had read in the morning paper, and write a song
around it. The chord structures were similar, a basic riff of G, Em,
C, D, in various combinations, and the lyrics journalistic: "Where
There's a Will, There's a Way," (*In the town of Bethlehem many
years ago . . .*), "Time Was" (*Time was when a man could
live alone . . .*), "Lou Marsh" (*My story is a sad one, it's*

ugly and it's harsh, about a social worker, his name was Lou Marsh), "On My Way" (*Well, sometimes I am happy, sometimes sad, Thinkin' of the good times I've had* . . .), "Talking Plane Disaster" (*Well, once I heard some people say, if you gotta travel, there's just one way* . . .), "How Long" (*How long, how long can we go on, How long, how long can we go on* . . .), "William Moore" (*Walkin' down an Alabama road, rememberin' what the Bible told, Walkin' with a letter in his hand, dreamin' of another southern land* . . .).

In a *Broadside* editorial, "The Need for Topical Music," Phil put it this way:

> Every newspaper headline is a potential song, and it is the role of an effective songwriter to pick out the material that has the interest, significance and sometimes humor adaptable to music. A good writer must be able to picture the structure of a song as hundreds of minute ideas race through his head. He must reject the superfluous and trite phrases for the cogent powerful terms. Then after the first draft is complete, the writer must be his severest critic, constantly searching for a better way to express every line in his song . . . It never ceases to amaze me how the American people allow the hit parade to hit them over the head with a parade of song after meaningless song about love. If the powers that be absolutely insist that love should control the market, at least they should be more realistic and give divorce songs an equal chance . . .

Sam Hood: "I first met Phil when he came to me and told me that he was a great songwriter and a great singer and that he wanted to play my father's club, The Gaslight, that he had been playing the coffeehouses and had developed an intense following.

"We'd heard about Phil around the Village. He was somebody who was singing and writing great protest songs. I don't know if it was because we were booked up or if he was really nervous when he auditioned for me, but I told him to try again a couple of weeks later. At the audition Phil was very, very nervous. He tried hard to be slick, but he wasn't pulling it off at all. It was weird. The Gaslight had a reputation for being the premiere showcase, but you have to see that in the context of the times. Nothing like The Bottom Line is today. It was very small and catered to the artists. We weren't involved in the music business. It was strictly

rock and roll. Which hadn't touched this area at all. It was important to perform at The Gaslight, that's where Bob Shelton of the
Times hung out a lot, either there or Gerde's or The Bitter End. It
was the place you had to perform if you wanted to go any further
with your work, to reach the public. The headliner was responsible for bringing the audience in. We developed a policy around
this time of a guarantee to be paid to the headliner, or a percent-
age of the gate, whichever was larger. The second act would be
paid not a whole lot, maybe $100 a week. Our headliners were
Van Ronk, Jack Elliott, Tom Paxton, Jose Feliciano, Buffy
Sainte-Marie, and maybe a dozen or so others that could make
money.

"Phil came back for the second audition a couple of weeks
later. He was great, just terrific. It was all enthusiasm, some really
solid writing, some really poor writing, but that could be excused
because it was politically correct. After his audition, he was sending people to see me to tell me I should book him. He was so
funny, he created this crusade."

Hood, young and tough, was able to deal effectively with the
folkies as well as with the street-tough Italian neighborhood where
The Gaslight was located. The further erosion of the Village by
outsiders brought intense pressures on the club owners from the
neighborhood. It was to the credit of people like Sam Hood, dip-
lomats as well as head-on fighters, that the Village clubs were able
not only to survive, but flourish as the new songwriters took contemporary music out of the hands of Tin Pan Alley, and, as one
club owner expressed it, "put it into the hands of the poets."

Local pressure was kept up on the clubs, trying to drive them
out. One owner was murdered in front of his club, the killers
never apprehended. Rumors were strong that he had resisted
neighborhood "protection." The Gaslight was receiving sum-
monses daily for operating without a cabaret license. Legal battles
centered around zoning laws, which had to be changed if there
was to be legitimate entertainment in the cafes. The residents were
furious over the proliferation of mixed couples who frequented the
coffeehouses. It was, after all, Greenwich Village, but it was also
New York, where neighborhoods changed each time you crossed
the street.

The club owners attempted to walk the uneasy line between

those who lived in the neighborhood and those who came down to hear the music. They tried to hold the noise down after a certain hour. There was little tolerance shown to drunks. The Gaslight was starting to draw the boisterous "uptown" crowd on weekends, a nonspending, noisy group which came to be known by the regulars as "the tourists." Seeing someone vomiting in the street was a sure way to tell it was Friday or Saturday night on MacDougal. The Gaslight put in a weekend cover charge of $3.50 (not including drinks) for the "tourists."

Recalls Van Ronk: "One night Phil was sitting across from me at The Kettle of Fish, which was upstairs from The Gaslight, and the next night I knew him fairly well. I didn't really mark his entry until I heard him perform for the first time, at The Third Side, where he was still passing the hat, following Tiny Tim and Richie Havens. For one thing, he was obviously a man of the Left, and I liked that. He was very quickly picked up by the people at *Broadside,* and I didn't much care for that. Roughly speaking, they were the direct descendants of the People's Artists and the old Communist Party cultural front. My background was anarchistic and Trotskyist. So there was no love lost. Phil saw politics essentially as white hats and black hats. That included unreconstructed Trotskyites like myself. There was no question that Phil was major, from the very outset, at least as far as everyone on the street was concerned."

Alice considered him pretty major also, if not in quite the same way. She was pregnant. When she told him, he put his hand to his forehead. It was the last thing in the world he wanted. He made Alice swear she wouldn't tell anyone, not even Jim and Jean.

She continued to work at Rafeo's. One night, after his show at The Gaslight, Phil stumbled home drunk on white wine, and as he sat at the kitchen table, the sun coming up, he made a list of Alice's assets and liabilities. On the plus side was the fact that she was wealthy, or at least from a wealthy family, which meant that if he married her she wouldn't be after the money he was sure he was going to make when he became famous. She was a good cook. She wasn't really in show business. Her liabilities were headed up by the fact that she was pregnant.

As Alice started to show, Phil became increasingly concerned.

She put no pressure on Phil to marry her, or even to stay with her once the child was born. Phil called Sonny, who had moved to Far Rockaway once her divorce was finalized. He explained his situation to her. She told him that if Alice wanted the baby, he should marry her, he owed her that. He could always get divorced, but at least the child would have his name. Since Alice was Catholic, she probably wouldn't keep the baby if she wasn't married. Phil hung up, more confused than ever. He'd take a trip, go to Florida, maybe pick up a few gigs down there, make up his mind along the way.

Later that night the phone rang.

"It's Sonny. Your father dropped dead an hour ago, Phil. Now you have one day to make up your mind, not one month. You better think fast about Alice. The family's coming to Rockaway tomorrow."

"What for?"

"The funeral."

"Do I have to come?"

"Phil, it's your *father!* Of course you have to come. What kind of shit is this? Your father is dead and you have to come to his funeral."

Phil couldn't understand why he had to go. It was almost as if he were afraid. He fell back onto the bed and thought a long time about Jack. He remembered how his father had shrugged his shoulders when Phil began to play the guitar. Jack wanted Phil to pursue a profession; music was a hobby. Phil hardly knew his father when he was alive, in death he'd be farther away. And the trip to Florida was out. Shit.

The body was flown in from Cleveland. Phil and Alice arrived in Far Rockaway early. They spent the day watching Jack being put into the earth.

In the car, on the way back to New York, Phil talked with Gertrude.

"I'm going to marry Alice, Ma."

"Why?"

"Because I have to."

"Why?"

"Because she's pregnant."

"Why?" Gertrude was numb. She was too tired to deal with this new situation. She liked Alice well enough, but she couldn't understand why Phil would go and get married if he were so interested in building a career. What was so great about marriage? And if he wanted to be married so badly, why couldn't he at least have picked a Jewish girl? She sipped her tea silently.

That night Phil went to Carnegie Hall to see the farewell performance of The Weavers.

Back in his apartment. It is late. He sits at the kitchen table alone. Tearless, he hears the melody in his head. It is his eulogy. "The Ballad of Davey Moore":

Hang his gloves upon the wall
Shine his trophies bright and clear
Another man will fall before we dry our tears
For the fighter must destroy as the poet must sing
As the hungry crowd must gather
For the blood upon the ring
The blood upon the ring.

For the father must destroy as the poet must sing. He gets up quickly, emerges into the night, walks the city trail along Thompson. It is time to sing.

They were married at City Hall by the Justice of the Peace. Jim was best man; Jean, the bridesmaid; Suze Rotolo, Bob Dylan's girlfriend, the witness. Phil and Alice were cracking up during the ceremony, unable to keep straight faces. The judge stopped in the middle of the ceremony and ordered Phil to take his hands out of his pockets. "In case you don't know, young man, this is a serious occasion."

"We know, sir," Alice shot back. "We're just nervous, that's why we're giggling."

"Did you two just meet or something?" asked the judge, who then rushed through the rest of the ritual.

They left the chambers. Mr. and Mrs. Ochs, one acorn on the way.

They moved to 178 Bleecker, a larger place with enough room for the baby and George the cat. Copies of the New York *Times* soon carpeted the floors. About this time Jim and Jean announced their engagement and accepted a national tour. There was a possibility of their signing on with Andy Williams' Good Time Singers. Jim wasn't really sure it was the direction to go for Jim and Jean, but Jean insisted they try for it.

The Bleecker Street apartment, centrally located, became a meeting place and major hangout for Village musicians. The door was always open, the traffic constant. Al Kooper, Danny Kalb, John Sebastian, Eric Andersen, Eric Jacobsen, Dave Van Ronk, Pat Sky, Joe Butler, Zal Yanovsky, and Bob Dylan. Discussions might start at The Kettle and continue back at the apartment. Songs were sung constantly. David Cohen would lie in front of the door, anyone entering or leaving had to step over him. Alice, Suze, and Betsy would talk about the coming baby and make sure there was enough wine and bread for the boys.

As June approached, Phil decided to take up an offer Eric Jacobsen had made—to open for The Knob Hill Upper Lick 10,000 in Fort Lauderdale, Florida. Jacobsen, one of the Village regulars from the earliest days of Folk City, liked Phil, thought he was a very talented songwriter, a nice young kid. His own group, The Knob Hill Upper Lick 10,000, was doing well, and he thought the exposure would be good for Phil. He enjoyed Phil's enthusiasm, especially when Phil assured him that Phil Ochs was going to be the biggest star in the world. Recalls Jacobsen: "I remember Phil telling me he was going all the way, he was going to sell a million copies of his first album, even though he didn't as yet have a record contract. I didn't want to seem negative but I took a bet on every album he made with him, for a hundred dollars an album, up through the last one. He never paid off. He always claimed they could take off at any time."

It would be his first paying gig since coming to the Village. Alice was to stay behind and sit by the phone.

In Florida, during the day while the others were sleeping or at the beach, Phil would sit in his hotel room and write. By his chair were sheets of paper filled with new lyrics. He would sit and look over his guitar to the floor, reading the words as he composed the melodies.

Meanwhile Jacobsen had discovered groupies and decided Phil needed a little recreation, time away from his guitar. Eric required one of his personal fans to bring along a friend for Phil. Late that afternoon, while all four of them were in bed (this only after the girl, with no clothes on, had poured several drinks into Phil and led him by the hand), the phone rang. Alice. Phil's girl picked up the receiver—a no-no when sober, a goof when drunk.

"Who's this?" Alice asked.

"Who the fuck is this?"

"Alice."

"Alice who?" Eric grabbed the receiver, but it was too late. Alice told Eric to expect her in a day or two. Eric uh-oh'd Phil until Alice arrived, but she never once mentioned the phone call. They went for a walk one night on the beach, and Alice told him it was okay, it was something musicians did. Phil went for a swim in the midnight ocean. When he came out of the water and sprawled out on the gray moonlit sand, he told her that he hadn't done anything, that he was having "problems." He told Alice there was something "wrong" with him, he was suffering from several "diseases." From time to time during the months that followed, Alice would try to turn him on, but he would only apologize, saying as soon as he was better he'd be great again.

After Jack's death, there was no reason for Gertrude to remain in Cleveland. She and Sonny had managed a reconciliation during the funeral and Gertrude decided to move to Far Rockaway permanently. Michael enrolled at Adelphi University on Long Island and lived with Gertrude.

It was the summer of '63. Michael spent a lot of time in the Village, where it seemed everyone knew who his brother was. He hung around with Phil after shows, upstairs at The Kettle. It was understood Michael was not to participate in any discussions, only to watch. He got the message. To be in the presence of royalty was a privilege.

He would hang out at the Bleecker Street apartment with Alice, sitting around and drinking coffee, talking about how great it was that Phil was working, even if Alice saw less of him now that he was performing all the time—at The Third Side, Gerde's, and The Gaslight. For Phil, work was the most important thing.

He would come off the stage flying, join Dylan for a few drinks, sit in for a few hands of poker and be chased quickly. The others,

knowing he didn't like to lose, would push every hand. Dylan was
the natural leader of the group; Phil was considered number two.
One night shortly after Dylan had signed with Albert Grossman,
they were sitting around at The Kettle, Phil telling Dylan he'd really
made it. "Bobby, you really are the biggest thing right now."

"Naa, nobody knows who I am." Dylan decided to test his
popularity. Blind drunk, he staggered down the stairs to the
front door of The Gaslight, leaning against the gigantic coffee urn.
Everybody who entered the club was questioned by Dylan. "Do
you know who I am?" He'd mark their answers in his notebook.
When someone would say, "Yeah, you're Bob Dylan," he would
squint his eyes and burn into theirs, sneering, "You don't know
who I am."

*It is 5 A.M. Phil and David Cohen stumble up to the Bleecker
apartment, drunk. Alice in the bedroom, sleeping. They sit around,
their heads thrown back. There is a knock on the door, Phil gets
up to open it. Dylan rushes in, hot and fresh. In the living room he
asks Phil to play something. Phil reaches for his guitar and does
"The Power and the Glory." David Cohen does a song. Then Dylan
plays, for the first time anywhere, "Mr. Tambourine Man." It slaps
Phil sober. He sits up and tells Dylan, solemnly, it is without question the greatest song he's ever heard. Alice, awakened by the
music, is standing in the hallway, smiling. Breakfast will be ready
in a few minutes.*

Newport was anticipating its most popular festival ever, even
though as recently as 1960 the folk festival had been canceled for
lack of interest. Manny Greenhill, one of the founders of the original Newport Folk Festival and the man responsible for bringing
many of the best-known traditional acts to it in the fifties, was able
to revive the annual event in 1961 as the interest in folk music grew
with the success of The Kingston Trio. Within two years, Newport
became the most important single showcase for folk singers, especially those with little previous exposure.

Scheduled to play Newport '63 were Bob Dylan, Tom Paxton,
Sam Hinton, Bob Davenport, The Freedom Singers, Jim Garland,
Ed McCurdy, Peter La Farge, Joan Baez, and Phil Ochs. The fes-
tival program, edited by Sis Cunningham, hailed the new singer-

songwriters as creating a "renaissance in folk music," and dubbed them "Woody's Children." Articles began to appear everywhere, from *Sing Out* magazine to the New York *Times,* about the new music. And all as a result of three hot days in July.

Phil was nervous, biting his nails to the knuckles. He'd come to Newport with six-months-pregnant Alice, Betsy Dotson, and Michael. As the time drew closer for Phil to perform, he developed a crushing headache, so severe tears came to his eyes. After first refusing any help, he finally gave in, was rushed to a nearby hospital, diagnosed as suffering from heat prostration and given salt tablets. He took them, determined to return to the festival and perform. A few hours after he left the hospital, the headaches started again, this time worse than before. He was taken, by ambulance, to the Women's Hospital, where they decided to administer a spinal tap immediately. The next morning the doctors told him he was all right and could be released as long as he promised to curtail physical activity until he fully recovered from the effects of the treatment. He ignored the advice, and backstage at the festival a couple of hours later, the pain in his head and back was so intense he could barely make it to the bathroom.

When it was time for Phil to perform, Pete Seeger suggested he forget it, he was in no shape to go on. "I'll sing," Phil insisted, his face beaded with sweat. Seeger helped him get to the stage, and left him clutching a makeshift curtain. He went out to explain to the crowd that Phil wasn't feeling very well, but insisted on singing. They applauded as Phil staggered out.

He began his performance with "The Ballad of Medgar Evers" and followed with "Talking Birmingham Jam." As if by magic, his strength began to return. By the end of "Birmingham Jam," he was dipping and waving his guitar, holding his head high, crisply singing in the clear and warm July breeze. He did another song, this one about the John Birch Society. The enthusiasm was boisterous, contagious. Phil returned for an encore and sang "The Power and the Glory," bringing the people to their feet, stomping and clapping. He left the stage and collapsed. Michael, Betsy, and Alice brought him over to a nearby tree and raised his feet against the trunk so they were above his head, propping him up to try to relieve the pain.

A couple of hours later, when Phil was feeling a little better, he received a folded note. Seeger had been sending all the young performers short messages about their sets. His note to Phil referred to the John Birch Society song, criticizing it harshly, calling it "sophomoric." The note concluded: "I wish I had one tenth your talent as a songwriter. My comments here are harsh, but I thought that they'd be useless to you if not frank. Pete Seeger."

Phil read Seeger's criticism with a combination of amusement and outrage. There had been a professional distance between the two caused by Phil's expressed desire to become a pop star, and Seeger's continual insistence that Phil remain committed to politics. It seemed ironic to Phil that Seeger was acting as the voice of conscience while riding the charts himself; The Kingston Trio's version of "Where Have All the Flowers Gone?" and Peter, Paul and Mary's "If I Had a Hammer," had both gone top ten.

Seeger closed the historic festival in a duet with Dylan of "Ye Playboys and Playgirls" (*ain't a-gonna run my world*). Phil, barely able to stand, watched from the sidelines and cheered along with the rest of the crowd.

The reaction to Newport was immediate. The festival affected the careers of all those who'd performed. Suddenly the "straight" media was paying attention. "New Folk Singers in 'Village' Demonstrate a Pair of Trends," the New York *Times* announced shortly after the festival ended. The feature cited the strong country influence in popular music, and the trend toward "new" performers writing their own material. At the end of the piece, Phil was mentioned: "Mr. Ochs, who prefers to be called a topical singer rather than a folk singer, performs only his own material. A former journalism student, he has become a sort of musical editorial writer. His satire is trenchant and his opinions are controversial in 'Fifty-Mile Hike,' 'William Worthy,' 'Talking Cuban Crisis,' and 'The Ballad of Billie Sol,' a few of the sixty songs he has written to meet his self-imposed topical deadlines."

Phil was ecstatic. He was sure now there had to be a connection between his family and the Ochs family which had founded the New York *Times*. He spent hours in the New York Public Library researching the Ochs family tree. Although he could never find a link, he was always sure one existed.

Officially, the Hollywood blacklist had been broken by Otto Preminger's screenplay credit to Dalton Trumbo for the 1960 movie *Exodus*. Trumbo, one of the original "Hollywood Ten," had been a victim of "Red Channels," a fifties pamphlet which first published the names of the officially undesirable, among them Pete Seeger. Once Hollywood grudgingly began to let those blacklisted work again, it seemed the issue was finally a dead one; in reality, it was a time for retrenchment and replanning. The new blacklisting would be more devious, more clever. The basic mistake of "fifties" blacklisting was that it brought the issues to the public; it gave the people too much information; it made them choose sides. You were either *for* John Garfield or *against* him, that type of thing. The new blacklisting was more sophisticated. It took the choice away from the public, giving it instead to the performers themselves.

Late 1962. Ed Sullivan invited Bob Dylan to appear on "The Toast of the Town." Sullivan had made his reputation on television by booking the hottest acts first, before any other TV show. At dress rehearsal, Dylan sang his "Birch Society Blues." After the run-through, Sullivan was in conference with the network, and Dylan was informed CBS wanted him to sing something else, that "Birch" song not "acceptable." Dylan walked, talking loudly about how he would never appear on any TV show where he couldn't perform a harmless satirical piece of fluff like "Birch Society Blues." He was off the show.

After Newport '63, "Hootenanny" became ABC's most popular show. Joan Baez, another of the "controversial" performers who'd never performed on network television, was invited to appear. She eagerly accepted "Hootenanny" 's invitation when word somehow got to her that Pete Seeger and The Weavers had been "excluded" from the series. It was never made quite clear who originally brought up the issue, whether in fact the network made a blanket announcement that Seeger would never step foot on an ABC sound stage, which seems highly unlikely, or whether Irwin Silber's *Sing Out* magazine first pointed out the Seeger-less programs. At any rate, Baez announced she would never participate in a show

that wouldn't have Seeger or The Weavers. A statement was issued
by the producers of "Hootenanny" questioning Seeger's "artistic
level." This was a mistake on the part of the program, for it
justified a position no one was sure until then it had actually
taken. *Broadside* magazine and *Sing Out* printed demands that
Pete Seeger be allowed on the show. *Sing Out* cried "McCarthyism." Harold Leventhal, Seeger's manager, charged the network
with "political blacklisting." Jack Newfield, then writing for a
Manhattan newspaper, *The West Side News,* reported: "Richard Lewine, producer of the show, denied the blacklisting
charge, saying, 'They [Seeger and The Weavers] were not invited
because we wanted better folk singers . . . We used The Smothers
Brothers because they are far better than The Weavers.' . . .
[Leventhal] termed Lewine's comparison of The Weavers and
The Smothers Brothers 'nonsense,' and added, 'How can they say
Pete, who originated the term 'Hootenanny' in concerts fifteen
years ago, and The Weavers, with six million records sold, are not
as good as other groups?"

Baez's refusal to be on the show prompted other acts to do the
same. Tom Paxton, Barbara Dane, and The Greenbriar Boys,
among others, refused to appear. At Rutgers University, where
one of the shows was being recorded, four hundred students pick-
eted, joined by many folk singers. In fact there was more and better talent on the picket line than on the show. ABC was deluged
with angry letters. Once again, the network denied any involvement, insisting the show was an independent production, in effect
putting the responsibility on Lewine.

Phil was energized by all this. Along with Paxton, he went to all
the performers he knew and insisted they not appear. In effect they
were blacklisting themselves over the issue of Pete Seeger's alleged
blacklisting! Phil wrote a strident ballad chronicling the troubles
that had plagued John Henry Faulk, the "country-bumpkin" performer blacklisted during the fifties; "The Ballad of John Henry
Faulk":

> *And you men who point your fingers*
> *And spread your lies around*
> *You men who left your soul behind*
> *And drag us to the ground*

> *You can put my name right down there*
> *I will not try to hide*
> *For if there's one man on the blacklist*
> *I'll be right there by his side.*

It would be many years before Phil would make his only appearance on network television.

ABC sent Seeger a loyalty oath to sign as a requisite for appearing on "Hootenanny," and of course Seeger refused to sign. *Broadside* wrote that the request by ABC "affirms the existence of the oft-denied blacklist. At least Pete seems to have overcome his lack of talent and proper repertoire given as earlier excuses." Leventhal, quoted in the magazine, stated, "No one I could contact at ABC knows anything about who might have sent the loyalty oath affidavit to Pete Seeger." Seeger had just come off a seven-year court battle which had grown out of his refusal to sign loyalty oaths back in the fifties.

The boycott grew. Bob Dylan; Peter, Paul and Mary; Jack Elliott; even The Kingston Trio, all refused to appear. Ironically, Seeger was against boycotting the program. He analyzed the situation politically. Any appearance of a "controversial" performer on the networks was a victory. He called Phil's and Paxton's organizational tactics "undisciplined." Almost before he realized what had happened, Seeger was once again in the center of controversy. He saw little use in forcing insignificant victories, which usually led to further defeats. "Hootenanny" was canceled by ABC, effectively cutting off the network showcase from those performers who could most benefit from national exposure. What had begun as a tentative step toward incorporating the new folk music into a major American pastime ended in controversy, innuendo, and accusation.

Phil approached Harold Leventhal about the possibility of visiting Woody Guthrie in the hospital. Leventhal, Woody's manager, tried at first to discourage the visit. Woody, paralyzed and near death, wasn't able to recognize the visitors any more, but every folk singer who came to New York wanted to visit the dying legend. Phil persisted, and Leventhal reluctantly set it up. Leventhal was sure Woody wasn't even aware Phil had been in the hospital room. Phil said little during the visit, mostly staring at Guthrie stiff and silent in his bed. Shortly after, Phil wrote one of his most beautiful ballads, "Bound for Glory":

> *Now they sing out his praises on every distant shore*
> *But so few remember what he was fightin' for*
> *Oh, why sing the songs and forget about the aim*
> *He wrote them for a reason, why not sing them for the same?*
> *For now he's bound for a glory all his own*
> *And now he's bound for glory.*

Phil asked Leventhal to manage him. He tried the same tactics he'd used with Sam Hood: coming on strong, insisting he was going to be a star, bigger than Dylan, sure his albums would all be million sellers, telling people to call Leventhal and say how great Phil was. Recalls Leventhal: "He kept on saying then that he was going to be bigger than the others, bigger than them all." Leventhal was turned off by Phil's approach. He sensed a lack of organization, of professional focus. Any one of the careers Phil predicted for himself was a full-time pursuit. Phil was going to be a movie star, a rock star, a folk hero, a political force greater than any politician. Leventhal's resistance was gentle but absolute. He said he wouldn't have enough time to devote to Phil's career, being too busy managing his other performers, which included Theodore Bikel, Alan Arkin (then a folk singer), and Pete Seeger. However, he did agree to handle Phil's publishing. "Appleseed Music" was set up to handle all of Phil's songs.

Phil then approached Albert Grossman, Dylan's manager. Grossman had come to the folk scene early, gobbling up as many acts as he could, convinced folk music was the next big commercial wave. He would hang out nightly at Gerde's or The Gaslight, sniffing for talent. He knew Phil, liked his songs, saw possibilities. He signed him, adding him to his growing stable—Dylan; Peter, Paul and Mary; and Ian and Sylvia. Next on Phil's list was signing a recording contract. Columbia, Dylan's label, was his first choice. Grossman told Phil to be patient.

Sing Out magazine announced a fall hootenanny at Carnegie Hall to be hosted by Theodore Bikel and Izzy Young, and to feature many of the performers from the Newport '63 Festival; Len

Chandler, Buffy Sainte-Marie, Dave Van Ronk and The Jug Stompers, and Phil Ochs. One purpose of the show was to test their commercial drawing power on a larger scale in New York than the Village coffeehouse circuit, or a summer weekend in Rhode Island. Robert Shelton wrote in the *Times* that the show, considered by many to be a landmark, was "too much of a good thing." It was a sign perhaps that the first euphoric wave of excitement over the sixties folk boom had begun to subside.

The feeling among the performers was different. The show was a complete success, every seat sold out in advance. As for Shelton's review, they shrugged it off, describing it as the expected "straight media reaction." About Phil, Shelton wrote, "Ochs was a tart satirist."

A few days later, another, smaller hoot was held at Town Hall, with Phil, Peter La Farge, Guy Carawan, and Buffy. This one was billed as a HOOTENANNY FOR STUDENTS AND WORKING PEOPLE.

Phil was happy. He'd managed to play Carnegie Hall and Town Hall in a single week.

Alice was due anyday, her condition confining her to the walk-up apartment. Phil would come home late, usually high on wine, and collapse on the bed, asking, as his body fell, if she'd had the baby yet. Letters were arriving every day from Phil's draft board. He'd written back a few times explaining he was exempt by marriage, and that he was about to be a father. They insisted he come down for a physical and an interview. He sent letters back saying he was "on the road" or "ill."

Jim and Jean were gone, off to the West Coast preparing for their debut as part of The Good Time Singers on Andy Williams' TV show. Jim was sure they'd never be back in New York. Jean wasn't as confident and decided to sublet the Thompson Street apartment to a friend. Phil was preparing for a series of concerts in the Midwest which Grossman had set up. He stuffed his dirty underwear into his guitar case and took the subway to Far Rockaway, so Sonny could do his laundry. The next day, he said goodbye to Alice and was gone.

He called her from Michigan a couple of nights later. Alice gasped into the phone that she was going into labor. Phil didn't know what to do. Alice told him to call back later and hung up.

She called Eric Jacobsen, who rushed over and took her, by cab, to a nearby clinic for unwed mothers. She'd made no plans for having the baby and didn't have enough money to check into a private hospital. The clinic was the only place Eric could think of to take her. She felt at home, as unwed as the other girls there. Eric stayed with her through the night. A few days later, after a temporary stay for the baby in an incubator, he brought mother and daughter, Meegan, home to Bleecker Street.

Phil and Dylan were hanging out all the time now. Alice would cook dinner for Dylan and his girlfriend Suze two or three nights a week. During coffee one time, Alice gave Dylan Meegan to hold for a second. He reacted as if he'd been handed a porcupine; his fingers stiffened, his eyebrows pushed up nearly to his scalp. He held the baby upside down by the ankles until Alice took her back. Afterward, Dylan climbed down the fire escape to avoid the crowd of fans who pursued him constantly.

Phil and Alice were having dinner one evening, when the door-bell rang. Outside stood a young, skinny boy wearing a torn sweater and faded dungarees, carrying a large pad and pencil. He introduced himself as a Phil Ochs fan. He wanted to meet the great Phil Ochs. Phil invited him in and asked him if he'd like to join them for dinner. Alice set a place for the fellow, and they all ate, talking as if they'd known each other for years, going on about music, politics, and Bob Dylan. When it was time for Phil to go to The Gaslight, he and his fan climbed out the window and down the fire escape, even though there was no one waiting at the front door.

Topical music needed issues, controversy, for persuasion. The stronger the issue, the better the argument. What was happening in Hazard, Kentucky, was perfect material for the new crusaders. Hazard—its very name suggesting the drama of the miners' strug-gle—was attracting national attention. In the Village, concerts were being organized, and demonstrations were being planned. The general co-ordination of events was being handled by a young man fresh out of NYU, Arthur Gorson.

Gorson had been a leader of the 1960 NYU campus chapter of

Students for Kennedy. This led to his becoming the chairman of NYU's division of Americans for Democratic Action. He soon became a member of the board of directors of ADA and national chairman of Campus ADA, giving him two votes on the board, while Hubert Humphrey and Joe Rauh, also directors, had only one vote each. Meetings were held monthly in Washington, D.C., where the Administration's courtship of the country's youth was centered.

As head of Campus ADA, Gorson was aligned with Students for a Democratic Society. Through SDS he met Stokely Carmichael of the Student Nonviolent Co-ordinating Committee (SNCC). Together they began to question the objectives of the Kennedy administration, particularly in terms of how it chose to deal with the problems of the working class and minorities.

At the ADA National Convention of 1963, Gorson introduced a resolution condemning discrimination in trade unions, confident it had enough votes to pass. The resolution blew everything apart. David Dubinsky tried to have Campus ADA thrown out of the national organization. Gorson was offered a bribe by a well-known labor representative to revoke the resolution. As a result, he dropped out of the ADA and, together with SNCC, began organizing full-time for civil rights.

Gorson on Hazard: "There was an ongoing, indigenous movement that radicals and artists hooked on to. SNCC was very self-conscious about whether it was too black. It was a different time in history. They were interested in being involved, if only incidentally, in an organized white southern project.

"The Kennedy people were trying to launch their war on poverty legislation, and what they needed was a real heavy test-case focal point, a crisis situation to push on poverty legislation in order to bring funding into the Appalachian area. We were, strangely enough, aligned with the Kennedy War on Poverty because we were relying on it ourselves.

"Hazard wasn't a good test case because we were dealing with older people who had no experience with democracy. Even if you set up a local organization, it immediately reverted back to the leaders dealing with the clothes that we raised and sent down by the truckload as patronage. It was always John L. Lewis or the company store. You'd leave them alone, and immediately they'd become bosses on their own. Local dictators."

But it was ideal for the topical-song movement. Gorson met with Hamish Sinclair, the Scottish filmmaker and senior organizer of events in Hazard. Sinclair was involved on every level, hoping to develop material for a major documentary. He was instrumental in bringing the coal miners' strike to the attention of the New York artistic community. Sinclair recruited Phil, who got high thinking about being able to reach into the federal government, being on page one of the New York *Times,* instead of page fifty-one where the hoot reviews were.

Phil sang at church rallies to raise money for Hazard. He became involved with the "Affairs Committee of the Ethical Society" and the "Pennsylvania Committee for Another Winter." Sinclair, secretary of the "National Committee for Miners," introduced Phil to union leaders, influential politicos, and to Arthur Gorson, now organizing monthly "sings" at The Village Gate to raise money for the miners in Hazard.

They liked each other from the beginning. Phil was impressed with Arthur's ability to organize. He saw Gorson as soft-spoken, yet persuasive; articulate without excess. Effective. At The Village Gate rallies, Phil sang with Judy Collins, Buffy Sainte-Marie, Bob Gibson, Hamilton Camp, Eric Andersen, David Cohen, and Bob Dylan. Recalls Gorson: "The miners' movement was the favorite cause of folk singers for a while. It had all the appeal that songs are made of. It was romantic, heroic, dramatic."

Gorson's next step was to arrange trips to Kentucky, bringing performers down to see for themselves what the situation was like. Phil, Dylan, Judy Collins, Eric Andersen, and Arthur spent five days with the miners, singing, picketing, eating, sleeping. Phil talked to the miners. He visited their families. Whenever he had time, he'd be on the streets of Hazard selling copies of *Broadside,* taking whatever he could get—twenty-five cents, fifty cents, a dollar—and keeping that money separate, handing over every cent to Sis when he returned to New York.

Phil and Eric Andersen drove back together, traveling through West Virginia. Phil was flooded with the romanticism of their adventure, their flirtation with danger, the luxury of safety. As Eric drove, Phil wrote "The Hills of West Virginia."

It was the only time Alice ever saw him cry. She'd gone down to do the laundry. When she returned, she found him at the kitchen table, his forehead flat against the formica top, his arms dangling at his sides, his body silently convulsing. She dropped the laundry and knelt beside him.

"Phil . . . Phil . . ." He kept on shaking. The TV was on. Walter Cronkite. There were tears in his eyes too. It was November 22, 1963.

Phil loved Kennedy. He was civil rights, he was the Peace Corps. He was Marilyn Monroe singing "Happy Birthday" in Madison Square Garden. He was the son of a movie mogul; a football player, a war hero. "That Was the President." When Phil finished writing the song, he fell into bed. Unable to sleep, he stared at the ceiling.

"What's wrong, Phil?"

"I think I'm going to die tonight, Alice. I'm going to die."

Two weeks after Kennedy's assassination, Phil was booked to play The Gaslight. Sam Hood was concerned about Phil doing the gig because two of his songs, "Talking Vietnam" and "Cuban Missile Crisis," contained material critical of the late President. The afternoon Phil was to open, Sam sat down with him and suggested he consider dropping the two songs from the show. Hood had good reason to be concerned. After Kennedy's murder, Van Ronk had played the following evening and sung a farewell to Kennedy to the tune of "Good-time Brodie." In effect, good riddance. The club had been filled with tourists, and there was nearly a riot. People were shouting, screaming, demanding in rapid succession: (1) their money back; (2) Van Ronk's assassination; (3) the bombing of The Gaslight.

Phil was outraged at Hood's suggestion, accusing him of censorship, insisting the two songs were even more important since Kennedy was dead.

Against Hood's advice, Phil sang the songs. Some people in the audience stood up, disgusted, and walked out. Others shouted at Phil to "get lost" or to "respect the dead." Phil continued to sing, seemingly oblivious. Hood watched from the bar. He raised a drink to his lips and thought how foolish he'd been. They were both right.

Phil was writing for *Broadside* all the time now, bringing songs to the office every day. He'd write down ideas on scraps of paper and late at night, after his shows, put them to melodies. Being around Sis and Gordon gave him the idea of reviving The Almanac Singers. He tried to talk the Village folkies into putting out a "Broadside Ballads" album. After all, didn't they all owe a lot to *Broadside,* Dylan included? Phil got commitments from The New World Singers, Pete Seeger, Peter La Farge, Gil Turner, Happy Traum, and Mark Spoelstra. Seeger, in particular, nodded favorably at this type of activity, the true spirit he felt the new folk movement should embrace.

The only one who resisted was Dylan. Phil became relentless, insisting Dylan owed something to *Broadside* and all the folk singers of the past. "Bob, think of all the songwriters you'll inspire."

"Are you crazy? I don't want to inspire any songwriters. If I'd made the basketball team in high school, do you think I'd be here now?"

On "Broadside Ballads, Vol. I" Phil hoped to perform "The Ballad of William Worthy," his first recorded material. The song told the story of a reporter convicted of illegal re-entry to the United States after visiting Cuba without a valid passport:

> *William Worthy isn't worthy*
> *To enter our door*
> *He went down to Cuba*
> *He's not American anymore*
> *But somehow it is strange to hear*
> *The State Department say*
> *"You are living in the Free World;*
> *In the Free World you must stay."*

Shortly before the "Broadside" album was released, Phil received a phone call from William Worthy, and immediately invited him to the apartment for dinner. Worthy accepted the offer. After dinner, they all went to The Gaslight to watch Phil perform. Before doing the song, Phil introduced Worthy to the crowd, which greeted him with a standing ovation.

A few days later, Phil received this letter:

Dear Phil Ochs,
   Last night I certainly enjoyed hearing your ballad on my passport case.
   Dick Gregory has told me that he plans to start cracking jokes about the case on his circuit. So perhaps between Ochs and Gregory the whole sorry business can be laughed out of court.
   This quick note is written on the run. My regards to your wife.
                                                         Cordially,
                                                         William Worthy

A few months later, Worthy's conviction was overturned in the U. S. Court of Appeals. Presented by William Kunstler, Worthy's defense successfully established that in the United States it was not a crime to come home.

By December, the "Broadside Ballads" album was finally ready to be recorded. Dylan would only appear billed as "Blind Boy Grunt." Michael wanted desperately to go to the session. Phil took his brother aside. It was a small recording studio: there just wasn't going to be enough room. He couldn't come along. Michael was disappointed, but accepted Phil's explanation outright. Phil always knew best. Later, at The Kettle, where the performers were gathering before heading for the studio, a friend of Phil's popped in unexpectedly. He was an open-tuned guitar player, and Phil, on the spot, invited him to join the session. Without saying a word, Michael left, walking up MacDougal, over to the park, and back again, shaking his head slowly, a half-smile set on his face. He dropped in on Alice for some coffee. Over a cigarette he told her what had happened, and, after some wine, began to complain loudly of the way Phil always treated him. His own brother didn't want him around. Alice confided that she felt like a cook and a message-taker. Phil was getting a little too popular for wives and little brothers.

The next night Michael came staggering up to the apartment. He looked Phil in the eye and said: "I wouldn't have you as a friend, so I won't have you as a brother."

Michael quit Adelphi and moved back to Columbus, Ohio, to finish college at Ohio State.

Phil spent Christmas in Hazard, performing "No Christmas in Kentucky" for the miners. There was no Christmas on Bleecker Street for Alice and Meegan, alone in the cold brick apartment. The next day, Alice read in the New York *Post:*

> Hazard, Ky, Dec. 26 (AP):
> *They don't have Christmas in Kentucky*
> *There's no holly on a West Virginia door*
> *For the trees don't twinkle when you're hungry*
> *And the jingle bells don't jingle when you're poor.*

The article described how a band of New York students and organizers had decided to sacrifice their Christmases to try to make a better one for those in Hazard. "With them was twenty-three-year-old Phil Ochs, a folk singer from Greenwich Village and composer of the carol which inspired the mission of mercy." Alice wrapped herself in Phil's red jacket and fed the baby.

> *When the wind from the Island is rollin' through the trees*
> *When a kiss from a prison cell is carried by the breeze*
> *That's when I wonder how sad a man can be*
> *Oh, when will Celia come to me.*

Dear Phil Ochs,

I can hardly find the words to tell you how much I appreciate that song you composed and sang for the sake of my husband's reunion with me. As I listened to your song when played on a tape recorder, I could not hold back my tears. The melody was hauntingly sad and plaintive and the words conveyed so eloquently our plight of separation then. Bill and I had the song played and replayed several times, and I think I'll never get tired of it. It is so beautiful and splendidly sung by you.

It is heartening to find in this world people like you who go out of their way to contribute their share in the cause of humanity and the correction of injustices. There is no doubt you have great talent, and I am so glad that you are using it for good purposes. I wish you success and good luck along the line you have chosen to devote your energies.

With every hope that I would someday have the privilege to meet you in person, I thank you with all my heart.

Sincerely yours,
Celia M. Pomeroy

By January of 1964, Phil almost never went home to Bleecker Street, preferring to play cards at The Kettle with Dylan, Ed McCurdy, Tom Paxton, Clarence Hood, and Burt Ziegler, who ran The Figaro, or hang out with Bob Gibson at his studio on Fifteenth Street. He and Gibson would sit around, getting high on cheap wine, writing songs, sometimes rewriting songs, using the same chord constructions, laying out new lyrics. "Too Many Martyrs" became "That's the Way It's Gonna Be":

> *If you say that all the good times are gone*
> *If you say this rain will keep raining on*
> *I'll walk along with my head held high*
> *Find that song and I'll sing it to the sky*
> *I may be wrong, but I'll live until I die*
> *That's the way it's gonna be.*

At The Kettle, Phil and Dylan would argue music constantly, Phil insisting songs with messages could attract a larger audience if they were pretty, Dylan shaking his head, sucking on a cigarette, telling Phil melodies weren't important, it was the words. Through the smoke of their rap a strange paradox began to emerge. Dylan's songs, not Phil's, were being covered by pop groups. Peter, Paul and Mary hit with "Blowin' in the Wind," going top ten; Sonny and Cher did "All I Really Want to Do"; The Zombies had "It Ain't Me, Babe"; and The Byrds destroyed them all with "Tambourine Man."

Phil's songs were also being covered, but only by folk groups. The Good Time Singers covered a couple of songs, as did The Back Porch Majority. Ronnie Gilbert did "The Power and the Glory." A new acoustic group with short hair and button-down shirts came out with an album of "tender and soulful ballads," including Phil's "New Town." The album was a flop. Two years later the group changed its image, had a hit single, and was on its way, as Frankie Valli and The Four Seasons.

Dylan would recognize earlier than the others who his audience was. Already he was changing his music, becoming less topical, more personal, while Phil and the others were still Christmas-caroling in Kentucky.

Late at night, after cards, Phil, Dylan, David Cohen, and Van Ronk would all pile into a cab and head for Forty-second Street, to catch a Western double feature at the Lyric, OD on dry pop-corn, and shoot back at the screen with finger pistols—their feet up on the chair in front, their dialogue better than the lines in the film. Except if they were lucky and got a John Wayne, or an Audie Murphy, in which case they would sit in quiet awe of the big guys.

They all loved the movies and tried to learn from them. Dylan's use of the landscape as a metaphor for the soul (*down the backroads of my mind*) couldn't be learned any better than by watching the cinematic technique of dramatizing internal conflict through visual images.

One friend recalled how Dylan, Neuwirth, and David Cohen used to go to see comedies in order to discipline themselves not to laugh. Laughing, even smiling, went against the image of the angry young man. Only Phil openly displayed his sense of humor. One time he ran into Dave Van Ronk at Minetta's. It was early on a Friday night. The waiters and waitresses from several clubs were picketing on MacDougal for a raise in pay. Van Ronk suggested that he and Phil join the demonstration. "Aah," Phil sighed as he drank a glass of white wine, "let 'em eat cake."

One Saturday night at The Kettle, while sitting with David Cohen at a table, Phil charted his career. He took out a piece of graph paper he kept folded in quarters in his jacket pocket and spread it out in front of him on the checkered tablecloth. "This is where I am now," he said, pointing to a dot on a line. "And this is where I'm going to be in six months. Here's where I should be a year from now." He looked at David. "What's so funny?"

"You can't chart your career. That's the difference between you and Dylan. You operate from your head. Charts, plans, ideas, crusades. Dylan operates from his cock. Have another drink."

Dylan walked in. "Phil," he said, "how'd you like to meet someone important?"

"Who?" Phil asked. Dylan wouldn't tell him. Phil, Cohen, and Dylan went outside and got into a cab.

"The Dakota," Dylan told the driver.

They took the elevator to the fourteenth floor. They found the right apartment, and Dylan rang the doorbell. Standing on the other side of the entrance was Marlon Brando, and what appeared to be an Indian princess behind him.

Michael and Phil, 1961 (*Photo by Harry Phin*)

Michael and Phil, a few years later (*Photo by Sandy Thompson*)

Jim and Jean
(*Alice Ochs*)

Phil posing for Alice on the fire escape
of the Thompson Street apartment
(*Alice Ochs*)

Bob Dylan, 1963
(*Alice Ochs*)

(*Alice Ochs*)

Phil and Alice shortly before Meegan's birth (*Courtesy of Alice Ochs*)

Phil, Alice, and Meegan in the Bleecker Street apartment (*Courtesy of Alice Ochs*)

Arthur Gorson (at right) with Dr. King and Berman Gibson, 1962 (*Courtesy of Arthur H. Gorson*)

An early publicity shot of a Phil Ochs image soon to be discarded (*Courtesy of Arthur H. Gorson*)

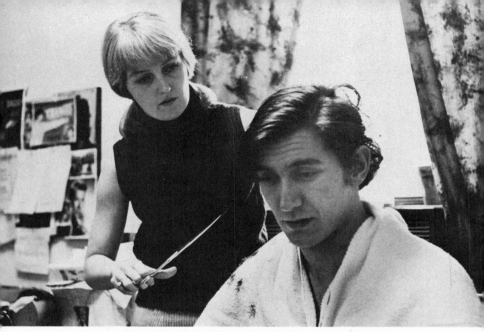

The afternoon of Phil's Carnegie Hall concert, Susan Campbell gives Phil a haircut (*Courtesy of Susan Campbell Harris*)

VARIETY

Wednesday, November 10, 1965

WHY
IS
PHIL OCHS
APPEARING AT
CARNEGIE HALL
NEW YORK

JAN. 7, 1966

?

artist management
ARTHUR H. GORSON, INC.
850 Seventh Avenue
New York, New York
JU 6-5124

NEW YORK POST, FRIDAY, DECEMBER 3, 1965

ARTHUR H. GORSON presents

Elektra Recording Artist
PHIL OCHS CONCERT
FIRST N.Y.

at **CARNEGIE HALL** 7th AVE. & 57th ST., N.Y.C.
Friday, JANUARY 7th, 1966, 8:30 P. M.

TICKETS: $3.25, $2.75, $2.50, $2.00
Available at box office or by mail from:
ARTHUR H. GORSON, Inc. 850 7th Ave. N.Y. 10019
All checks payable to Carnegie Hall
Enclose self-addressed, stamped envelope

Before the concert with David Blue (*Courtesy of Arthur H. Gorson*)

After the concert with (from left to right) Mother Ochs, Gertrude, Sonny, and Robin Tanzman (Sonny's daughter) (*Courtesy of Arthur H. Gorson*)

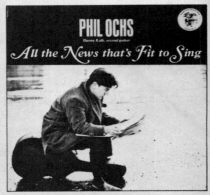

"Come on in, boys."

Phil was dumbstruck. He was in *Terry Malloy*'s living room! Brando invited them to join him on the floor, where they all sat in a circle and passed a joint.

"Why don't we all go down to The Gaslight and blow everybody's mind?" Dylan suggested a few minutes later.

Brando hesitated, not sure he wanted to leave the reservation. Dylan pressed him, but he politely refused. When it was time to go, Brando thanked them for dropping by and told them to come again.

As soon as the door closed behind them, Dylan and David Cohen cracked up, laughing, holding their sides.

"What's so funny?" Phil asked.

"He thinks he's an Indian," Dylan replied. "We passed the peace pipe around."

"An Indian," David Cohen echoed.

Phil rode down the elevator with his hands stuffed in his pockets, his lips pressed tightly together, not finding anything funny.

In the street, David Cohen lit another joint.

"A goddamned Indian," Dylan said once more, quietly.

Phil was approached by Jac Holzman of Elektra Records, who signed him almost on the spot. Holzman had started his label with Theodore Bikel. While Vanguard "New Folks" included Baez, Eric Andersen, Leon Bibb, Odetta, Doc Watson, The Weavers, Pat Sky, and others, Elektra had Judy Collins (Holzman's Joan Baez), Tom Rush, Freddy Neil, Tim Hardin, and Phil Ochs. Holzman, through Grossman, offered Phil no money to sign, only the opportunity to record his songs without corporate censorship.

Grossman announced the Ochs-Elektra deal in the trades. Phil went out of his mind with excitement. He started planning the album immediately, trying out material on whoever happened to be around, playing his songs over and over again, hour after hour. He stayed up nights planning the cover, the liner notes, the design of the album, the order of the songs. In February he went into the recording studio, and in three sessions completed "All the News That's Fit to Sing," with Danny Kalb on second guitar.

The album was produced by Jac Holzman, with Rothchild listed as "recording director." It was recorded at New York's Mastertone Studios. The cover showed Phil sitting on his guitar case, in the middle of a wet city street, reading the New York *Times* ("All the news that's fit to print"). Sis Cunningham did the liner notes, promising that the album had "an awful lot more . . . than what you'll find in *Newsweek* or even the *Times*."

Phil conceived the album as a musical newspaper. He chose "One More Parade" as the headline; continued with page one material, "The Thresher," "Talking Vietnam," "Lou Marsh"; sidebar'd with "The Power and the Glory" and "Celia"; and closed out the back page with his musical adaptation of Poe's "The Bells." Side Two contained the feature stories, beginning with "William Worthy," continuing with "Automation Song," "Talking Cuban Crisis," "Bound for Glory," and ending with an editorial, "Too Many Martyrs." As a coda, "What's That I Hear," his most Dylan-like song, a mirror-image of "Blowin' in the Wind":

> *What's that I hear now*
> *Ringin' in my ears*
> *I've heard that sound before*
> *It's the sound of Freedom ringing*
> *Ringin' up through the skies . . .*

It became Phil's most covered song.

The initial sales of the album were mostly in New York. Phil set out to concentrically widen his territory. Throughout the winter Grossman booked him into new clubs. He did a lot of one-nighters in New Jersey ("From New York's Greenwich Village, Union Junior College presents . . . PHIL OCHS singing Songs from the Headlines!!"). At the same time, he continued to play at benefits. In March, a benefit for Appalachia was organized by Arthur Gorson, featuring Judy Collins, Dave Van Ronk, and Phil Ochs. Speaking at the affair was Berman Gibson, leader of Kentucky's unemployed miners' movement, all proceeds to be used for the continuation of The Committee for Miners.

Phil went to Boston, where he played Club '47. While there, he ran into Manny Greenhill, one of the key figures in the Boston folk scene and a friend from Newport. Phil and Manny spent long hours arguing politics into the night—Phil from a sixties perspective, Greenhill from the forties. Manny enjoyed Phil's enthusiasm, seeing in him an excitement reminiscent of the old days. Phil sensed the gamesmanship in Manny's arguments, and almost always took an opposite extremist position, forcing Greenhill to a more spirited defense of his perspective ("Look how far we've come").

In April, Phil appeared at the City University of New York's City College bookstore, where he sat all day on a stool, playing songs from his album, stared at by students who, for the most part, had never heard of him.

Off to a gig in the Interlude coffeehouse in Kew Gardens, New York, playing to the tourists. Back to The Unicorn in Boston. *Boston Broadside* ran a poll to find out who were Boston's favorite visiting performers. Van Ronk came in first, Bob Dylan second, Jean Redpath third, Phil Ochs fourth. Honorable mention to Jose Feliciano, Jack Elliott, Doc Watson.

Reviews of Phil's album began to appear. *Variety:* "The LP gives a fine example of the use of modern folk music for the purpose it was originally styled, the making of social comment."

Off to La Cave in Cleveland.

Josh Dunson, writing in *High Fidelity* magazine on Phil's album: "As important in 1964 as Bob Dylan's 'Freewheelin' album was in 1963."

Back to New York for another benefit for The Committee for Miners, "Folk Music at the Gate," featuring Phil with Bob Gibson, Carolyn Hester, Tom Paxton, Brother John Sellers, and a new, unknown black comedian by the name of Flip Wilson.

The L.A. *City Press:* "Mr. Ochs is certainly no genius although he might be a hero, and he isn't much of an artist. His songs are lacking in imagination and taste and tend to be overly emotional."

He travels alone. The whole country his back yard, everyone his brother. Image. Dylan's "Girl of the North Country." Phil's "City Boy." No roots, no home, no family, loneliness. Sixties mythology.

Alice was left behind, but she certainly wasn't alone. She knew every musician in the Village, most of whom spent a night or two on her floor, crashing. John Sebastian, Al Kooper, David Cohen, and Danny Kalb were over all the time.

When Phil did come home, it was only to sleep. He had little to say to Alice, and Alice had even less to say to him. She'd gotten a camera while he'd been away and was into photographing everyone and everything, even selling some of her pictures for album covers. When Phil was around, she was always taking pictures of him; catching him on the phone, playing with Meegan. He didn't like Alice photographing him. He never wanted to be captured unposed. He only wanted "official" pictures showing him with an intense, squinty look on his face, his lean jaw jutting in front of his mouth, his lower lip tucked in. Phil on the fire escape, Phil in the park, Phil staring away into creative space. Alice kept snapping, her own image in her mind's eye as the Nikon focused on Phil.

Late one night in June. Phil calling from the Midwest, long distance, collect.

"Ochs here."

"Hi, Phil."

"I think I want a divorce."

It was all right with Alice. She wasn't seeing much of Phil, and she wasn't about to sit home and wait. She was tired of competing. Phil only made love to his audiences.

He called again the next night to make sure the conversation had really taken place. Alice assured him it had. "I'm a lousy father, a bad husband. You deserve more than this." Alice agreed.

He came back to New York and stayed at the Chelsea Hotel for two weeks before returning to Bleecker Street. Alice wasn't alone. Phil excused himself and went downstairs to wait on the stoop until the guy left. He went back upstairs and told Alice he'd changed his mind, he'd thought it over, they should have another child. Alice shook her head slowly. She discouraged him. He made an offer. Stay together for three months; if it works out, have another baby. Alice made some coffee, but by the time she brought Phil his cup, he was out, fully clothed, across the bed, George the cat curled up next to him.

Newport '63 was the explosion; Newport '64 its fallout. Protest music was now being played everywhere. The program of events included an extensive article written by Phil, "The Year of the Topical Song":

"I wouldn't be surprised to see an album called 'Elvis Presley Sings Songs of the Spanish Civil War' or 'The Beatles with the Best of the Chinese Border Dispute Songs.'" He wrote about his own trips to Hazard, and included a nod to Dylan for his contribution to protest music, acknowledging him as the king.

Newport was divided into various segments: protest music, bluegrass, gospel, and something called a patchwork of American music. A City Showcase presented Phil, Judy Collins, John Sebastian with Joe Butler and Zal Yanovsky, all members of a new group called The Lovin' Spoonful, and Chuck Berry, out of jail and looking for a way back. Richie Havens made his festival debut, as did Eric Andersen. Phil had been instrumental in bringing Eric to the festival, and had planned something special for the occasion.

Phil was on before Eric, and at the end of his set, as the applause began to fade, Phil said, "I'd like to bring Eric Andersen up here." Phil's guitar strummed under the patter. Eric bounded onto the stage. Phil spoke quietly into the mike, his voice going up slightly at the end of each sentence, halfway between word and song, "I'm Phil, he's Don . . . I wanted to bring him up here to do one thing which is very much out of character with this whole program. This is a songwriter's hoot. I'd like to do a song by the two most successful songwriters in the world, Paul McCartney and John Lennon . . . no relation." As Phil played rhythm and Eric melody, they began "I Should Have Known Better." When they got to the "hey hey hey's," the audience screamed in mock frenzy. *"That when I tell you that I love you . . ."* More screams. They finished, and the crowd was on its feet.

Newport '64 was the most successful folk festival yet, attendance topping seventy thousand. An album was immediately announced by Vanguard.

Riding the top-forty charts that week was a record called "The Eve of Destruction." It was a bad song, universally hated by the folkies, a feeble imitation of the music they were making. Phil told reporters he was happy a protest song, even that one, had found its way into top ten, but privately he made fun of it. "Wouldn't it be great if, instead of singing, 'Love thy neighbor,' he'd written, 'Eat thy neighbor.'"

Off the energy of the festival, Phil, Eric Andersen, Pete Seeger, Jackie Washington, Gil Turner, and Carolyn Hester headed for the Mississippi Caravan of Music, one of a number of summer projects coming under the supervision of the Council of Federated Organizations. Concerts were being staged to encourage voter registration among the blacks. Phil drove down with Eric Andersen, leaving a day ahead of the others.

Phil was a terrible driver, often drunk, and scared to death of other cars. Eric persuaded Phil to take a break, and took the wheel himself. Phil, feet hanging out the window, head against the seat, talking nonstop, made predictions about how much his album was going to sell, what a big star he was going to be, how sorry Grossman would be for not working harder. Eric smoked and drove. If Phil's head was in the future, Eric's was right there, in "southern town." Mississippi, the graveyard of progress.

They were there only two days when the bodies of Chaney, Schwerner, and Goodman were found—the three civil rights workers who were murdered and buried in the swamps, their necks stretched in the name of God, the Bible, and the Ku Klux Klan. It had its sobering effect on Phil.

For the whole week they were in Mississippi, Eric and Phil traveled together, talking to the people, performing and getting off the stage quickly. He told Eric, "I'm afraid they're going to kill me while I'm singing, while I'm on stage." While he performed, he made Eric promise to scan the audience and the wings, looking out for assassins.

Phil wanted to talk to "the average Mississippian." Eric tried to discourage him, but it was impossible. Phil would walk up to strangers, notebook out, ask a question, and write down what people said.

They played The Gaslight that fall—Phil the headliner, Eric the opening act. One night Phil sat at the bar, holding a glass of wine with both hands, hair spilling off his head into the top of his glass, telling Van Ronk how awful Mississippi had been, how he couldn't believe the things he'd seen and heard about "niggers" and "lynchings," Schwerner and Goodman and Chaney "getting what they'd deserved." Van Ronk shrugged his shoulders. He'd been there before, and worse, he assured Phil. Mississippi couldn't put a claim on ugliness.

They continued arguing, even as Phil approached the stage, strumming his guitar. He began his set with "William Worthy," and went into "The Power and the Glory." He turned away, tuned his guitar, and came back to the mike asking the crowd to raise their glasses, to join him in a toast. "Here's to the State of Mississippi"—

> *For underneath her borders the Devil draws no line*
> *If you drag her muddy rivers nameless bodies you will find*
> *And the fat trees of the forest have hid a thousand crimes*
> *And the calendar is lying when it reads the present time,*
> *Here's to the land you've torn out the heart of*
> *Mississippi find yourself another country to be part of.*

There was a stanza quoting a Mississippian (*The folks up North, they just don't understand*); one about the schools of Mississippi (*where they're teaching all the children that they don't have to care, all the rudiments of hatred are present everywhere, oh every single classroom is a factory of despair*); the cops of Mississippi (*chewin' their tobacco as they lock the prison door, behind their broken badges there are murderers and more*); the judicial system (*When a black man stands accused, the trial is always short, While the Constitution's drowning in an ocean of decay, 'unwed mothers should be sterilized' I've even heard them say*); and finally, the churches (*where the cross once made of silver now is caked with rust, and the Sunday morning sermons pander to their lust, Oh the fallen face of Jesus is chokin' in the dust, and Heaven only knows in which God they can trust*).

The house went crazy—standing, cheering, whistling, stomping. Phil finished with a flurry of strums and a sideways glance at the audience. Van Ronk stood. He was shouting now, the noisy approval in the room subsiding.

"Philly," he shouted, arms spread, drink in hand, "I'm trying to tell you. Why single out Mississippi from the other forty-nine? It's just as bad down the block as it is across the river. Poor boy, you're reducing the problem to a liberal's mentality, so totally unimportant."

Phil stared at Van Ronk.

"Death to liberals, and *Broadside* magazine," Van Ronk shouted, downing his sauce.

During the days, Phil was always searching for new places to visit, new things to do. Anything to keep him out of the apartment, away from Alice and the baby. If there were no political rallies happening, he could always go up to Forty-second Street and hit five or six movies, going to the first one at noon, for sixty-five cents, emerging from the last one at two or three in the morning.

One time he read in *The Village Voice* about a group of committed, disenchanted educators from various colleges around the country who'd decided to form their own, alternative institution. He figured he'd check it out.

The Free University, located in a converted factory on Union Square, was established by Sharon Krebs. It offered courses in "alternative lifestyles" and "radical politics," taught by a mostly radical faculty, eager for an outlet to share ideas, to meet new people.

Phil sat in on a few classes of Stew Albert's, one of the early organizers of student and civil rights demonstrations. Albert invited Phil to speak to the class one evening. Sitting in that night, also at Stew's invitation, was Paul Krassner, at the time struggling to keep his own satirical magazine, *The Realist,* alive. Krassner used *The Realist* to support his other career, as a stand-up comic, or he used comedy to support *The Realist,* whichever was working at any given time.

After class, at The Kettle, they all got drunk and sat in for some fast poker.

By January 1965, Phil and Alice officially separated. He'd taken an apartment on Fifteenth Street, letting Alice keep Bleecker. Just before he left, he sat down with her at the kitchen table and made a list of people she wasn't to sleep with. She took the list, smiled, and kissed him on the cheek. She kept the list in her purse, checking the boys off, making sure she got every last one of them. She had the first one over the night Phil moved out.

The first Sunday in January was set for a hoot to support *Broadside* magazine. Harold Leventhal came down to see Seeger play. Albert Grossman was there also. Phil cornered Grossman, asking why he wasn't doing more for him. Grossman told Phil the time still wasn't right. Phil asked about a concert at Carnegie Hall. Grossman suggested Phil talk to Leventhal about getting a booking at Town Hall. Phil insisted he didn't need Town Hall. He had a solo album out, was on the two Newport Festival albums and the "Broadside" record. He was ready to move.

A few weeks later he had a gig at The Unicorn in Boston and invited Arthur Gorson along for the ride. The day after Phil opened, he and Arthur walked along Wingaersheek Beach. Phil talked about how Grossman always made him feel he was in Dylan's shadow. He needed someone else to manage him, someone who understood organization, political organization, getting things done. "Think of it, Arthur, I'd be leaving Grossman, the biggest manager in the business, for you, an unknown. I'll create my own Albert Grossman. Think of it as a bold step. Leaving Grossman for Gorson!"

Arthur had no idea what show business was all about. He wasn't interested in finances at all. He was a political activist and full-time organizer, making the princely sum of twenty-five dollars a week. He had no professional ambitions, no business sense. Phil figured he was perfect for the job.

And Arthur accepted, of course.

V

Show me the whiskey that stains on the floor
Show me a drunken man as he stumbles out the door,
And I'll show you a young man with many reasons why,
And there but for fortune may go you or I.

Show me a country where the bombs had to fall
Show me the ruins of the buildings once so tall,
And I'll show you a young land with so many reasons why,
And there but for fortune may go you or I.

Phil Ochs, "There but for Fortune"

1965. Civil rights began to give way to Vietnam as the prevalent liberal, radical, student issue. North Vietnam was being bombed daily, code name "Rolling Thunder." Student protests erupted on campuses across the country.

Camelot became Dodge City. The Beatles said Norwegian Wood was good. The Rolling Stones pledged their souls to Lady Jane. Phil Ochs dared to eat a peach. Judy Henske: "He was always buying trousers that were too long, the cuffs falling under his heels. He thought he was two inches taller than he really was."

There were attempts to incorporate civil rights into the Anti-war Movement. Martin Luther King came out against the war. He and others insisted that the Vietnam War was a race war. Dissent became "protest," either on college campuses or in the streets of Washington. Everywhere, it seemed, people were marching for something; demonstrating against something else. "Protesting" as a theme began to infiltrate the commercial avenues of com-

munication. "It's what's up front that counts." Violence as a form
of protest reflected the Johnson administration's policy of justify-
ing might (the war in Vietnam) in the cause of right (democracy).
John F. Kennedy, in retrospect, seemed idyllic. He'd encouraged
student participation in the government, understood the necessity
for dealing economically with the problems in Latin America after
unsuccessfully trying to invade it at the Bay of Pigs. Johnson
coated his maniacal foreign policy with a heavy dose of domestic
progress, his "Great Society."

Civil rights had gained strong national support during the early
sixties; the Anti-war Movement had little away from the campuses.
Those who'd championed civil rights were American heroes, folk
heroes, folk singers; those against the war were traitors. Traitors
didn't have hit records. It was all over now, Baby Blue.

From an interview with Phil in *The Village Voice:*

> There's nothing noble about what I'm doing. I'm writing to
> make money. I write about Cuba and Mississippi out of an inner
> need for expression, not to change the world. The roots of my
> songs are psychological, not political. I can tell I'm just beginning
> to write decent stuff. I feel the images and words coming more
> easily. As I reach new levels, I can begin to fathom what Dylan's
> songs are all about . . . I'm beginning to read poets like Brecht.

Phil's second album was released in February. The cover
showed Phil, in a peacoat, sitting against the side of a building filled with torn political posters (KEATING, NEW YORK'S
OWN . . .), his head directly underneath a graffiti'd peace symbol.
Next to him, in the street, a torn fragment of a Goldwater poster.
Scrawled in white ink across the bottom of the cover: "I Ain't
Marching Anymore." Was Phil Ochs saying he was giving up protesting? On the back of the album was a letter from Phil: "And so
people walk up to me and ask, 'Do you really believe in what your
songs are saying?' "

He followed with a list of the most common complaints about
his songs:

> There's nothing as dull as yesterday's headlines,
> Don't be so ambitious.
> Sure it's good; but who's gonna care next year?

I bet you don't go to church.
Don't be so negative.
I came to be entertained, not preached to.
That's nice, but it really doesn't go far enough.
That's not folk music.
Why don't you move to Russia?

And yet every once in a while an idea grabs me and the familiar excitement returns as I turn myself on with the birth of a song. And I know again that I'll never kick the habit of writing.

And so people walk up to me and ask, "Do you really believe in what your songs are saying?"

And I have to smile and reply, "Hell, no, but the money's good."

Phil described each song on the album:

SIDE ONE

I AIN'T MARCHING ANYMORE: This borders between pacifism and treason, combining the best qualities of both. The fact that you won't be hearing this song over the radio is more than enough justification for the writing of it.

IN THE HEAT OF THE SUMMER: Scenes and images of the riots last summer in Harlem. As is usually the case, the loudest bursts of outrage came from those most responsible for the debacle.

DRAFT DODGER RAG: In Vietnam, a 19-year-old Vietcong soldier screams that Americans should leave his country as he is shot by a government firing squad. His American counterpart meanwhile is staying up nights thinking of ways to deceptively destroy his health, mind, or virility to escape two years in a relatively comfortable army. Free enterprise strikes again.

THAT'S WHAT I WANT TO HEAR: There are many fine sentimental out-of-work songs floating around, but as unemployment figures grow larger, so grows the need for more realistic songs and, consequently, actions. I can spare a dime, brother, but in these morally inflationary times, a dime goes a lot farther if it's demanding work rather than adding to the indignity of relief.

THAT WAS THE PRESIDENT: My Marxist friends can't understand why I wrote this song, and that's probably one of the reasons why I'm not a Marxist. After the assassination, Fidel Castro aptly pointed out that only fools could rejoice at such a tragedy, for systems, not men, are the enemy.

IRON LADY: A century from now, intelligent men will read in amazement about the murder of Caryl Chessman and wonder what excuse for a society flourished in these times. The idea for the song was given to me by a social worker in Ohio who had taken the phrase from a poem written by a man on death row.

THE HIGHWAYMAN: I never could follow poetry in school, but this work by Alfred Noyes has completely captivated me since my childhood. It is a classic study of romantic narrative that seemed to have been made for music.

SIDE TWO

LINKS ON THE CHAIN: Historically, labor unions have been a catalyst to social change, and in my opinion have a definite responsibility to be in the vanguard of important battles. When the civil rights struggle came to a head, they had become such a part of the establishment that the old lions of the Left were the new pillars of the segregated structure. But I'm sure they'll be able to straighten out this embarrassment at one of their many White House meetings.

HILLS OF WEST VIRGINIA: On one of my trips to Hazard, Kentucky, I drove through West Virginia with Eric Andersen and found myself renewing an old habit of pretending I was taking pictures with my mind. When the trip was over, I set down these images which really don't have any special message.

THE MEN BEHIND THE GUNS: I saw this in a collection of bland patriotic poems, but there were so many ringing phrases in this one, I found myself rereading it several times and reaching for my guitar. My apologies to the author, John Rooney, for changing a few lines, but the discipline of music had to win out in the end.

TALKING BIRMINGHAM JAM: In Birmingham, tourist city of the South, you can bomb the church of your choice with the apparent blessing of Governor George Wallace. Birmingham is one of the cities that made the FBI what it is today.

BALLAD OF THE CARPENTER: The State Department has a nasty habit of blocking the entrance of Ewan MacColl into this country, and undoubtedly one of the reasons is songs like this. All political consideration aside, if you take a serious look at the quality of culture in America, you can see that the State Department can ill afford such a tactic.

DAYS OF DECISION: The American politician has developed into a gutless master of procrastination with a maximum of non-committal statements and the barest minimum of action. This moral vacuum is exceeded only by the apathetic public who allows him to stay in power. How feeble is the effect of a song against such a morass, but here it is.

HERE'S TO THE STATE OF MISSISSIPPI: This song might be subtitled, "Farewell to Mississippi," for in order to write a few more songs like this, it might be wiser for me to stay away for a while. I was down there last summer and must admit that I met some nice people and that the state isn't as bad as my song implies, unless you are a Negro who had forgotten his place, or unless your last name was Chaney, Goodman, or Schwerner.

Eventually, the album sold better than forty thousand copies. It was released the same month as Dylan's "Bringing It All Back Home," which included "Mr. Tambourine Man" and "It's All Over Now, Baby Blue." Dylan's album went gold.

In an interview in *The Village Voice* entitled "Dylan Meets the Press," by J. R. Goddard, Dylan was asked about his relationship with Baez. He replied, "She's my fortune teller."

Q: Bobby, we know you changed your name. Come on now, what's your real name?

A: Philip Ochs. I'm gonna change it back again when I see it pays.

Journalists began to "analyze" Phil's work in print. *Boston Broadside* dragged Phil's work through the academic mud:

In "I Ain't Marchin' Anymore" Ochs' writing reaches its most pathetic point; it is, ironically, a better indictment of his poetastry than any critic could brew. . . . A piece (like Marchin') can not be unhypocritically written or sung by an individual who has not taken a formal stance as a Conscientious Objector . . . an indication of one's sentiment is not sufficient; anyone can Howl! . . . The measure of Ochs' success is the measure of the taste, the intelligence and sensitivity of his audience.

Phil played The Gaslight in March. One night, just before he was about to go on, he swallowed one of his contact lenses. He'd put it in his mouth to wash it, and as he stood in the kitchen directly offstage, the lens went down. He panicked. Sam tried to calm him, but Phil insisted he couldn't go on without his contact lens. He had prescriptions all over town because he lost a pair a week, but it was too late to get a new one now. He looked around, his lips pinched on both sides, and cleared everyone away. Standing over a butcher block, he stuck his finger down his throat and threw up. He then dove into the green mess with both hands until he found it. "I've got it!" he cried, and, after rinsing it off and putting it in, strummed his way onstage.

Alice decided to move to California with Meegan to start over. Jim and Jean were gone, off to Hollywood pursuing careers in television. Betsy Dotson moved uptown when she began working in the New York office of The Rolling Stones. Alice received postcards from Betsy whenever the Stones flew her to England, which was often. Alice had come of age and, with the money she inherited, decided to buy a house in Mill Valley, California, for sixty thousand dollars. Cash. Gertrude gently tried to talk her out of it. The money didn't matter to Alice. She wanted a great big house with lots of windows, and a color TV for herself and Meegan.

Alice was dressed in black for the flight west. As she kissed Gertrude goodbye, her mother-in-law whispered in her ear how beautiful she looked. "Thank you," Alice said softly, clutching her baby and turning her back on New York.

Phil was over at Judy Collins' place, on the West Side, where everyone now seemed to hang out. He'd come in on fire from The

Gaslight, full of songs and wine, when he first saw Tina Date.

She was an Australian folk singer and a close friend of Judy Collins. In New York for the first time, she was anxious to meet all the New York folkies. Phil corralled her early that night, against the living room wall. It was like a scene from *The Jolson Story:* celebrity picks out girl at party, charms her with showbiz pizzazz, proposes at dawn.

Tina had never heard of Phil Ochs and was annoyed by his constant buzzing and stuttering, understanding little of what he talked about. Phil had no idea Tina was resisting him. When he tried to take her to his place, she turned him down.

He called her the next day and invited her to see him perform at The Gaslight. His songs were pleasant enough, but he was so . . . scruffy, with dirty shoes, an ugly, ill-fitting tweed jacket with a belt in the back, a gray, seamy shirt, and the oiliest hair she'd ever seen.

Phil was sure he'd found the woman of his dreams. He started carrying her picture in his wallet, showing it to everybody, explaining she was the true love of his life.

From the Denver *Post* of March 14, 1965: "Don't be fooled by the title [of the album], Mr. Ochs is still marching, against war, against intolerance, against the South, and nearly everything else that troubles people today, but you have to be in tune with this kind of music to like it."

Record World: "Folkster Ochs writes and sings a bitter song, but his accusations ring too true to ignore. He seems to respond to the violence of the everyday world and implies that anyone who doesn't concern themselves deeply is apathetic and worthless."

The idea for the Berkeley teach-in was Jerry Rubin's. The hope was to draw attention to the growing Anti-war Movement by staging the largest demonstration to date against the war in Vietnam, on the site where the Free Speech Movement had begun. It would be a spectacular, with music, dancing, celebrities.

Rubin was able to get commitments from a wide range of people, including I. F. Stone, Norman Mailer, several senators, speakers from the Left, others from the Right, Isaac Deutscher from Europe, and Paul Krassner from New York. It was Krassner who suggested that Phil Ochs be invited. Rubin had never heard of him. Krassner assured him that Phil would be perfect for the type of event being planned.

Phil broke his commercial engagements to appear at the teach-in. Rubin: "The first thing I learned about Phil was that he knew where the action was. . . . I remember taking him on a tour of the campus the day before the teach-in began, and genuinely liking him. He was totally unpretentious. He listened as much as he talked. He was really there, he was fascinated by the Berkeley campus, the students, the political activists, the Free Speech Movement. That night we stood together on the balcony of the student union overlooking where the event was going to be held."

The next three days brought the phenomenon of the teach-in into the national media. Stories appeared on the network news and in every major newspaper in the country. Rubin became an immediate media symbol of the Anti-war Movement.

It was Phil's job to come to the mike and sing whenever the speeches became too rhetorical. He would sit on a panel next to Rubin. At a given signal, he was to get up and perform one or two songs, then turn the microphone back to the speakers. He did this for three days.

Berkeley was a revelation for Phil. Singing for those people had been a privilege. Now he wanted to sing in every college in the country, for every student, every teacher. Whenever he heard about a campus demonstration taking place against the war, he wanted to be there, even if it meant giving up a paying gig.

He went to Haverford College to participate in the "End the Vietnam War" demonstration; he traveled across the country, taking only his guitar; rallying students, singing for them, loving it when they yelled for more. On May 7, he brought it all back home when he showed up at a rally sponsored by the Free Speech Front, an anti-war coalition at Ohio State. Thousands showed up to see and hear him play. *The Lantern* ran a picture on its front page of Phil, surrounded by students, his guitar in hand, smiling broadly.

Krassner ran a piece by Phil about it in *The Realist,* "How I learned to love the folk scene and stop worrying about music":

> . . . Dallas isn't really all that bad if you stop and think about Columbus, Ohio; at least Dallas almost admits it. And Dallas

doesn't have Ohio State University, which is still discussing the right of freedom of speech while other schools are arguing about pulling out of Vietnam.

When I was a student at State, I was so suffocated by the provincial patriotism that in a fit of madness I wrote a violent pro-Castro article for a dormitory paper. The next day I realized that few people had a sense of humor, as Fidel was hung in effigy with me as the dummy.

It's not every college dropout who can take revenge on his alma mater, I thought, as my train slipped into Ohio under cover of darkness. When I got to campus the next morning, the soporific spirit still prevailed: the art students were doing a bust of Robert Taft; Ray Bliss was recruiting new faces for the shotput team; and the fraternities were building floats out of Regimen tablets. . . .

He began to talk to his audiences more, between songs. No longer the shy country boy, he began to talk more about his experiences in the Anti-war Movement, expressing his dissatisfaction with America's war machine:

Now, for a change of pace, here's a protest song. . . . A protest song is a song that's so specific that you cannot mistake it for bullshit. . . . Good word, bullshit . . . ought to be used more often . . . especially in Washington . . . Speaking of bullshit . . . I'd like to dedicate this song to McGeorge Bundy.

Not everyone appreciated Phil's enthusiasm. He was scheduled to give a concert in Baltimore. The board of School Commissioners tried to have it canceled on the grounds that Phil was a "Communist." Phil's response made the Baltimore newspapers: "I don't feel put down by it. It's a joke, really."

In England, Baez's single of "There but for Fortune" reached No. 13.

With two thousand dollars borrowed from his father, Arthur set up "Arthur H. Gorson Management Inc.", two small rooms at 850 Seventh Avenue. He and Phil went to Albert Grossman to tell him his services were no longer required, thank you. Grossman shrugged his shoulders. He told Arthur it was a mistake for Phil to leave Albert B. Grossman Management. He, Grossman, could do something with Phil's music. He had power in the industry because he had Dylan. He sat back in his chair, lifted one to Phil and said, "It's the right move, but it's a mistake. Ah, well, the world has lost a great manager. Good luck."

Arthur knew nothing about show business. He was a political organizer and assumed that managing a career was the same as organizing a political campaign. Phil knew nothing about managing either, but was sure Grossman had done everything wrong. He would lecture Arthur constantly about what he wanted them to accomplish and the way he thought they should go about accomplishing it.

The day Arthur signed the lease for the office, he and Phil walked over to Carnegie Hall. They slipped through an open door and stood on the empty stage together. Phil spoke softly, "We'll have this place. We'll get Carnegie Hall."

Arthur approached Harold Leventhal about the possibility of producing Phil at Carnegie. Leventhal refused, offering instead to produce a Phil Ochs concert at Town Hall. If the results there were favorable, he would think about Carnegie. That was the logical progression, that was the way it was done. Arthur tried every promoter in town and was turned down by all of them.

So Arthur and Phil decided to produce the concert themselves. They scraped together six hundred dollars for a deposit on the hall, got an advertising agency to agree to bill later, and never thought about what would happen if they failed. They had thousands of handbills and posters made and hung them everywhere— lampposts, the sides of buildings, subway stations. It seemed impossible to walk down a single block in Manhattan and not know that Phil Ochs was coming to Carnegie Hall. Tickets for the concert started at $2.50. Neither of them figured things like cost-versus-profit. They just wanted the house filled.

Arthur hired Suzie Campbell to help him run the office. Suzie was the sister of David Cohen's girlfriend, Sally. Arthur met Suzie when she came with Phil to a party at Arthur's tiny Lower East Side apartment the night his Ukrainian neighbors tried to kick his door down for playing music too loud. Suzie helped Arthur make final preparations for Phil's Carnegie Hall debut, set for January 6, 1966.

Phil saw the office as a base from which to launch his world crusade. There were no limits to how far they could go. The West Coast, Canada, England, Europe; Phil's attitude was, "Let's do it." He was out to conquer the world.

He and Arthur formed "Barricade Music" to keep the rights to Phil's publishing within the organization. This time Phil wanted to retain the rights to his new songs rather than sell them, as he had done with his earlier material to Harold Leventhal. It was a crucial move. This way, profits would begin from record sale number one. Phil was anticipating a lot of money from what he was sure would be a long string of hit singles.

In June, while Arthur continued organizing the office and making preparations for Carnegie, Phil played Canada for the first time. He was a smash at Toronto's Gate of Cleve, enthusiastically received by the largely expatriate audience, and raved about in the press. "Here's to the State of Mississippi" was nominated by the Canadian Federation of English Teachers for "Song of the Year."

Phil appeared with Oscar Brand and Judy Collins in a gymnasium in Ontario, the temperature in the arena below zero. After the show, Phil and Brand discussed the mood in America toward the war in Vietnam. Phil told Brand he couldn't believe the people of the United States knew what was really going on, that "if the public knew, they would stop it."

"Phil," Brand replied, "the public is doing it."

That summer Phil was not invited to perform at Newport, but he went anyway with Arthur. He was there when Dylan made his historic appearance, picking up an electric guitar and changing the course of rock music. Dylan played "Like a Rolling Stone," with Al Kooper on the organ, to the outrage of the crowd, and was booed. He came back with his acoustic guitar to play "It's All Over Now, Baby Blue," and left.

So did Phil and Arthur. *Broadside* magazine, which had previously admonished Dylan for the "Bringing It All Back Home" album, was outraged, as was *Sing Out!*, which was even stronger in expressing its disgust with this "new" Dylan. The folk community, which had thrived on Dylan's success, was suddenly without a leader. Dylan had been the king of protest music, and Ochs the pretender to the throne. Only when Dylan abdicated, he took the throne with him. Everyone in the folk community was sure Phil was outraged at Dylan's selling out to rock and roll. They were wrong.

In a letter to *The Village Voice,* responding to an article the paper had run after Newport, Phil described the "real Bob Dylan":

> I feel I must protest. Because of the nature of Bobby Dylan's songs and mine, I am periodically being used as ammunition against him. He is erratic while I am normal, he has forsaken his principles while I'm dedicated to the cause, etc.
>
> But it ain't me, babe. I'm not the white hope against neurosis; I'm only a writer who as a matter of fact goes out of his way to defend Dylan and his changes. . . . I'd like to straighten out a couple of other common misconceptions that have been floating around. Dylan and I are not in competition with each other; we're in competition with our individual creative processes, trying to stimulate our minds to produce the greatest amount of quality we can. Of course, I hope someday to write ten times better than Dylan; but I also sincerely hope that Dylan will someday write ten times better than Dylan. . . . I can't emphasize strongly enough that there must be no shackles put on any writer to force him to cover certain subject material or use certain styles. Dylan is being violently criticized for using amplified rock 'n' roll as his medium on the Newport folk stage. . . . I understand that even most of the festival directors were quite upset at his performance there, and I think the best way to judge for yourself who was making the most valid musical point is to listen to a couple of Newport records of previous years and then listen to Dylan's new single, "Like a Rolling Stone." . . . The people that thought they were booing Dylan were in reality only booing themselves in a most vulgar display of unthinking mob censorship. Meanwhile, life went on all around them.
>
> As for the reasons for my not being invited to Newport, I wouldn't presume to guess their motivations, but I couldn't help but wonder, perhaps it's my breath?
>
> Phil Ochs

Before the summer was over, rock-and-roll groups began replacing the suddenly out-of-place folk singers in the Village clubs. The Blues Project headlined at the Cafe Au Go Go, The Lovin' Spoonful were packing them in at the Night Owl. Dylan's influence was so strong that by going electric he had shorted the careers of dozens of would-be spokesmen for their generation.

In August, Phil returned to Canada to headline the Mariposa Folk Festival. It was Saturday night. As he started to sing, the rains came. Thick Canadian rain pelted the four thousand people sitting on the ground. No one moved. The lights failed, then the sound. Phil went wild as hundreds of flashlights shone up from the crowd, lighting him in a Riefenstahlian tableau. Someone rushed to the stage with a portable public-address system. Phil sang, his voice projected through the single bullhorn. It was an inspired moment; the audience was on its feet, splashing the rain with their hands as they cheered him on.

Phil played Carnegie Hall that September as part of the mammoth Sing-in for Peace. It was the first major New York concert protesting the war. Everyone in the folk world participated, including Dylan. Although he performed "Blowin' in the Wind" that night, he was much more interested in what people would think of his newest single, "Sooner or Later." Backstage he sang it twice for Phil, who wasn't impressed. He told Dylan he didn't think it was a very good song. Dylan was pissed off. He walked away from Phil, saying nothing. Later, he and Phil were going uptown sharing a cab when Dylan ordered the driver to pull over. He told Phil to get out, expelling him from Highway 61.

In November, Phil was invited to do a week at Toronto's Faim Foetale. He and Arthur were watching Canadian TV early Tuesday evening when a bulletin announced that New York City and most of the East Coast had been blacked out by a power failure. After watching for a while longer, switching channels, getting as many details as possible, Phil told Arthur he was going for a walk and would be back soon. He returned before long, flushed, excited, out of breath. He'd just written a new song. He played it for Arthur, and then played it over and over and over. "Changes" marked a breakthrough for Phil as a songwriter. He'd written his first abstractly lyrical song; a song with no political message, no sociological lesson; a wistful song about romance, if not about love. "Listen to the melody . . . listen to the melody, can you dig it?" he murmured, his chin slouching on his guitar.

Sit by my side, come as close as the air
Share in a memory of gray
And wander in my words, and dream about the
Pictures that I play of changes . . .

The world's spinning madly, it drifts in the dark
Swings through a hollow of haze
A race around the stars, a journey through the
Universe ablaze with changes . . .

Your tears will be tremblin', now we're somewhere else.
One last cup of wine we will pour
And I'll kiss you one more time and leave you on the
Rolling river shores of changes.

Still later that night, Phil tried to call Tina, but couldn't reach her. So he called Alice instead and sang the song for her over the phone. Alice was happy to hear from Phil, and invited him out to California to see her. He said he would, asked about Meegan, and sang the song for her again, after which he asked her if she thought it was great.

"It's great, Phil," Alice said, twice, before hanging up.

Although Phil's Carnegie concert was sold out weeks in advance, Arthur continued running ads, putting a "sold out" stripe across all of them, a mark of his pride and his triumph.

Gertrude was proud of her son. She made arrangements for everyone in the family to be at the concert, including Fanny, who, although she was well past eighty, insisted she come along to see her grandson perform on the great Carnegie stage.

As curtain time approached, Phil grew increasingly agitated. The excitement had been building inside of him all day. Telegrams were arriving from as far away as England:

> Socialists worldwide join me in wishing you an artistic but nonetheless financial success. Please confirm or deny the following rumors for Tass Soviet News Agency: 1. You have signed a three-million-dollar contract with Brian Epstein. 2. You will lip-sync tonight's concert. 3. B. F. Sloan is a personification of your

wildest nightmare. 4. You are Lyndon B. Johnson's political philosophy twin. 5. You lease, at great personal profit, the town of Woodstock, New York, to Albert Grossman. 6. Elektra will deduct the cost of the go-go dancers for your concert from royalties.

Betsy

Just before he was about to go on, he lost his voice. He was clearing his throat every two seconds, rasping and hacking, trying to get it back. He drank water, he washed his face, he changed his socks, but his voice remained a harsh scratch. Arthur paced back and forth, silently. Suzie Campbell had given Phil a haircut earlier in the day at the office, and was now contantly brushing hairs off his jacket and trying to fix his collar.

Finally, the moment arrives. He walks onstage strumming his guitar. Although facing his audience, the follow-spot obliterates the people from his sight.

Oh I marched to the battle of New Orleans . . .

Even with a sore throat, he makes the songs sound pretty. The young men in the audience study him, their chins held in their hands. The women want to mother him.

He sings of the romance of rebellion. To rebel is the duty and the privilege of the young:

Oh, I am just a student, sir, and I only want to learn
But it's hard to read through the risin' smoke
Of the books that you like to burn
So I'd like to make a promise and I'd like to make a vow
That when I've got something to say, sir
I'm gonna say it now . . .

The audience approves. Applause for performance marks the alliance. They will understand, he will teach. They will listen, he will sing . . .

Wade into the river, through the rippling shadow waters
Steal across the thirsty border, Bracero
Come bring your hungry body, to the golden fields of plenty,
From a peso to a penny, Bracero . . .

"We'll do a song then about revolution. What's been true of all revolutions from the beginning, the French, the American . . .

this is a fictional song, a cinematic song, you've got to picture this mansion on the top of the hill housing the last of the idle rich, the last of the bourgeois, the last of the folk singers . . . as they're being circled tighter and tighter by the ringing of revolution . . . all the people on the inside spiritually resemble Charles Laughton . . . and all the people on the outside physically resemble Lee Marvin . . . as a matter of fact this song is so cinematic that it's been made into a movie . . . it stars Senator Carl Hayden as Ho Chi Minh . . . Frank Sinatra plays Fidel Castro . . . Ronald Reagan plays George Murphy . . . John Wayne plays Lyndon Johnson . . . and Lyndon Johnson plays God . . . I play Bobby Dylan, a young Bobby Dylan . . ."

> *In a building of gold, with riches untold*
> *Lived the families on which the country was founded . . .*

Are there any who still fail to understand what it's all about?

> *Is there anybody here who'd like to wrap the flag*
> *around an early grave?*
> *Is there anybody here who thinks they're standin'*
> *taller on a battle wave?*

"The other night, a voice came to me. Turned out it was God. Said, 'Ochs, wake up, this is God here. Over.' I said, 'You're putting me on of course, Dylan.' So he did a few tricks, moved the bed back and forth. Trembling, I asked, 'What is it you want, Oh Lord?' He said, 'Well, frankly, Phil, I went downtown the other day. Saw *The Greatest Story Ever Told*. Couldn't believe it. It's gone too far. Something must be done about Christianity.' Then, woof, in a puff of smoke he disappeared. The next morning I woke up, had a few drinks and realized it was all true. I decided to do something about Christianity. But what could I do? Me, a poor, humble boy from the sticks. Then I remembered, I was a songwriter. Aha. So I sat down with pen in hand . . . over to my typewriter . . . and ended up writing this next song which is about Christianity. Actually an anti-hymn, the first anti-hymn, folks."

> *Christian cannons have fired at my days*
> *With a warning beneath the holy blaze*
> *And bow to our authority*
> *Say the cannons of Christianity . . .*

Act Two.

> *Come, get out of the way, boys*
> *Quick, get out of the way.*
> *You'd better watch what you say, boys*
> *Better watch what you say . . .*
> *We've rammed in your harbor*
> *And tied to your port*
> *And our pistols are hungry*
> *And our tempers are short,*
> *So bring your daughters around to the fort*
> *Cause we're the cops of the world, boys*
> *We're the cops of the world . . .*

"There's been a drastic change in American foreign policy in recent months. Take the Dominican Republic, which we did . . . a little while ago, killing a few people here and there, mostly there . . . saving the day for freedom and democracy in the Western Hemisphere, once again, folks. I was over there, entertaining the troops. I won't say which troops. Over there with a USO group including Walter Lippmann and Soupy Sales . . . I played there in a small coffeehouse called The Sniper . . . and this was my most unpopular song . . . with the poetic, symbolic title, 'The Marines Have Landed on the Shores of Santo Domingo.'"

> *. . . and the crabs are crazy, they scuttle back and forth*
> *The sand is burning.*
> *And the fish take flight, and scatter from the sight;*
> *   their course is turning.*
> *As the seagulls rest on the cold cannon nest*
> *The sea is churning*
> *The marines have landed on the shores of Santo Domingo . . .*

"In every American community there are varying shades of political opinion . . . one of the shadiest of these is the liberals. An outspoken group on many subjects . . . ten degrees to the left of center in good times, ten degrees to the right of center if it affects them personally . . . so here then is a lesson in safe logic . . ."

> *I cried when they shot Medgar Evers*
> *Tears ran down my spine*
> *And I cried when they shot Mr. Kennedy*
> *As though I'd lost a father of mine.*

But Malcolm X got what was coming,
He got what he asked for this time.
So love me, love me, love me,
I'm a liberal . . .

Then, the revelation. "Changes." The metaphor for revolution is the reality of young love. Or is the reality of revolution the metaphor for love?

A final thought closes the show. It is not political; it is philosophical. It is not about living; it is about life.

There's no place in this world where I'll belong
When I'm gone
And I won't know the right from the wrong
When I'm gone
And you won't find me singin' on this song
When I'm gone
So I guess I'll have to do it while I'm here . . .

Then he's gone.

In many ways it was the last performance of "Phil Ochs, the singing journalist"; the final edition of all the news fit to sing. While he would continue to use social and political issues as a springboard for many of his songs, his themes were evolving, his songs becoming more personal, more politically abstract.

Clearly, Phil was influenced by Dylan's metamorphosis, from political nihilist to mystical androgyne, *like a rolling stone.* Woody's children were growing up. For years, Phil had written songs about the romance of politics. Now he was starting to write about the politics of romance. It was inevitable; Dylan's abandonment of protest music was an assassination of style. Phil Ochs, the singing journalist, was executed in the name of rock and roll.

The album finally released contained all Phil's between-songs patter and most of his new material, omitting any songs which had appeared in the earlier albums. Arthur had arranged with Jac Holzman to have the concert recorded for release as a live album. Although they went to considerable expense to capture Phil live, the album almost never got made.

Most of the tape from Carnegie was unusable. That night Phil had been hoarse, nervous, stumbling over lines. The reviews of the show were mixed. Shelton, in the *Times,* noted: "One suspects it was a bad case of nerves that kept [Ochs] from bringing the many fine things he has in his verbal-musical arsenal to the auditorium." *The Village Voice* agreed: "In trying to judge Phil Ochs' first Carnegie Hall concert last Friday night . . . it's necessary to separate his material from his performance . . ."

Arthur persuaded Phil to go to Jordan Hall in Boston, to repeat the show for the sake of the album. Most of what ended up on the record came from that show, but even much of that wasn't good enough. There were bits and pieces included from Carnegie, and from Jordan, but most of the album was actually recorded, with no audience, in Judson Hall, across the street from Carnegie, and the least expensive place they could find to approximate the acoustics at the concerts. Nearly every line of the vocals was punched in, audience reactions heavily augmented. The idea was to capture a live Phil Ochs performance; what they got was one of the most doctored "live" albums ever recorded.

When the album was released, there were new problems. Phil insisted that the back of the album carry a series of poems by Mao Tse-tung, underneath which would appear, "Is This the enemy?" Phil couldn't wait for the album to be pressed. He sent the first copy he received to Mao. He wanted him to know the name of Phil Ochs; he hoped the Chinese leader would write back to him. Elektra Records stood by Phil, even when half the distributors of the album refused to carry it because of Mao's poetry. It was a courageous move on Jac Holzman's part; Elektra was a small company with a lot of money invested in the album. At one point before the jackets were printed, Holzman called Arthur to ask if Phil would consider changing the liner notes. The answer was no, and Holzman went along. In fact, Phil had Holzman send Mao a fifty-dollar royalty check for the use of his poetry. It was never cashed.

Arthur quickly culled the best from the reviews and released a flyer to the press, filled with raves from as far away as Canada. The Toronto *Globe:* "Phil Ochs sings the frightening truth, and in such an enjoyable way that there is no alternative but to listen." Arthur was hoping to overcome the resistance to distribute by the one factor that meant more than politics in the record industry. Sales.

Reviews of the album continued to appear. Some, like the one in *Variety,* begrudgingly approved of Phil's talent, while questioning his politics. "Could he sing his songs in China?" *Billboard* awarded the album a Special Merit Pick. By April, it was No. 24 in the "Looking Ahead" section of *Cash Box.* By July, "Phil Ochs in Concert" reached No. 150 on the *Billboard* listing of best-selling albums across the country.

It would have gone higher if a hit single could have been broken from it. For, by 1966 album sales were heavily influenced by the top ten. The Beatles, The Rolling Stones, and Bob Dylan had revolutionized the concept of the rock-and-roll "album." Singles were taken from albums and made into hits, resulting in increased sales of the albums they came from. The Beatles' and Rolling Stones' albums always outsold Bob Dylan's because, until 1965, Dylan had never recorded a hit single. After "Like a Rolling Stone," sales of Dylan's albums soared.

The fact that "Phil Ochs in Concert" broke into *Billboard*'s top 150 was impressive, for no single had been released from it. What probably helped sales was Joan Baez's hit version of "There but for Fortune," released as a single, backed with Bob Dylan's "Daddy, You've Been on My Mind." Baez recorded the song after Jackie Washington, a Village folkie and friend of Phil's, had brought the song to her in Boston. A much more successful recording in England than it was in the United States, it was nevertheless the first "hit" record with only a single acoustic guitar accompaniment. Phil loved the fact that "There but for Fortune" was the hit, and Dylan's song the B side. The next goal was to have a hit record written and performed by Phil Ochs.

As the Seventh Avenue crusade continued, Arthur H. Gorson Management began to sign on additional acts. The group moved upstairs to a larger office, and took on Eric Andersen, David Blue (David Cohen), Jim and Jean (fresh from quitting Andy Williams and back in New York), Judy Roderick, and Tom Rush. Arthur H. Gorson Management took 15 per cent from all its acts, most of which Arthur put right back into the financing of the office and new shows. It was becoming the hottest management office on the East Coast, challenging Albert Grossman for the best stable of folk acts in the country. Phil and the others performed constantly. Expenses were high, especially traveling and promotion. They should have been making a lot of money, but they were barely keeping their heads above water. Arthur grouped his performers and offered packages for a very attractive price, enabling smaller clubs and universities, normally unable to afford so many acts on a single bill, to book Phil Ochs, Eric Andersen, David Blue, Judy Roderick, Jim and Jean, and Tom Rush for an evening of folk music. The idea was to reach new audiences.

As Phil traveled around the country, performing, ideas for songs kept coming to him. He would write down lines on scraps of paper, on tablecloths, on his wrist if he had to. One night, in a cafe, he got into a heated political discussion with a stranger. The other fellow sat back in his chair, waved one hand, and sighed, "It wouldn't really interest anybody outside of a small circle of friends." Phil jumped out of his seat, laughing, "Great line for a song!" It would serve as the title for Phil's ironic description of the fear and apathy surrounding the murder of Kitty Genovese.

Phil's songs continued to be covered by a wide variety of performers—some, perhaps, not fully aware of who he was. Anita Bryant, about to embark on a tour with Bob Hope for the boys in Vietnam, was gathering material for an album of patriotic songs. Someone suggested she sing "The Power and the Glory." At the recording session she kept interrupting the takes, asking if it was really a patriotic song, and what did "only as rich as the poorest of the poor, only as free as a padlock prison door" mean? She recorded it anyway.

Phil's main diversion while touring was going to the movies. He saw *The Spy Who Came in from the Cold, Black Orpheus,* and *The Umbrellas of Cherbourg,* while playing the Faim Foetale, prior to his appearing at the Mariposa Folk Festival, in Canada; saw *T.N.T.* in Ohio, the same day he met Donovan for the first time; played an engagement with The Butterfield Blues Band, met P. J. Proby, taped a promo in San Francisco for a radio program on KQED: saw *The Young and the Damned* (*Los Olvidados*), Renoir's *Monsieur Lange,* while doing a series of concerts for SDS of Michigan, SDS of Chicago; met Muddy

Waters, saw *Morgan, Children of Paradise;* ate at New York's Artists and Writers Restaurant because it was where the old *Tribune* writers used to hang out; got drunk at the Astor bar after meeting and arguing with Tina, saw *East of Eden* for the twentieth time, met Bo Diddley, saw *The Group* and hated it; was invited to the mansion of Manfred and Renata Clynes, broke up laughing and had to leave, walked down the road and played miniature golf with himself, then went to see *Years of Lightning, Days of Drums;* saw *La Notte* and *The Agony and the Ecstasy* in Detroit; saw *Inside Daisy Clover,* was interviewed in New York by *Newsweek* magazine, and then went to a Preminger double feature, *The Man with the Golden Arm* and *The Moon Is Blue,* wound up that day guesting on Bob Fass's all-night WBAI talk show along with Eric Andersen and Arthur; returned to Chicago for a political benefit and to play the club Poor Richard; did another folk festival in Berkeley, went to see *Red Desert;* returned to New York, spent a few days with Tina which ended in a brawl; wrote "I've Had Her (She's Nothing)," and wound up at the Newport Folk Festival.

Phil was away from the office a lot, leaving Arthur to run things. Arthur wanted to move into record production. He formed Wild Indigo Productions, still another branch of the management firm. The first album produced was Jim and Jean's "Changes," which contained several Barricade-controlled Phil Ochs songs.

Arthur had come a long way that first year. The pressure on him was enormous and began to spill over into his personal life. He broke a cardinal business rule and became romantically involved with his assistant, Suzie Campbell. Quickly, they were engaged to be married. They began to bring the tension and problems of running the office home with them. Their bickering over little things soon developed into full-scale arguments. They started fighting all the time, throwing each other out of cabs, rooms, restaurants.

Arthur went on the road with Phil for a short time, and when he returned, found Suzie living with his concert manager. The two men talked over the situation in the office. Two nights later, Arthur broke a chair over his former concert manager's head in the Cafe Au Go Go. Suzie married Paul Harris, the piano player.

Phil was aware of what was going on, and it bothered him. He was concerned, not about Arthur's feelings, but about his ability to continue to run the office effectively. Perhaps, he thought, if Arthur had concentrated more on Phil's career than on Suzie Campbell's affections, "Changes" might have been a hit.

Arthur suggested to Phil they go to England in order to introduce Phil's music over there and possibly open up a foreign branch of the management office. Phil wanted to go to England for a lot of reasons, one of which was to see Tina, who had flown to London after their last fight.

Upon landing at Heathrow, Phil bought up every newspaper and magazine available. He insisted that Arthur and he check into the best hotel, and ordered a huge dinner for both of them.

Arthur had several people to see. One of them was Tito Burns, an executive of the Grade Organization, a British-based management firm which he wanted to handle tours in Great Britain for Phil, Eric Andersen, Jim and Jean, Judy Roderick, and Tom Rush. Arthur also had several meetings with David Platz of Essex Music, who was the Stones' publisher, to discuss his handling Wild Indigo and Barricade copyrights in the United Kingdom and Europe. It was agreed that Essex would administer copyrights if it could produce a British hit of a Barricade product; otherwise, all rights would revert to Arthur. To lock up the agreement, David Platz handed Arthur a check for five thousand dollars against future Barricade royalties.

During all of this, Phil very much wanted to meet The Beatles. One afternoon he walked over to their office, introduced himself, and was brought in to see John Lennon. They sat around and talked, Lennon knowing who Phil was, Phil knowing who Lennon was. After a few polite moments, Phil left. He walked to Hyde Park, sat alone, and fed the pigeons.

Melody Maker: "If Bob Dylan is the king of protest—and some say he's already abdicated—Phil Ochs, who arrived in London at the beginning of this week, is the President."

The President of Protest decided to look up Betsy Dotson, now Betsy Asher, married to Peter Asher, of Peter and Gordon. Betsy introduced Phil to Peter, and the three of them traveled around London, seeing shows, going to discotheques, eating in the finest restaurants, drinking. With Peter's help, Phil was finally able to locate the hotel where Tina was staying. He and Arthur checked out of their present hotel and into Tina's. In fact, they reserved the adjoining suite. Phil wanted to see her, but she refused to ever talk to him again.

It was late at night. Arthur was in the next room when he heard the crash. Phil was breaking up the room, throwing chairs into walls and mirrors, thrashing about, enraged, his hands bleeding from the flying glass. He was in a fury because Tina ("that bitch!") wouldn't see him. Phil and Arthur were thrown out of the hotel and "warned" never to come back. They checked into their third hotel of the trip.

Arthur was able, with Tito Burns's help, to put together for Phil a brief tour of several British pubs, folk clubs, and universities in Birmingham, Manchester, Cardiff, Nottingham, Liverpool, Cambridge, and finally London. It was an exploratory tour designed to see just how Phil and his music would be received in England. The reactions were mostly curiosity combined with an inability to crack Phil's American vernacular.

They traveled by lorry. Late one night, while Arthur was driving and Phil was in the back, watching the stars, the song came to him. From nowhere. He would later describe "Crucifixion" as "only the greatest song I've ever written." It was about Kennedy, but it wasn't like "That Was the President." It was about Christ, but it wasn't religious. And it was about Phil's fascination with the night; the ultimate journey, death. It was, at last, his fade-in to greatness.

> *And the night comes again to the circle studded sky*
> *In loneliness they gather, in emptiness they lie*
> *Till the universe explodes as a falling star is raised*
> *Planets are paralyzed, mountains are amazed*
> *But they all glow brighter from the brilliance of the blaze*
> *With the speed of insanity then he dies!*

When they arrived back at Kennedy, Phil picked up a copy of *Cavalier* magazine—*Esquire* with tits. In it was a feature about Phil written by Robert Shelton. Shelton was one of those critics who'd been angered by Dylan's rock and roll and had turned to Phil as the new leader of topical songwriting. Also in this issue was an article Phil had written, "That Was the Year That Weren't."

Shelton's profile contained Phil's opinion of The Beatles ("a sexual outlet for young, overenergetic people. The Beatles masturbate their audiences, but the music is great!"), of Vietnam ("The Vietcong are right because they provide an extreme answer to the extreme problems of poverty, famine, disease. We should support Ho Chi Minh as the last workable bulwark against Communist China in Asia."). Phil's article was much more tongue-in-cheek. He wrote about a new game he'd invented, "Album Titles." Cover: A color close-up of a large female breast; title: "More Judy Henske." Cover: A leering, bearded man aiming a rifle out of a window; title: "Another Side of Dave Van Ronk." Cover: A dungareed, half-smiling, long-haired boy walking down a snow-covered street with Suze Rotolo; title: "The Free-Stealin' Phil Ochs."

Phil told Arthur he wanted to perform at Carnegie Hall again. With the success of the live album, he'd gained more confidence and wanted to return to Carnegie to give a better performance than the first one. Arthur arranged for a Thanksgiving Eve concert. Once again Gertrude brought the family to see Phil perform. It snowed heavily that night, but even this didn't deter Fanny, who took the bus and subway in to see the show.

During the intermission, Phil introduced Gertrude to David Blue. He told her, privately, David was going to be a star, much bigger than Dylan. Gertrude wasn't impressed. She thought he was too well dressed, and when he said hello to her he hardly moved his mouth. During the second part of the show, Phil introduced David Blue to the audience and let him sing a song. Then, Phil's final song of the evening. His first public performance of "Crucifixion." It was like nothing they'd heard before:

Phil lowering his head for the quiet parts,

> *The Spanish bulls are beaten; the crowd is soon beguiled,*
> *The matador is beautiful, a symphony of style . . .*

raising his head, shaking it to crescendo,

> *Then this overflow of life is crushed into a liar*
> *The gentle soul is ripped apart and tossed into the fire . . .*

toning his accompaniment as an alternating bass,

> *Time takes her toll and the memory fades*
> *But his glory is growin' in the magic that he made.*
> *Reality is ruined; there is nothing more to fear*
> *The drama is distorted to what they want to hear*
> *Swimming in their sorrow in the twisting of a tear*
> *As they wait for the new thrill parade . . .*

holding his guitar as if it were a woman, one hand on her neck, the other around her waist, leading, dipping, rocking to the chorus,

> *So dance dance dance*
> *Teach us to be true*
> *Come dance dance dance*
> *'Cause we love you . . .*

Coming in off the beat, imposing the final stanza, a repeat of the opening, now a fade-out,

> *And the night comes again . . .*

> *They are on their feet, their hands above their heads, clapping, their voices demanding more.*
> *He gives them everything. All he wants in return is their love in the form of a hit record. Just one. With a bullet.*

VI

My rhymes are all repeating
My ballad's growing blind
My words have turned to water
The women turn to wine.
Sorry, I can't stop and talk now
I'm in kind of a hurry anyhow
But I'll send you a tape from California.
            Phil Ochs, "Tape from California"

Arthur produced a "Baroque Beatles Concert" at Carnegie Hall, a program of classically performed Beatle music. It was a financial disaster, the first time he'd actually lost money for the company. He then signed Joni Mitchell, an unknown folk singer from Canada. Phil insisted they couldn't take on any more acts, they had too many already. He was afraid his pivotal position was being threatened; he began to complain that his career was being ignored, that Arthur was paying too much attention to the others. Joni Mitchell was let go, her publishing returned to her. Eventually, it would be worth millions.

There were other problems; arrangements for Phil's first large-scale tour of England had broken down. The British Government was demanding a complete accounting of Phil's expenses for the previous pub tour. Essex asked for the same from Arthur. Before Phil could return to England, any back taxes which were due had to be paid. The details were finally worked out, and Phil did tour England, but the trip was plagued. There were misunderstandings about dates, confusion regarding transportation, and problems with hotel reservations. Small annoyances became large ones. Phil lost a contact lens somewhere in Birmingham. A telegram had to be sent to the New York office, requesting a replacement set of lenses to be forwarded "as fast as possible."

Essex Music was also having difficulties. It hadn't been as easy as everyone thought it would be to get British pop stars to record Phil Ochs. His lyrics were too obscure, his melodies lacked the eclectic appeal of the "British Sound" of The Beatles, The Rolling Stones, and The Dave Clark Five. After weeks of negotiation, Crispian St. Peters, who'd had a hit record with "The Pied Piper," released his version of "Changes." It reached the top twenty in England. The only other Phil Ochs song to be recorded there was the B side of a Peter and Gordon single. Peter Asher chose "Flower Lady" for the other side of "Lady Godiva" in return for the British publishing rights to the song. It was less than a smashing success.

Back in New York, the office continued to have its problems. Eric Andersen was lured away by Brian Epstein with the promise of stardom. Epstein was going to personally manage his career. Judy Roderick's career had never gotten off the ground. Jim and Jean were fighting with each other. When Phil returned from England, he wanted to know why he couldn't get a shot on network TV. Arthur tried to explain to Phil that no one was getting TV exposure since "Hootenanny" had been canceled. And anyway Arthur was becoming annoyed with Phil's constantly reminding him of how it was Phil Ochs who'd set him up in business, how it was Phil Ochs who was responsible for his success, how without Phil Ochs there was no Arthur Gorson. Arthur preferred being in the studio to tracking down contact lens prescriptions.

They sat in the office one night, sharing a bottle of wine. They'd decided to end it. Arthur would retain a slight interest in the Barricade songs, but that would be all. He wanted nothing more. As they worked out the details, they avoided each other's eyes.

Michael and Phil hadn't spoken to each other in years. After graduating from Ohio State, Michael had moved to Los Angeles, hoping to make it as a photographer. It had been difficult. He'd taken a number of jobs to support himself. He worked for a while as a night janitor, mopping floors in order to survive.

The photo assignments came slowly, and the money wasn't much, but his pictures were good, and he began to get work. While negotiating with Bob Krasnow of Buddah Records to shoot the cover for the new Sopwith Camel album, Krasnow asked if the rumors about Phil were true, that he'd left Arthur Gorson and Elektra Records. If they were, he wanted him bad. It was the first Michael had heard about it. He told Krasnow to get in touch with Phil right away. Krasnow asked him to call his brother as a personal favor. Because Michael needed the album cover assignment, he decided to make the call. He got Phil on the phone that night. "I'm just calling to tell you that Bob Krasnow is very interested in signing you to Buddah. I hear you're shopping, and you should get in touch with him because he's real enthusiastic about the possibility of . . ."

"Wait a minute, wait a minute," Phil said quickly. He'd been caught completely off guard by the call. His mind raced as he spoke. "What are you doing now? What's happening?"

"I'm into photography."

Phil lowered his voice. "Look, uh, I've left Arthur. I need a manager. You're the only one I can trust. Would you be willing to come back to New York?"

"No."

"Look, I've really changed. I'm not into the same trip I was when you left. I think we'll get along now. I guarantee you I'm different. I met this girl, Tina, who destroyed me. I now know what it's like to be treated that badly. We'll definitely get along. How are you making out?"

"Breaking even."

"Okay, then, you can make a lot of money. I need someone I can trust. It'll be great for the both of us. We can be brothers again."

Michael paused, taking a deep breath. "I need a month to wrap things up here."

"One week and you got a deal." Phil gave Michael 25 per cent, unheard of in the industry.

In January 1967, they set up an office at 1697 Broadway. It was a show business building, in the heart of Tin Pan Alley. They had "Aquarian Age Inc.," the name of their new company, painted on the door, and they were in business.

Michael's first assignment from Phil came quickly. "Find me a woman and get me an apartment."

"Is that what managers do?"

"Yes. You're my personal manager. That's why you're getting 25 per cent."

Michael picked up a copy of *The Village Voice* that Wednesday at five-thirty in the morning. He started circling apartments listed for rent. He took the IRT to Spring Street to check out a couple of places, figuring to start in that neighborhood and work his way north. He looked at a great duplex on Prince Street, with large square rooms and wide sheets of light streaming in through the windows. The super told him he'd just rented it to someone else.

"Are you sure it's rented?" Michael asked, crushing a fifty-dollar bill into the fellow's hand.

"Actually, you were here first."

Michael knew a girl from college who'd recently moved to New York. He invited her to go with him to the opening of the new discotheque Cheetah. He wanted to know if she had a friend for Phil. She did.

Phil hated Karen from the moment they met. "She's the downest chick I've ever met in my life," he told Michael.

"Yeah," his brother said. "But she is gorgeous."

That she was. "What do you think of the place?" Phil asked her as they sat sipping drinks, watching the other couples dancing.

"Very sixties," she shouted back over the blast of rock and roll. Phil blew air threw his lips. She was beautiful, but a definite down.

A week later they were living together on Prince Street.

The first Phil Ochs concert arranged by Michael was set for a Saturday night in Potsdam, New York. In the flushed excitement of getting the office together, they'd both forgotten to make arrangements for transportation. Michael called every train and bus that went even close to the upstate New York town, but there was no way to get there in time unless they hired a plane and flew.

Phil was totally against this. He never flew. He remembered Buddy Holly.

"Come on, Phil. It's safer than shit. We've got to do it, it's the

only way to get there. Do you want the first concert we do together to be a no-show?" Michael worked on him for hours. Phil
marched around the office—his brother, in step, behind him.
"Have you ever missed a concert?"

"No."

"Come on, we gotta do it. Come on, man, no problem. There's
nothing to be afraid of." Michael was scared shitless. He'd flown
only once before himself. But he wanted this concert. He finally
convinced Phil to charter a plane.

They boarded the two-engine Cessna late that afternoon. "I've
got to get drunk for this," Phil said, as he brought a bottle of wine
to his lips. They arrived on time. Phil did three encores while
Michael was busy arranging for two seats back to New York on
the last commercial flight. When Phil finally came off the stage,
Michael grabbed him by the coat and practically had to drag him
away from the fans, who were waiting for Phil by his dressing
room, to a hired car.

They just made it to the plane, flopping into their first-class
seats like two conquering heroes. They'd done it. The Ochs
boys. Michael smiled and turned to Phil, who was already asleep,
his mouth open, his head cocked to one side.

Michael's goal was to make Phil a star. The first step was
choosing a new record label. It was clear that Phil's relationship
with Elektra was over. Holzman had signed a number of rock acts
to the label, including Clearlight and The Doors. The folk acts were
offended, Phil among them. Holzman had always claimed there was
simply not enough money to pay large advances to Elektra's artists, or to sponsor promotional tours to sell albums. The combined
production costs of Phil's three albums on Elektra had been under
ten thousand dollars, less than Holzman gave The Doors as a bonus
to sign. When it was time for Phil's contract to be renewed, he'd
made a list of demands for Arthur to present to Holzman. Holzman had suggested a budget of ten thousand dollars for the promotion of the first new album, with an additional fund of ten cents
from every new album sold to be used to promote the first three
Phil Ochs albums. Phil demanded fifteen thousand dollars and fifteen cents per record. He also expressed his dissatisfaction with
Paul Rothchild as the producer of the first three albums. Phil

wanted the right to choose his next producer. He also wanted an
escalating scale of royalties: 5 per cent until all session costs were
recouped, to a ceiling of 8 per cent on all sales over seventy-five
thousand albums. These figures were based on the fact that the unit
cost of an album decreased as its sales increased.

Phil wanted, as a bonus, the difference between the amount
budgeted for production and the amount actually spent, nonrefundable and up front. He wanted 60 per cent of all subsidiary and
foreign rights.

Holzman, on the other hand, wanted a commitment from Phil
for three albums in the next two years. Phil preferred to record on
"inspiration." He wanted a one-year contract with two one-year
options.

Holzman felt Phil's demands were harsh. His record sales
hadn't been that great; the total sale of all three Phil Ochs albums
was approximately forty-two thousand units. Holzman mentioned
this to Phil, who argued that sales weren't higher because the albums had been poorly promoted. Thirty-five per cent of all his
record sales came from New York. His second biggest market was
Canada, where he'd appeared in several folk festivals and at numerous coffeehouses. His sales in that country amounted to 11
per cent of all albums sold. San Francisco, the center of the student anti-war Free Speech Movement, was responsible for only 2
per cent, about the same as Los Angeles, while Philadelphia, not
exactly a liberal stronghold, was right behind Canada, with 10 per
cent, followed by Boston, with 9 per cent. It was clear to Phil his
sales were related to personal appearances, not financed by Elektra, rather than the minimal advertising of his albums the company had done.

Unable to come to terms, Phil and Elektra parted company.
Phil rejected Buddah quickly, feeling the label wasn't big
enough for him. He wanted Columbia, and after Columbia,
Warner Brothers because of its connection to the movies. It
looked as if Phil was going to sign with Warner. Mo Ostin, its
president, offered him a twenty-five-thousand-dollar bonus to
sign. Just before the deal was finalized, Phil decided he had to
have Columbia, if only because Dylan was there. Michael set up a
meeting with two representatives from the label, David Swainey
and David Rubinson, both of whom had worked on the Anita

Bryant recording of "The Power and the Glory." They met for drinks at The Tin Angel, in the Village. Phil asked Swainey how tight he was with Clive Davis.

"Real tight."

"Good," Phil said, sipping a glass of white wine. "Call him up. I want to go over to his apartment. I want to speak to Clive. To-night." Without hesitating, Swainey called Davis.

"Sure," Davis said. "Come on up."

It was after eleven when they arrived. Davis greeted them dressed in a formal dinner jacket. The apartment was set in candle-light. Phil shook Clive's hand, and a few minutes later, with Davis sitting on the sofa, played all eight songs he'd written for the pro-jected "Pleasures of the Harbor" album.

When he finished, he put his guitar down and had a glass of wine. "Okay, I want you," Clive said. "How much do you want to sign with Columbia?" Michael spoke for Phil, looking directly at Clive. "We want twenty-five thousand dollars." Davis agreed on the spot.

The next day Michael and Phil's lawyer met with the attorneys for Columbia Records. At the meeting, one of the company's law-yers said the figure was too high and Columbia wouldn't pay it. Michael reminded him that Davis himself had okayed the deal, verbally, the night before, in his home. Incredibly, Phil's lawyer decided to try and negotiate with Columbia, at which point Mi-chael stood and said, "There is no negotiation. Either we get what was promised to us or we leave."

They left. Outside Columbia's building, Michael fired Phil's lawyer.

Back at the office, they tried to figure out what had gone wrong. Maybe Columbia was using Phil to undercut Davis' authority. It was possible, also, that Davis had had second thoughts and de-cided to pull a move that would force Phil to pull out of the deal. At any rate, it was off.

Low on Phil's list was MGM's Verve-Forecast, formerly Verve-Folkways, because, while it had The Blues Project, Tim Hardin, Richie Havens, and Janis Ian, it hadn't been able to develop any of its acts into superstars. They'd had a shot at Dylan, but he'd re-signed with Columbia. Jerry Schoenbaum, president of MGM, offered to let Michael name his price. He asked for thirty thousand. Shoenbaum agreed. Phil freaked at the thought of actually signing with MGM; he just couldn't do it.

Michael flew to California, to talk with A&M Records, another label interested in signing Phil. Its stable included Burt Bacharach, The Baja Marimba Band, Claudine Longet, Herbie Mann, Jimmy Rodgers, Procul Harum, Chris Montez, Liza Minnelli, and Wes Montgomery. Phil Ochs would be its ultimate *non sequitur.*

Jerry Moss, president of A&M, offered twenty-five thousand dollars, but he wanted the publishing rights to Phil's music included in the deal. Michael said no, the publishing had to be separate, there was no way it could be thrown in. He went to see Mo Ostin, at Warner Brothers, and it seemed a deal was still possible there. He met one more time with Jerry Moss, and finally a deal was worked out where Phil could retain the publishing rights to his material. Moss assured Michael that Phil would be free to record his songs without any censorship problem from the label, and he would be included on all production decisions. Michael told Phil the A&M deal was the best they could get. "Okay," Phil said. "Let's take it."

A&M planned a cross-country promotional tour for Phil, beginning in March at Philadelphia's Academy of Music, and continuing through July, taking him into clubs and arenas he'd never played before. He did a concert at the Westbury Music Fair on Long Island, a pop-music tent usually reserved for the Steve and Eydie crowd. While Phil toured, Michael assumed the role of public spokesman. He answered all the mail which came for Phil. For requests to have Phil speak at a rally, Michael would write back, "Phil Ochs speaks through his songs." For interviews, Michael would request a list of questions, submit them to Phil, and mail back the answers. Political appearances were carefully chosen, so as not to interfere with commercial commitments.

The tour brought Phil back to New York in April, where he met Jack Newfield. Newfield had written often about Phil in *The Village Voice,* and was now working on a book about Robert Kennedy. Newfield was flying to Washington the next day to see Kennedy deliver his first speech on the floor of the Senate against the Vietnam War, after vacillating for a year about whether or not to speak out. He had decided to break with Johnson and divide the Democratic Party. Newfield asked Phil if he'd like to come along.

They flew down together on the Washington shuttle and, after staying in Kennedy's office for a while, headed for the floor of the Senate. Afterward, they all returned to the office, where, prompted by Newfield, Phil sang "Crucifixion." He hadn't brought his guitar with him, so he sang it acappella, tapping his foot to keep the rhythm.

After the first three verses, Kennedy blanched. He realized Phil was singing about his dead brother. Unable to speak, he just shook his head, as tears filled his eyes.

On the plane back to New York, Phil asked Newfield if Kennedy was into music. "Of course," Newfield replied. "He likes a lot of it. He knows your songs, Phil. He knows you've sung at a lot of anti-war rallies. He's sympathetic with what's happening on the campuses." Phil leaned back in his seat and closed his eyes.

> *They say they can't believe it, It's a sacrilegious*
> * shame*
> *Now, who would want to hurt such a hero of the game*
> *But you know I predicted it; I knew he had to fall.*
> *How did it happen? I hope his suffering was small.*
> *Tell me every detail, I've got to know it all,*
> *And do you have a picture of the pain?*

The new office was filled with people all the time. Michael would spend hours on the phone, arranging concerts, setting up personal appearances, taking care of Phil's day-to-day schedule, while Michael J. Pollard might drop by to see what was happening, or Zal from The Lovin' Spoonful might pop in to see if Phil was in town. Jerry Rubin came by a lot; so did Paul Krassner. Newspapers, *Time, Newsweek, Playboy,* and *Cavalier* piled up on the floor. Michael furnished the office with huge oak furniture he'd gotten by giving the janitor of the building a couple of bucks for any pieces left behind in other offices. A great upright pump organ was the centerpiece of the place. Phil loved it, and would sit down by it whenever he came into the office, trying to find a way to get it to work. A giant wood-framed map hung on the wall, something Phil and Michael had picked up on Canal Street for two dollars.

With a red crayon, Phil colored in all the countries which had "gone Commie." Michael contributed a giant collage he'd made out of dozens of pictures of Elvis. Though it was originally for the office, Phil loved it so much he hung it in the living room on Prince Street.

In the office, Phil was constantly in motion, like a pinball, moving from person to person, room to room, grabbing his guitar, playing his latest song, asking everyone if it was great, making a million telephone calls ("Ochs here"), eating Chinese food out of white containers with his fingers, running his hand through his hair, laughing at everything.

Phil was back in New York again in May, between scheduled concerts on the A&M tour. He was in The Dugout, on Bleecker, participating in a sparerib orgy with Eric Andersen, David Blue, Bobby Neuwirth, and Dylan, when Andy Wickham and P. F. Sloan came through the door. Wickham and Sloan had been wandering about the Village searching for the notorious Phil Ochs to find out "what maketh him to protest." They looked for Phil between plugging tunes for Don Kirshner's Dunhill Records, an assignment Wickham landed because he was British, and being moptop was all the credentials needed. Sloan, composer of "The Eve of Destruction," was Wickham's sidekick for both the "mission" and the plugging.

They spotted Phil at the table. Wickham decided to walk over and introduce himself. The others ignored him, but Phil was full of questions, firing them, clipping Wickham's answers to get to the next question. Who are you? Why did you come looking for me? What does your father do? Where did you go to school? What's Lou Adler like? Do you like surfing? Why do you live in Los Angeles and not New York? Wickham told Phil, in response to one of the questions, that his father was an Air Commodore in the Royal Air Force. Phil bolted upright, grinning. "Really? Great!"

Nobody could have understood why Phil was so interested in Wickham. They wouldn't have been able to make the connection, because standing before him was, incredibly, the image of Dave Sweazy! The lofty elegance, the perfect youth languishing on the grass, the immaculate pretty boy. "Come and see me when you're

in Los Angeles," Wickham said to Phil, and left. While the others
at the table still huddled, their backs keeping away the underprivi-
leged, Phil looked out, toward the door.

They got to know each other quickly. Wickham would tease
Phil about his politics, putting down the Left and its "heroes."
The more Wickham tried to get Phil angry, the harder Phil would
throw his head back and laugh, silently, at his new friend.

They made a striking pair. Wickham, British down to his her-
ringbones, thin, almost emaciated, neck wrapped with expensive
silk scarves, skin lightly freckled, wavy brown hair. Phil, a bit
overweight, sloppy, rumpled clothes, greasy hair over his eyes,
dirty fingers constantly touching his face, words crashing into each
other on the way out of his mouth. Walking together down the
street, they looked like an animated number 10.

Andy's politics were no joke. His revulsion with the Left was
real, coming out of the same England that so impressed Pete
Seeger in the late fifties and early sixties. The British working class
repulsed Wickham, but he still felt they had a lot more to complain
about than America's overfed, college-educated, pampered nou-
veau-lefties who marched against the war during the day and went
home to watch the news on their color TVs at night.

Andy was suspicious of the musical protest "industry," and
those capitalizing on it. Wickham's persistent questioning of Phil
evolved into a long, meandering political debate which in turn became a philosophical search-and-seizure mission into the other's
values, opinions, and passions. Each represented an extension,
rather than a reiteration, of the other's turf. They were, in fact,
private partners in an adolescent passion play.

There was a desert, it seemed, in the Greenwich Village oasis.
As Jack Newfield pointed out in his "Notebook for Night Owls"
column in *The Village Voice* that May, reviewing a "mind explosion" concert at the Second Avenue Theater:

> The audience was dominated by mindless fan-club types who
> screamed just on seeing their idols, and didn't care about the
> words or music . . .
> This is true of the Mamas and the Papas, The Stones, and The
> Byrds. When they recorded "Turn, Turn, Turn" and "Mr. Tam-

bourine Man" they were pioneers; now they are parasites, leeching off a scene and their own reputations . . .

There is a breakdown of standards today. Anyone with long hair (preferably blond), a freaky lifestyle, electric instruments, a press agent, and three friends can become a pop star.

The most personal vision of this generation is being expressed, and acted out, in its music. Dylan, The Beatles, Donovan, Janis Ian, Phil Ochs, Tim Hardin, Eric Andersen—they are doing the work of novelists and dramatists.

Newfield's evaluation was interesting, since Dylan was incapacitated, The Beatles had stopped touring, Donovan was banned from performing in the United States because of a drug bust in England, Janis Ian was a novelty, Tim Hardin was almost completely unknown outside of New York, and Eric Andersen had never had a hit record. In truth, by 1967, the New York folk-pop sound was dying.

Phil spent that summer in Los Angeles, preparing to record his first album for A&M, "Pleasures of the Harbor." He arrived sometime in May, and rented a small house in Laurel Canyon.

He was immediately uncomfortable. Every place that should have been a bar was a health club. He drifted to the offices of the Los Angeles *Free Press,* a paper which at the time resembled New York's *Village Voice.* It was at the FREEP that he first got the idea for the "War Is Over" rally.

It came out of something the late John Carpenter said to Phil, something Carpenter had first heard from Allen Ginsberg. Over a beer, Carpenter, who worked at the FREEP, told Phil Ginsberg had suggested the paper simply declare the war over, to demonstrate the power of the press. Phil slammed his beer mug on the table and grabbed Carpenter's shoulders with both hands.

> *Silent soldiers on a silver screen*
> *Framed in fantasies and drugged in dreams*
> *Unpaid actors of the mystery*
> *The mad director knows that*
> *Freedom will not make you free*
> *And what's that got to do with me?*
> *I declare the war is over*
> *It's over*
> *It's over . . .*

Cardboard cowboys of a new frontier
Drowning Indians in vats of beer
The troops are leaving on the Trojan train
The sun is in their eyes,
But I am hiding from the rain
Now one of us must be insane
I declare the war is over
It's over
It's over . . .

One-legged veterans will greet the dawn
And they're whistling marches
As they mow the lawn
And the gargoyles only sit and grieve
The gypsy fortuneteller
Told me that we've been deceived
You only are what you believe
And I believe the war is over
It's over . . .

There were at least another dozen verses to the song. It was like
an epic World War II movie: Lyndon Johnson, the mad director,
marching his men to hell.

In the FREEP, Phil wrote:

Now some of you may not believe the war is over—and that, essentially, is the problem. The mysterious East has taught us about
the occult powers of the mind, and yet we go on accepting our
paranoid President's notion that we actually are involved in a war
in Asia. Nonsense. It's only a figment of our propagandized imagination, a psychodrama out of 1984.

Below Phil's article was a full-page ad announcing "VD Day,"
in Cheviot Hills Park, June twenty-third. Everyone was invited to
come and celebrate the end of the war with Phil and his friends.

Phil began to make preparations for the event. He worked night
and day, but no matter how much he had to do, his Saturday
nights were reserved for Andy Wickham. They'd meet for dinner at
any one of a number of sleazy Chinese restaurants they liked, after
which they'd go either to the races or downtown, where Wickham
liked to watch local prizefights, or perhaps a good wrestling

Meegan
(*Alice Ochs*)

Paul Krassner (*Photo by Grace Moceri*)

Tom Paxton and Phil Ochs (*Photo by Michael Ochs*)

The afternoon of the first "War Is Over" celebration in Los Angeles, June 23, 1967 (*Ron Cobb*)

VD DAY

NOV. (1PM) 25TH

WASH- SQUARE PARK

★ A CELEBRATION ★

THE END OF THE WAR!

Phil and Andy Wickham (*Photo by Michael Ochs*)

Larry Marks (*Courtesy of A&M Records*)

An idea for a lyric

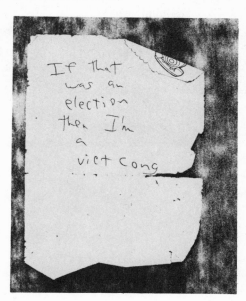

(Courtesy of the Phil Ochs estate)

The Elvis collage in Phil's apartment (*Photo and collage by Michael Ochs*)

Phil and Karen in New York (*Photo by Michael Ochs*)

Phil and Karen at The Troubadour in Los Angeles
(*Courtesy of Michael Ochs*)

match. Wickham, an amateur pugilist, regarded fisticuffs as a skill which, in its highest form, approached art. He would tell Phil how great it was to see two young black men fighting it out in the ring for the glory of being a winner. "You can take all your songs about the plight of the oppressed and they don't mean anything when you compare it to fifteen bloody rounds in the ring, where two men literally fight for survival."

They would talk about the fights, debating techniques, Wickham re-creating entire bouts, waving his arms, playing both fighters at the same time. While Phil explained to Wickham the ideological battles of the Left, Wickham unlocked for Phil the ideology of battle.

A couple of days before the demonstration, Phil was having breakfast at Schwab's Drugstore on Sunset Boulevard, when he ran into an old friend, Village expatriate Judy Henske. Henske had moved to the Coast, married, and settled in Pasadena. Six feet tall, one-time Broadway actress before and after playing folkie in the Bleecker theater of the early sixties, she threw her arms around Phil, engulfing her old drinking buddy. She wanted to know two things: why he'd referred to her in print as a big breast, and what he was doing in Los Angeles. In response to the first question Phil only grinned. To the second, he told her about the album and the demonstration. Henske was eight months pregnant, but she swore she'd be there.

He needed someone to take pictures. He looked up Ron Cobb's phone number and address in the L.A. phone book and, Friday evening, went to Cobb's house. "Hi, I'm Phil Ochs."

Although they'd never met, Phil was anxious to talk with Cobb, who had a considerable reputation as a political cartoonist, drawing extremely intricate pen-and-ink cartoons which expressed mental confusion through physical distortion. The underground press was filled with his political observations. After a few bottles of beer, they went for a walk into the neon L.A. night. They wandered up and down Sunset, stopping to get something to eat at Ben Frank's, then out again, walking for hours, talking about politics, music, photography, love, death, Bob Dylan, The Beatles,

Herblock, John Ford, and the "War Is Over" rally. In the morning they went for breakfast. Ron would be at the rally with his camera.

The demonstration was to take place in the empty lot across from the newly erected Century Plaza Hotel, in Century City. Lyndon Johnson was scheduled to speak that day at a five-hundred-dollar-a-plate dinner in the hotel after The Supremes had entertained the guests. So Phil announced a one-penny-a-plate dinner to be held in the empty lot. It was all in fun, an expression of the joy of peace, rather than a demonstration of the madness of war. As Phil put it, "The old standbys of the Left and the attitudes they encompass should be avoided. Classics like 'Hey, hey, LBJ, how many kids did you kill today?' are as dated as the M-16. Since the war is over, we should have positive signs, like 'Johnson in '68 —the Peace President,' 'Welcome Hanoi to the Great Society,' or 'Thank you, Lyndon, for ending the war.'"

Phil was nervous and a little drunk. He put his hand to his throat every few minutes, checking, humming a few notes. He spent a lot of time tuning his Gibson. Leaflets were passed out declaring "VD Day," using the famous picture of the sailor kissing the nurse in Times Square on "VE Day" at the end of World War II.

Earlier, he'd driven to Pasadena to pick up Judy. She asked him to stop along the way. She wanted to pick up a friend, Diane, a famous Hollywood full-time whore and part-time go-go dancer whose main claim was that she'd gone to bed with every rock star in the world. She was a tall, gorgeous blonde who's only operative emotion, it seemed, was a fluffy giggle. Phil's eyes opened wide when he saw her, and he grinned. He proposed marriage to her several times that morning, and insisted she accompany Judy and him to the rally.

The place was flowing with people. There were police everywhere, mounted and in patrol cars. Phil was leading the parade along the Avenue of the Stars, Henske on one side of him, Diane on the other. The crowd began to chant, "The war is over!" They marched to the front of the hotel, shouting and singing. When they arrived at the flatbed on the other side, Phil jumped on top and someone handed him his guitar. The crowd roared. Henske, standing at the foot of the stage, looked up at him. He looked smart, quick, street-tough. "Ochs, you made it . . . you're in the big time." He looked down at her once, smiled, and began to sing.

Silent soldiers on a silver screen . . .

Without warning, the police mounted a full-scale attack, charging into the sides of the crowd, demanding, over bullhorns, that they disperse immediately. Phil had forgotten to arrange for parade permits! "You have two minutes to disperse," the atonal warnings repeated.

No one moved. The people in the back couldn't hear what the cops were saying and those up front had nowhere to go. Helicopters began circling above. Sirens went off. TV cameras, there to cover Johnson's visit, turned toward the action. People were pushing and shoving each other. Henske, afraid of getting crushed and losing her baby, shouted for help. Phil, his guitar still slung over his shoulder, managed to get to her, and then it seemed he was pushing her out of the way, as if to save himself. She called to him. He turned once and grabbed her hand. Diane, giggling, followed close behind. Ron's camera clicked like a time bomb. Somehow, they all managed to escape the clubbing and smashing that followed.

Later, at Judy's house, Phil was euphoric. He proclaimed the day a smash; everything had happened just the way he'd wanted it to. He turned on the TV to the news. There it was, in living color, his celebration of the end of the war, and the L.A. Police Department massacre that followed.

At the FREEP, Phil ran into another old friend from New York, Paul Krassner, on his way to make a guest appearance on "The Joe Pyne Show." He invited Phil to come along "for the fun of it."

Joe Pyne was a sensation on West Coast radio and television, appealing to a reactionary constituency which applauded his tough, no-nonsense approach to "lefty-creeps" like Krassner, who was the type Pyne liked—small, meek-looking, vulnerable. Sitting next to Krassner, Pyne looked bigger than he was, and he liked that. Now if he could only get a rise out of the little bastard. Phil watched, fascinated, from the audience as Pyne continued his interrogation. He was probing, looking for the type of reaction from Krassner which his ratings needed. When all else failed, Pyne asked Krassner about his acne scars. The audience gasped. The camera tightened on Krassner's face. He looked at Pyne and said, "Well, Joe, if you're going to ask me questions like that, let me ask you, Do you take off your wooden leg when you make love to your wife?"

Pyne's jaw fell to the basement. He'd lost a leg in the "big" war and was extremely sensitive about it, and Krassner had found Pyne's Achilles heel. Shaken, he turned to the audience for questions. The shopping bag ladies filed by, one after another, outraged, shouting at Krassner, calling for his blood. At the end of the line, waiting patiently, was Phil Ochs. When it was his turn, he calmly spoke into the microphone. "I'd like to point out in the midst of all this that what Paul Krassner does is in the finest tradition of American journalism . . ." The audience exploded into a renewed frenzy. Waving their hands, stomping their feet, they screamed for Phil to be ejected from the studio. His voice was drowned out by the shouting. Confusion reigned. Though no one seemed to be listening any more, Phil kept on talking.

"Pleasures of the Harbor" was recorded in August, with a budget of forty thousand dollars and a producer by the name of Larry Marks, assigned by A&M to help Phil create the type of new sound he was looking for.

Recalls Marks: "We'd decided to try and expand Phil's market and the people he was reaching. We talked about it a great deal. He was writing things at that point, among them the song "Pleasures of the Harbor," which was an extraordinary piece, unlike anything that I'd heard from Phil before. It was something that required more than I think Phil had been doing up to that time. Phil's writing always tended to be verse, chorus, verse, chorus, verse verse verse or chorus chorus chorus. He was very much interested in the lyrics, the storytelling. He was limited, to a certain extent, in his musical expansion of what he did. 'Pleasures' had a terrific melody, and although it was repeated over and over again, we decided we would take a shot at expanding it, and treat every chorus and verse differently with a kind of orchestral background without overdoing it.

"We went into the studio and it was a lot of fun, and painful for Phil. It wasn't something he was terribly comfortable with. He knew that some things worked out well and some things didn't, but he didn't quite know how to change them. In the initial stages I wasn't quite sure what Phil was looking for either, or what was right for him. Maybe it was going back to the guitar and the vocal now, and letting Phil go by himself, not having to worry about expanding the background so Phil would expand all by himself. But there were a lot of things that Phil couldn't change because he just didn't have the technical knowledge.

"One of the reasons Phil's vocals came out so well was the arrangements were totally foreign to Phil. He had to work very hard with the vocals, do them verse by verse, line by line. 'Pleasures,' for example, was a long song. Phil is punched in constantly all through the album, on everything. Not because he wasn't capable of singing his whole song, it's just that . . . it's like a piano player who plays and sings. We took the guitar away from Phil, so the rhythm Phil felt normally going from his hand to his mouth was totally disconnected. Now he's got a pair of earphones on, like anybody else. He's singing to a track so every verse and every line, because they're all slightly different, become really a tone poem. And it's not like Phil laid out everything exactly the same, rhythmically. There are some lines that are slightly longer, some shorter, the rhythm, the meter is slightly different. He'd have to organize his thoughts, and do each one slightly different, and fall into the arrangement and the orchestration that was done for that particular verse. And they were all different. So it took him a long time to get used to it. But he did. He loved it. He loved the whole process. We always kind of trusted each other."

Marks brought together some of the finest personnel available to work with him on the album. Lincoln Mayorga did all the piano work. Ian Freebairn Smith and Joe Byrd each arranged several of the songs. It was decided to begin the album with the potential hit single "Cross My Heart."

Marks: "The problem was to keep the variety going. We decided this particular time we would use various classical techniques to keep it going, ostinato patterns. The thing that was typical with Phil, you can see a tendency for effect, was to slow down for the bridge, and all of a sudden the orchestra is straining hard to follow him. He played the guitar originally and we pulled it off the cut. Now you have the whole orchestra straining desperately to keep a definite tempo, go through the retarded sections and then back into tempo. It was hard to do, and it's prevalent through the whole album.

"'Outside of a Small Circle of Friends' is an extraordinary cut. The arrangement added to the irony of the whole song. Tacky piano played by Lincoln and a banjo and small rhythm section, nothing more. It's almost like a saloon song you shouldn't pay any attention to, and the lyric means practically everything in the world. It goes right for the throat. In between each turn-around section we had Lincoln play a totally different thing, so we wouldn't get locked into a figure. Phil sang after the arrangements on most cuts. Sometimes he sang lightly with the guitar and then came back later to lay his voice down. We worked very hard on Phil's voice. He wanted to make sure, for the first time in his life, that he sounded like a singer as opposed to someone who was delivering his own material. He worked hard on it.

"On 'Cross My Heart' and a couple of others he was sweetened a bit.

"'Crucifixion.' We made loops for the opening. Toward the end it wears. Basically we did loops, electric harpsichord, some bells, some electronic effects, and one of the hardest parts for Phil was, again, doing this all in tempo. I did the longest click track in the history of music for this. To keep a tempo beat, I literally went through, bar by bar. I knew how Phil would try and sing it, and although I knew it would be perfect because Phil couldn't sit down and play it with his guitar, I laid it out, counted out the bar numbers. There were a thousand bars or something, an astronomical amount. We weren't sure how we were going to get through it. I recorded the click track on tape. I put it on one track of the tape and kept the rhythm all the time. I slowed it down, speeded it up, tried to follow Phil's normal way. When he slows the verse down, the whole thing slows down. As you cut the track there is some reference point on the tape. It was just incredibly difficult. He was drowned out at the end. We should have mixed him higher."

The opening moments of "Pleasures of the Harbor," a song Phil wrote after seeing John Ford's *The Long Voyage Home*, were filled with a sweeping, orchestral introduction; a windjammer at full sail, dissolving into the hushed voice of the sailor, Phil Ochs.

> *And the ship sets the sail. They've lived the tales*
> > *to carry to the shore*
> *Straining at the oars or starting from the rails.*
> *And the sea bids farewell. She waves and swells,*
> > *and sends them on their way.*
> *Time has been her pay, and time will have to tell.*
> *Oh! Soon your sailing will be over.*
> *Come and take your pleasures of the harbor . . .*

Phil's development as a songwriter had reached a dramatic stage. Gone was the urgent topicality in his lyrics, replaced by a growing sense of self-recognition; a shift in emphasis from the reporter's pen to the poet's eye. Phil's musical persona, till now the outspoken rebel ("Draft Dodger Rag," "I'm Going To Say It Now," "There but for Fortune") was indeed changing. Gone was the merchant marine wearing a peacoat on the cover of "All the News That's Fit To Sing," the social albatross beached on the streets, out of his natural element, the sea. With "Pleasures," Phil's self-image was ironically inverted. He was the sailor at sea, longing for the shore. The observer, responsible for protecting what can't be seen, what is just beyond the horizon, the pleasures of the harbor. It was Phil's version of The Protestant Ethic—the notion of the separation of pleasure and social responsibility. No longer the reportorial Everyman, he is alone, separate, the reflector. He is the artist.

> *And the sea bids farewell. She waves and swells and*
> > *sends them on their way.*
> *Time has been her pay, and time will have to tell.*
> *Oh! Soon your sailing will be over.*
> *Come and take the pleasures of the harbor . . .*

They finished recording the album Friday morning. Marks emerged from the studio with the tapes and took them to Contemporary Records, the best mastering facilities on the West Coast. It was a very long album, nearly an hour, and very tough to master.

By Sunday afternoon Marks, who'd gone sleepless for the better part of the week, finally boarded a plane headed east. He arrived at Kennedy Airport that evening, and, renting a car, drove home to

Connecticut. It was early morning before he was able to collapse into bed.

He wasn't home an hour when he received a call from Phil. He wanted Marks to come right back to the Coast. Something needed to be fixed on the album. Phil had listened to the final mix fifty times over the weekend, and kept hearing something he didn't like. By Monday afternoon, Marks was in the sky, headed for L.A.

He went over the "Pleasures" cut with Phil in the studio. There was one word where Phil thought his voice cracked. Marks tried to talk him into leaving it the way it was, suggesting the cracking added a sense of fragility. Phil insisted it had to be changed, and Marks fixed it. An hour later he was headed for the airport once again.

Phil supervised the design of the cover for the album. He wanted to be photographed standing on a dock, suggesting he'd either just arrived from or was preparing to leave for the sea. He wore a sailor's cap and a suede jacket. The jacket was a gift from Michael J. Pollard, who'd gotten it from Lenny Bruce.

Phil returned to New York that fall, and Michael immediately booked him into Carnegie Hall. He wanted Phil to go on a major tour to promote the album. Phil was against the idea. He'd just returned from what had amounted to three months on the road. He'd been away from Karen, away from New York. He needed a city hit before leaving again. Performing before a New York audience, Carnegie Hall, would provide it.

Phil was fantastic that night. His voice was crystal sharp, his guitar strummed passionately against the burst of new lyrics he'd put down. And the people were with him every minute, catching each nuance—laughing, humming, shouting, cheering. Next to Phil on the stage was a giant black bomb. It had been placed there before he came out, and never once, during the entire show, did he refer to it. He'd found it in an old antique shop and paid five dollars for it. He had no idea who'd made it, or why. But it was a perfect stage ornament, and completed the Phil Ochs tableau of a pair of microphones and a stool nearby with a glass of water.

He dedicated "Crucifixion," his final song of the evening, to Robert Kennedy. The audience listened breathlessly and, when he finished, burst into a thunderous ovation. Phil waved with his arms for them to be quiet, and when they settled down he made a joke about how his radical friends were rebelling against him because of his participation in the corporate world of recording. Therefore, in a gesture of conciliation, he'd invited Abbie Hoffman and Jerry Rubin to make a brief thirty-second announcement inviting the audience to come to Chicago that summer.

Rubin and Hoffman emerged from the wings and walked to the mikes, receiving a smattering of applause. Rubin began talking about Chicago, when Hoffman grabbed the mike away and shouted, "Fuck Lyndon Johnson, fuck Robert Kennedy, and fuck you if you don't like it." With that, he dove off the stage and ran up and down the aisles screaming, "Fuck Johnson," waving his arms over his head while Rubin cheered him on from the stage.

Phil was visibly shaken, as the evening disintegrated into a shouting match between Hoffman and the now angry audience. The Carnegie Hall management cut off the power to the lights and the sound system, restoring it only after Hoffman and Rubin left. Phil said goodnight into one of the microphones, and left the stage.

The album wasn't selling as quickly as Phil thought it would. Sales had been strong at first, but a lot of radio station resistance developed over "Outside of a Small Circle of Friends," because of its reference to grass:

> *Smokin' marijuana is more fun than drinkin' beer*
> *But a friend of ours was captured*
> *And they gave him thirty years*
> *Maybe we should raise our voices, ask somebody why*
> *But demonstrations are a drag*
> *And besides we're much too high . . .*

Ironically, the lyrics of the song were interpreted by station managers as Phil's advocating the smoking of grass rather than drinking beer. Actually, the lyric was more provocative than that, suggesting dope-smoking prevented more direct methods of dealing with the government—like demonstrating, for example. Although he smoked an occasional joint, Phil feared hard drugs. He saw the "chemical revolution" as something the government encouraged for the purpose of tempering the aggression of the revolutionary young; an effective method of letting them get high and drop out, dissipating the energy necessary for the Left to continue as a unified group. While official government policy was to ban all drug references in songs from air-play by bringing FCC pressure against those stations that didn't comply, tons of drugs continued to pour into the country from everywhere in the world, including the Far East, and from countries "hostile" to American foreign policy.

Despite the resistance, A&M felt the record had so much potential they issued it as a single three times, each version slightly different. The first radio version was two-sided, one intact, with the original verse; the other with the word "marijuana" deleted:

> *Smokin' is more fun than drinkin' beer* . . .

FM jockeys loved the first version so much they played it as soon as it came in. After management removed it from play lists, A&M issued a version with the entire verse omitted, and the single started to take off. In Los Angeles "Friends" reached No. 23, the album cited as a "mover." It broke into the national "Hot Prospect" listing of *Billboard* at No. 119, with a breakout noted in Seattle.

Phil now wanted to tour. He agreed with Michael that it was necessary to push the single into the top ten. Arrangements were quickly made, and, as Phil began to play the arranged dates, the single was chosen as the pick hit of KROY and KXOA, both Sacramento-based stations. The "Fabulous 50" from KJR showed it as No. 20, just behind "Words" by the Bee Gees, beating out Hugo Montenegro's "The Good, the Bad, and the Ugly."

Time magazine offered the album a begrudging plus surrounded by a lot of negatives:

> Ochs' melodic sense is so subservient to his lyrical exhortations that most listeners will feel that he might as well just stand up and talk . . . Nevertheless, Ochs is a talented rebel; his instrumentation is far out; and his songs defy most conventions, including the three-minute rule. Some last nearly nine minutes.

Billboard:

> A slightly different Phil Ochs—this one with more than just a guitar on numbers like the perceptive, haunting "The Party," which trills with piano, even an organ and violins on "Pleasures of the Harbor." The "Crucifixion" is very hip musically. He's still a pro-

tester deluxe. Take the chilling "Outside of a Small Circle of Friends," for example.

Variety noted:

Ochs sees himself primarily as an artist, not as a political leader. At the same time, however, he views politics as an art form. And, he says, he will continue to participate in anti-war demonstrations and write and perform songs that inform listeners where it's really at.

Derek Taylor, who'd done publicity for The Beatles, was hired by A&M, and one of his first assignments was to come up with ideas to promote "Pleasures of the Harbor." He sent a copy of the album to President Johnson at the White House. A couple of weeks later, a letter arrived at A&M from Washington, addressed to Phil, thanking him for the record, adding, "Your courtesy is warmly appreciated. With the President's every good wish, Sincerely yours, Juanita D. Roberts, Personal Secretary to the President."

At *Broadside* magazine, the album was seen as Phil's sellout, and a scathing review of "Pleasures" appeared:

"Cross My Heart" is both naive and pretentious . . . it suffers from the colorlessness of Ochs' singing; his one adventure, pulsating the word "flower" over seven notes, is a disaster . . . "Pleasures of the Harbor," except for occasional lapses in character, exudes Robert Taylor as Captain Hornblower, giving the order to set sail for England, now that he has single-handedly scuttled the Spanish fleet in the good name of the King . . . Phil Ochs came along when people wanted to protest. He was very good at writing protest lyrics, and whether or not he could sing or write good melodies was somewhat irrelevant. These songs, however, are not so good as his protest material and they do not compensate for his inability to do more than carry a tune. The arrangements are well-played and occasionally original, but the result is still of no consequence.

The magazine then published a lengthy interview with Phil, expressing, in part, his dissatisfaction with what was happening to the folk-music community:

. . . There has been a jump . . . a mass exodus of the New York folk crowd westward, leaving, let us say, the more intellectual

New York recording companies. Also there has been, at the same time, a big reaching out of such companies as Elektra and Vanguard for the commercial market. In a very blatant fashion, really. And I think in some cases they have gone too far, I really do. Consider the sudden success of The Doors. I'm not saying this to be bitter because I left Elektra. It's just that I don't feel comfortable, considering that Elektra was the company that put out such good music for so long, and it makes me uncomfortable to see a picture, a publicity shot, of Jim Morrison without a shirt on, and we're supposed to accept this as the "new wave" . . .

I think it ties in with a whole general movement, a whole desperate movement of people to "make it." At one point everybody wanted to be Elvis Presley. Now everyone wants to be the successful Bob Dylan. And, you know, they are all leaping across the moat hoping to get inside the castle, and most of them have slipped now and fallen in with the crocodiles, and have signed crocodile contracts. It's a fascinating study of human nature—how everybody has reacted in terms of grasping for riches, and reaching for wealth. That's what has happened. And it's a shame, considering how the future looked a couple of years ago with these companies.

If Phil were attempting to make peace with the "Broadsiders," it hadn't worked. In the following issue, the magazine published this reply from Jac Holzman:

In order to establish a more balanced perspective, some comments are required with regard to statements made by Phil Ochs in . . . his interview with *Broadside*. First, Elektra has never lost an artist that it wanted to keep . . . Phil is essentially correct in his feeling that California is a better place to record. We at Elektra concur and have for the past two years maintained an office in Los Angeles. Furthermore, we have just completed an Elektra-owned and -operated recording studio . . . In fact, Elektra maintains a larger staff in California than any West Coast record company maintains in New York.

Phil's comments about The Doors are just so much sour grapes. How can he refer to our "reaching out for the commercial market" as if this was some sort of sin? In my eighteen years as a record executive, never has an artist checked sales figures more carefully or more frequently than Phil. I say this in no condemnation of Phil, because an awareness of public acceptance is very much to be desired, but do I detect just a hint of envy?

Whether Jim Morrison sheds his shirt for a color photograph has absolutely no bearing on The Doors' music, and after all, isn't it the music that really counts?

Phil should remember that it was the open-mindedness of both Vanguard and Elektra that caused him to be heard on records at all, and without censorship of any kind!

Phil's final *Broadside* response was that Gregory Peck played Horatio Hornblower, not Robert Taylor.

Between dates on the tour, Phil decided, in November, to repeat the L.A. "War Is Over" celebration in New York's Washington Square park. It was typical of Phil Ochs to hire a publicity agent to promote the demonstration. Richard Gersh Associates prepared and released statements for the press, announcing:

PHIL OCHS, JIM AND JEAN, HENSKE,
KRASSNER, AND YANOVSKY
TO ATTEND "WAR IS OVER" CELEBRATION

The Diggers, an East Village commune with aspirations to create social revolution in the streets of New York, were enlisted by Phil to help promote the event by handing out leaflets.

This time, proper permits were secured, and there was no violence. The march received a lot of press coverage, especially in *The Village Voice,* which did a front-page feature story on it. Phil seemed at home as he led a parade of the curious, the disheveled, the drunk, and the sublime up Fifth Avenue, waving flags and singing songs.

The effective use of the media to draw attention to the absurdity of the Vietnam War wasn't lost on those planning to go to Chicago that summer and demonstrate against the war during convention week. Paul Krassner, who'd coined the term "yippie," was involved, along with Jerry Rubin, Stew Albert, Rennie Davis, Abbie Hoffman, and, when available, Phil, planning the events to take place in August.

Krassner's satiric talents blended well with Rubin's theatrical persona. The face paint, the wild hair, the tie-dyed tee-shirts, and the constant use of verbal obscenities were calculated by Rubin to offend America through his exposure by the media. Those in power had to conform to the media rules of acceptability. Poli-

ticians began to realize the United States had outgrown the sociological concept of neighborhoods, displaced by the technological
reality of networks. Rubin realized that to offend through the
media was also to offend the media. On a one-to-one basis, people
would always be surprised by Rubin, how "different" he seemed
from the person they'd seen on television, in the news. By recognizing the power of the media, Rubin—and by extension, yippie—
hoped to reject its influence. The violent reaction of the Los Angeles Police Department to the "War Is Over" demonstration
broadcast on the news was seen as a profound victory against the
media. It would form the ideological basis for what yippie hoped
to accomplish in Chicago, when it would surely confront the wrath
of Daley's Gestapo. If America could see it for themselves, they
might begin to wonder just what was going on. As Phil had put it,
"Ah, but in such an ugly time, the true protest is beauty."

Shortly after the New York "War Is Over" demonstration, Michael and Phil took off for the West Coast to continue promoting
the album. Michael had booked concerts throughout Washington,
Oregon, and California, winding up in Los Angeles, where Phil
looked up Ron Cobb. He wanted to tell Cobb all about the New
York demonstration. Cobb wanted to go to the movies. He got a
girl for Phil, and they doubled. Phil was moody that night, refusing
to talk to either Cobb or the blond hippie-type Ron had fixed him
up with. Later that night, after they'd taken their dates home, Phil
complained to Ron about the choice of girls. "Phil," Ron said,
"you don't have to be in love with every girl you date; you don't
even have to like her a whole lot to have a good time."
"Then, what's the point?" Phil asked.
"The point is, they don't have to love you either."

Michael had heard a lot about a club on Santa Monica Boulevard, just east of Beverly Hills, Doug Weston's The Troubadour.
Weston opened his club in 1957. After a shaky start, it had become the key spot in Los Angeles to break an artist. Labels
booked the club regularly to showcase acts, allowing Weston to
keep the bar while they rented out the club for a flat fee, making
sure the house was papered with reporters and critics. Weston

turned the traditionally dark Monday nights into "Hootenanny Nite," much like those that had originated at Gerde's.

Michael called Weston and asked if he'd like Phil to appear at the Monday hoot. Weston said of course he would, and after hanging up, told one of his assistants to have the marquee out front changed to read

HOOT NITE TONITE—PHIL OCHS

It was the first time in all the years of hoots at The Troubadour that any individual performer had had his name up in lights. When Phil and Michael showed up, they went crazy.

Phil was playing the hoot for free. He figured Weston was trying to use his name to make a fast buck. Phil waited outside while Michael burst through the front doors, demanding to see Weston immediately. Weston reacted to Michael with tart amusement, stating, simply, "He ain't performing. Take his name down."

Michael turned to leave, and then turned again. Weston was already receding into the blue-black interior of his club. "Wait a minute," Michael shouted. "Leave it up. He'll play."

Doug turned and smiled as he nodded his head slowly.

Phil began to hang out at The Troubadour, fascinated by Weston and his endless tales of the metaphysical and the lecherous. Weston would light a cigarette and through its silver smoke tell Phil tales of New York. "Tell me about James Dean again," Phil would say. Weston had been a bartender in Greenwich Village during the fifties and had become friendly with one of his regular customers, James Dean, then a little-known TV actor trying to break into the movies. Dean would come in, have a drink, and rap with Weston. After he'd leave Weston would hear a ripping screech of tires, and know it was Dean driving away. "What did he wear?" Phil would ask.

"A long gray overcoat." How did he comb his hair? Was he funny? Was he gay? Did he ever get into fights? Phil would shake his head, fascinated by Dean, enthralled by Weston.

Doug wanted to produce a Phil Ochs concert in Los Angeles. He'd made a reputation for himself as the best promoter in the area, specializing in exposing new acts. He'd produced successful shows for Joni Mitchell, Laura Nyro, and George Carlin, after the comedian had changed his image to that of a counterculture "freak." Michael was all for it, feeling it was the perfect way to end the "Pleasures" tour, which had been a lot of small clubs and college campuses, on the West Coast.

Phil wanted the concert to be held in the Santa Monica Civic Auditorium, the most prestigious spot in Los Angeles. Michael was against it, as was Weston, both feeling it was too big for Phil, that a smaller house would be better. Phil insisted, saying it was the only way he would do it. The show was heavily promoted, with lots of radio commercials and newspaper ads. In spite of the well-planned saturation campaign to sell tickets, the show was a financial disaster. The house was less than a quarter filled.

Phil, looking out on the empty seats, became more agitated than usual. Several times during the performance he forgot lyrics, and at one point, during "I Ain't Marching Anymore," decided his guitar was out of tune and stopped playing. "Sometimes," he sighed, "I suspect this guitar is fascist."

Afterward, Phil called Andy Wickham. He told Andy he was depressed about the turnout for the concert. Wickham met him for drinks. He decided Phil needed cheering up. They disappeared together for several days.

VII

My costume dropped to the floor
Naked at last, I couldn't fight it anymore
And the service was rendered
A poem fell from the wine
Buried the past the future was mine
The present surrendered
And the ballet master
Beckoning faster
The ballerina was posed
In the fragile beauty we froze
Let go, let go, let go, let go, let go
And the lady from the lake
Who helped me to escape
Left me with myself at last
Though I danced with the dolls in the doll house . . .
                    Phil Ochs, "The Doll House"

At a party somewhere on Flatbush Avenue after a concert at Brooklyn College. Phil Ochs, wearing a Marlon Brando black motorcycle jacket and yellow shades, is handed a glass of pale white wine as he heads for the big stuffed chair in a corner of the room. The Rolling Stones shout from the stereo speakers. Michael and Karen stand by the smorgasbord. Phil holds court. Always the same questions: What can we do? How can we stop this madness? How can we fight against the war? This time he has an answer for these middle-class children of the sixties. He takes the wine glass from his lips. "Come to Chicago."

Progress was being made. In January 1968, Robert Clark became the first black Mississippi state legislator in seventy years. Phil was part of the entertainment provided by the National Committee for Free Elections in Mississippi to celebrate the occasion. The program, produced by Ellis Haizlip, was held at New York's Tavern-On-The-Green restaurant. Besides Phil, Ossie Davis and Ruby Dee, Robert Hooks, Viveca Lindfors, and Diana Sands appeared. The Judson Poet's Theatre performed a mini-opera of "The Sayings of Mao Tse-tung."

Later that month, Phil appeared in another "Broadway for Peace" program, to help raise funds for those Congressmen who had taken a stand against the war and were now coming up for reelection. On the bill with Phil were Barbra Streisand, Leonard Bernstein, Alan Arkin, Paul Newman, Joanne Woodward, Eli Wallach, Harry Belafonte, and Tom Smothers. Michael told a reporter from *Cash Box,* "This is the first time Phil's been accepted by the establishment. This is the biggest break we've had all year."

There was no question Phil was continuing to shift toward the middle of the commercial road. He'd stopped producing material for *Broadside* magazine after the Holzman affair. Further signals came when Harold Leventhal failed to invite Phil to participate in the Carnegie Hall tribute to Woody Guthrie, which had brought Bob Dylan out of seclusion for the first time in seventeen months, following his motorcycle accident. Phil was hurt by not being asked to appear. He told a friend: "The Woody Guthrie Concert was the last straw. At the end of the concert they sang, 'This Land Is Your Land,' and I walked out in the middle of it because it wasn't my land. I should have been in that concert. I like Richie Havens, I like Judy Collins, and I like Odetta as performers, I think they're all very talented. But I can't quite see the logic . . . whoever decided they belonged in the Woody Guthrie Concert and I didn't, and Jack Elliott didn't . . . I'll go to my grave wondering about that. I think after seeing the Woody Guthrie Concert, I don't think Woody Guthrie would have been invited. He would have been out of place." Leventhal insisted the line had to be drawn somewhere; there were so many who'd wanted to participate, he'd had to pick and choose.

Late one night, Phil and Michael sat in The Hip Bagel, on Mac-

Dougal Street. Phil was having a steak with two root beers when Michael broke the news to him. "I'm moving to California."

Phil wasn't surprised. The Village was passing away. Everyone had either died or moved to the Coast. Or fallen off a motorcycle. Sam Hood had announced the closing of The Gaslight.

Michael urged Phil to come with him, that L.A. was where it was happening in the music business now. "Maybe so," Phil said. "But New York is still my home."

Michael agreed to continue to manage Phil. In fact, it would be better this way, he insisted. He was limited in New York; the building where their office was located was filled with toupeed tune pushers in blue-and-white striped suits and out-of-tune uprights with flattened keys.

Karen was excited for Michael. She wished she was moving to the Coast. She hated New York—the roaches, the cold winters, the isolation of Prince Street. She wanted to get into modeling, maybe break into the movies. Phil was against this, and didn't like it when she talked about it. A woman's job was to stay home, cook, clean, and look pretty for her man.

Yet, a couple of weeks later as Phil walked alone down Bleecker at five in the morning, he knew Michael had made the right decision. The Village was a cemetery. It was time for changes.

Phil and Karen packed whatever they had. Phil spent most of his final days in New York trying to find someone to sublease the Prince Street apartment. At the last minute, Jerry Rubin agreed to take it over. The only conditions Phil made were that if Rubin wanted to move he would find someone else to sublease, and whenever Phil came to New York he would be able to crash there.

Jim and Jean invited Phil and Karen to stay at their place in Topanga Canyon for a while. Karen and Jean pretended to like each other, Phil and Jim did The Sundowners for laughs, but it soon became clear it wasn't working. Phil would leave Karen at the house and meet Wickham downtown, sometimes not returning for several days. Jim and Jean were having their own problems, and Karen's presence, particularly when Phil was gone, made it even more difficult for the three of them. Everyone was relieved when Phil returned one afternoon, after being away for a day or two, and announced they were moving. He and Karen were going to share a house in the Hollywood Hills with Andy Wickham and his girlfriend, Frances.

Andy and Frances took the guest rooms in the rear, Phil and Karen had the front of the house. It was perfect for Phil and Andy, a nightmare for Karen and Frances. The women had to accept the peculiar living situation, and to understand that Phil and Andy were best friends, inseparable. Karen and Frances were permitted to remain with them as long as they enhanced the friendship, but were never allowed to challenge it.

Frances was younger than the others, almost ten years younger than Andy. She'd hardly dated before moving in with him. To her, this was the way all relationships must be. Karen, a bit older, resisted the notion that the men were absolute monarchs.

The men never took their women out on dates. They would stay up late at night and watch TV, getting drunk on wine; not Karen and Phil, or Frances and Andy; Andy and Phil.

The women had no opportunity to make other friends. The only people they saw, when the group went out, were either Phil's friends, or Andy's. Since Andy had very few friends, most of the time they were out with Phil's crowd. Recalls Judy Henske: "Karen's life with Phil was a life with his friends. I don't know of any time they ever went out by themselves. She really loved him. But you can only take so much. One time we were all sitting in The Troub, we used to have wonderful times at The Troub. On Monday nights it was like a club. Everyone knew everybody else. Nobody ever went into the hoots, everyone stayed at the bar. We were sitting there one night and I said, 'You know, everyone is like an animal. What animal do I remind you of?' and so on. When it came to Karen, she was easy. I called her a pedigree—small, thin, nervous, spoiled, flirty, the kind of woman Phil adored in his fantasies. Pedestal material. Everyone agreed Karen was like a gazelle. Finally, they got around to me. Karen looked right at me and said, 'A hyena.' It may have been the only time she enjoyed my company. I'll never forget it."

There was violence. The women were hit, smacked, belted around, punished. And yet they stayed. Karen was trapped by her inability to liberate herself from her emotional ties to Phil. She was hooked on the drug of Phil's swaggering narcissism. He was seasoned; he'd been there, he could afford to have it his way.

He'd already lived and rejected the traditional family life twice— once as a child, once as a father. Marriage, to Phil, was a microcosm of the American political power structure. The head of the house was the king of the castle; having a good job, being faithful to your wife, having lots of kids—the role of the American father. He understood the generation of World War II veterans who found themselves suddenly out of favor with their children over the issue of the war, who would go to any lengths to defend the moral security of the American family threatened by the spread of communism in Southeast Asia. Phil knew they were capable of killing for the preservation of the American way of life.

> *Missionaries will travel on crusades*
> *The word is given the heathen soul is saved*
> *Conversion to our morality*
> *Sigh the cannons of Christianity . . .*

Free love was linked irrevocably to the lifestyle of the New Left by the media's propagandistic coverage of the lifestyle of the hippies and yippies ("Make Love Not War!"). The effect was further outrage toward the radicals by the establishment, and the strengthening of its assumed link between communism and sex; a threat to democracy and marriage. Phil's fear of being trapped in what he perceived as the obsessive oligarchy of marriage was the basis for his agreement with Alice never to finalize their divorce, preventing either of them from getting married again as long as they lived. Karen, beautiful, refined, represented to Phil the conquest over his reverence for physical beauty which he always feared would lead to the relinquishing of his masculine throne. She was subjected to his lifestyle, she had to take it or leave it. She chose to take it.

Phil and Andy loved to get up early and meet David Blue for breakfast at Schwab's, to watch for movie stars. One morning, during eggs and sausage, Joseph Cotten walked in. Phil left his table and went over to Cotten to introduce himself. Phil was dressed in his usual Bowery-bum motif. Cotten was immaculate, wavy blue-gray hair tacked above his Protestant face. He looked at Phil and smiled without showing his teeth. Phil told Cotten how much he loved his movies. Phil was insane when he got back to the table. "Do you know who that was, man? Do you know who that was? Joseph Cotten, man, Joseph Cotten!"

Blue shrugged, ordered another cup of coffee, and continued to read the morning paper.

Phil was now inviting all his audiences to come to Chicago. Back in New York for a political benefit, he ran into Van Ronk at Minetta's. They proceeded to down a few and discuss what was happening. Phil invited Van Ronk to join the planned Chicago festivities. Van Ronk declined. "It's a mistake, Phil. If I were you, I'd stay clear of Chicago. It's a trap." Phil shook his head in disagreement. "It's a trap," Van Ronk repeated. "They'll use this to discredit the Left. You don't think the yippies, or anybody else, is strong enough to change anything, do you?"

"Yes."

"Phil, Daley's releasing hourly communiqués to the press about his ability to preserve law and order. It's a trap."

Phil continued to campaign actively for Eugene McCarthy. Rubin continued to chide Phil about it, labeling McCarthy an elitist, warning Phil he was becoming "more conservative than ever." Phil was convinced McCarthy was the answer to America's problems, if not politically, then charismatically. He had the potential to unify the Left, doing it like a rock star, appealing to the young, reading poetry to them, getting them to want to be involved.

Phil was at the opening of Eugene's, the cabaret created to raise funds for McCarthy's campaign. Located on New York's Second Avenue, on the site of the old El Morocco; exposed brick walls, beamed ceilings, checkered tablecloths, and lots of Democrats. Everything not nailed down was for sale, with proceeds going to the campaign. There for the opening, along with Phil, were poet Robert Lowell, playwright Neil Simon, and actress Myrna Loy. However, there was no exultation in the air that night. Twenty-four hours earlier, Dr. Martin Luther King, Jr., had been assassinated.

Later that night down in the Village, Phil ran into Jack

Newfield. They had a couple of drinks as they discussed the assassination and the upcoming Chicago convention. Newfield disliked Rubin and was concerned about Phil's admiration for the yippie activist. Newfield insisted to Phil that "yippie" was counterrevolutionary, in fact moronic. "It's a mistake, Phil," he said. "You don't get political change through rock and roll, long hair, and fucking in the streets. You wind up alienating a lot of people the movement has to reach. It's self-defeating, an artificial attempt to create a radical culture to match radical politics."

Phil insisted you could; his career was proof. Newfield urged Phil to get away from the "yippies" and to get away from McCarthy's campaign. "McCarthy's a loser." Newfield reminded Phil about McCarthy's campaign speech where he'd said he didn't care if Russia marched into Czechoslovakia—what Newfield called his "Dumb Polack" attitude. Nevertheless, Phil chose to stay with McCarthy, at least for the time being.

During this time, Michael was involved with the production of a Phil Ochs songbook. He wanted to do more than just put together a lot of sheet music. He had an idea for a book which would have songs, poetry, articles by and about Phil, lots of pictures and cartoons, and whatever else could be squeezed in. Ron Cobb contributed most of the photos and cartoons, and several of Phil's early *Broadside* articles were included. Between concerts, Phil helped with the overall design of the songbook.

The songbook was published in March of 1968. It had a picture of Phil on the cover, and "The War Is Over" printed along the side. There was no indication of what was inside. Nowhere did it say, "The Songs of Phil Ochs." Judy Henske wrote the introduction, "About the Author":

> I'll never forget the one time I saw Phil Ochs perform. It was in Hollywood and the crowd was tense with electric anticipation as the incredibly dapper figure walked out on the stage. Phil looked great that night; his crisp black hair had been freshly coiffed, his dark skin and eyes setting off both the startling brilliance of his freshly capped teeth and the red silk lining of his beautifully tailored tuxedo. In lightly accented English he introduced the first big hit, "La Bamba." A roar went up as the crowd started singing and clapping along. He followed this tour de force with "Lemon

Tree" and "If I Had a Hammer." What a performer! He was called back for encore after encore.

On the bill with Ochs that night was a sloppy long-winded protest singer whose name I forget. I left in the middle of his act.

The book contained lyrics from all Barricade-controlled Phil Ochs songs. Also included were pictures of Victorian nudes, posters of Che, photos of Andy Wickham and Eric Andersen, and the wax figurine Phil had picked up in an antique shop for a couple of dollars and named "Miranda," which eventually served as the inspiration for the song of the same name. The songbook was priced at $3.95. It sold over eight thousand copies in less than one month; more than 25,000 copies by the end of the year.

Michael was trying to get Phil onto network TV. He'd arranged for Phil to be interviewed in the trade publication *Amusement Business,* widely read by the network execs. In it, Phil was asked whether or not he felt there was a TV blacklist which was keeping him off the air:

> "The Tonight Show" terms my material "beyond its level of controversy." It wants snide jokes about the pill, but it's not to their interest to have someone say what a large portion of this generation is saying, and that is that this country is falling apart.

Phil claimed in the interview to have been turned down by Ed Sullivan, Merv Griffin, and the Smothers Brothers. Yet, he pointed out, CBS had shown him on the evening news singing "Draft Dodger Rag" at a rally, and ABC-TV had done a program entitled "Dissent or Treason," on which he'd sung "I Ain't Marching Anymore." Finally, Phil said he wasn't a protest singer.

> It's only one-fourth correct. I'm writing about social realism, not protest.

No interest was expressed by any of the networks in putting Phil Ochs on television.

American-International Pictures approached Michael about the possibility of having Phil star in a movie about a rock-and-roll singer who becomes President of the United States. Phil read the script and rejected it because he felt the screenplay portrayed American youth poorly. The rock musician who becomes President drops LSD into the water supply of Washington, D.C. Michael argued with Phil about his decision not to be in the film. He told Phil it would open the doors to other movies. There was the possibility that he might write some of the music for the film. Phil refused to reconsider. He was convinced it would be a disaster, and abort any future film work.

Wild in the Streets, starring Chris Jones, went on to become one of the biggest box office hits of that year, hailed by the New York *Times* as one of the top ten films of 1968.

The campaign heated up after Kennedy announced his challenge to McCarthy for the Democratic nomination. Phil wrote an article for *The Village Voice,* entitled "James Dean in Indiana," in which he commented on the race for the Party nod:

> Hubert Humphrey is a disgrace to his party and his country. If he bargains his way into the Democratic nomination, that will be the final moral death of that crusted party, the last old questionable cause of old men . . .
> I sang in Indiana for Eugene McCarthy ("Love Me, I'm a Liberal"), although my first instinct was for Kennedy, even after New Hampshire. It isn't easy to drag my guitar past the sensual photographs of a displaced prince (better-looking than Paul Newman; I'd like to see a shirtless candidacy shot of him saying, "Robert Kennedy is Hud"—then I'd vote for him) . . .
> America is two Mack trucks colliding on a superhighway because all the drivers are on amphetamines. On Primary Day I'll pay a visit to James Dean's grave and go to Indiana, watching the returns, not with a sense of amusement.

David Blue read the article and, while having lunch with Andy Wickham, said, "Ochs should go edit *The Village Voice,* that's the answer for him." When Wickham told Phil what David Blue had said, Phil replied, "The trouble with David Blue is that he has a BMI personality and an ASCAP mind."

"Pleasures of the Harbor" reached number five in Providence, Rhode Island, that week, behind "Magical Mystery Tour" and "John Wesley Harding."

A gala McCarthy rally was planned for Madison Square Garden in the spring. Phil was committed to appear, along with Alan Arkin, Larry Blyden, Arthur Miller, Robert Lowell, Elaine May,

Roscoe Lee Browne, Colleen Dewhurst, Jose Ferrer, Melvyn Douglas, Dick Van Dyke, Lillian Hellman, Dustin Hoffman, Eartha Kitt, Garry Moore, Tony Randall, Renee Taylor, and Gene Wilder. The following day he did a concert for McCarthy at Bowling Green University, at the invitation of the SDS. During the concert Phil told his audience, "Whenever the government senses you are trying to go deeper than just the surface meaning, they ban you from the air." The audience cheered. Why not? They had both been there before.

Phil was in New York for a couple of nights before returning to California. He ran into Newfield again, who suggested they fly to the Coast together. Newfield was going to be with Kennedy the night of the California primary. During the flight, Newfield tried to get Phil to switch his allegiance from McCarthy to Kennedy. Phil, drinking continuously on the flight, nodded in agreement with everything Newfield was saying. It was true that Kennedy had the ability to reach blacks and Chicanos, something McCarthy couldn't do. "Kennedy can bring Meany and Daley together, Phil; he can work with Chavez."

It wasn't until the day of the primary that Phil decided to support Kennedy, if he beat McCarthy in California. Phil watched the returns coming in on his color TV, placed at the foot of his bed just in front of the picture windows. He liked to watch television this way because, as he told Andy, "When they show the destruction of society on color TV, I want to be able to look out over Los Angeles to make sure they get it right."

That night, they got it right. Phil wept like a baby after Kennedy's brains were spilled on the industrial kitchen floor of the Ambassador Hotel. He cried through the night, without commercial interruption.

It was time for Phil to return to the studio. Jerry Moss was pressing for a follow-up album to "Pleasures." Phil had been writing songs everywhere; in planes, in the backs of cars, on his shirtsleeves. He had a lot of new material and was anxious to work with Larry Marks again.

They recorded the album in a week. Phil, still depressed over Kennedy's murder, wanted to get away from what he called "Old

America." He told Michael to book a tour of Europe while the album was being mixed. It was to be called "Tape from California."

Who's that coming down the road
A sailor from the sea
He looks a lot like me
I'd know him anywhere, had to stare
Feathers at his fingertips
A halo round his spine
He must have lost his mind
He should be put away, right away
In the corner of the night
He handed me his waterpipe
His eyes were searching deep inside my head
Here's what he said
"Sorry I can't stop and talk now
I'm in kind of a hurry anyhow
But I'll send you a tape from California" . . .

It was the return of the sailor, back from the sea, with new tales to tell and new places to see.

New York City has exploded
And it's crashed upon my head
I dove beneath the bed
Fighting, biting nails, turning pale
The landlord's at my window
And the burglar's at my door
I can't take it anymore
I guess I'll have to fly, it's worth a try
Someone's banging on the wall
But there's no party to recall
The singer of the shadows of his soul
So he's been told . . .

Phil had rejected his typewriter in favor of a tape recorder. His words would come in the form of a tape from California.

Half the world is crazy
The other half is scared
Madonnas do the minuet
For naked millionaires
The anarchists are rising,

While we're racing for the moon
It doesn't take a seer to see
The scene is coming soon . . .

The world was split, half crazy and half scared, presumably of the half that was crazy. It was a description of the physical state of the world, and a metaphor for the interior world of Phil Ochs: the singer/sailor the musician and the "shadow of his soul."

In concert, Phil was at his greatest when he performed this song, establishing the melody with a slick finger-pick intro, vamping chords during the verses. For the chorus, he would push the guitar up to the mike, and strum heavy, bassy chords, movie suspense music: vump, vump, vump, vump

"Sorry I can't stop and talk now . . .

vump, vump

I'm in kind of a hurry anyhow
But I'll send you a tape from California" . . .

Larry Marks: "We finished it rather quickly. Phil wanted to get away, to perform for a new audience. He was going to Europe, I believe . . . his meter problems with the long songs continued.

"We had meetings on the recording of 'The War Is Over.' Bob Thompson was brought in to arrange and orchestrate that particular cut. Phil was desperate to have that song done just right, and he usually got what he wanted."

Jack Elliott was brought in to play guitar on "Joe Hill," a song Phil had written to the same folk melody Woody Guthrie used for "Tom Joad." Marks remembers Elliott coming into the studio and immediately demanding something to drink. Keeping him sober long enough to finish the song was Marks's responsibility.

The longest piece on the album was "When in Rome," considered by many to be Phil's masterpiece, better even than "Crucifixion." It was recorded with a single guitar, Phil's, and it told the story of hatred gone wild, visualized as an uprising against the master race by a band of their slaves who fall prey to the same corruption of power as their tormentors, eventually to die by self-inflicted wounds. It was a song influenced by Elia Kazan's *Viva Zapata*.

In the fire blue forests faded and forgotten
I crawled through the cotton fields picking for cotton
The overseer sneered, his whipping was rotten
With ecstasy
In child-like terror I tore for the tap roots
The cards of the lash were calling to follow suit
I dashed for the swamps the hounds in hot pursuit
Jealously
All through the night a figure of fright as I hid my
*   head*
And they buried their nose in a cut of my clothes
*   now torn in shreds*
And they never would leave until they believed
*   that I was dead*
But I'd never curse their names
Oh who am I to blame
I know I'd do the same endlessly
And all the high-born ladies
So lovely and so true
Have been handed to the soldiers
When in Rome do as the Romans do . . .

Now nothing remained for building or burning
The losing of lovers was all I was learning
A time for escape and a time for returning had come to me
Back through the ashes and back through the embers
Back through the roads and the ruins I remembered
My hands at my side I sadly surrendered
Do as you please
The hero was home, proven and grown
I fell on the floor
Mad with romance they started to play
Their star was born
I bled like the rain I exploded in pain
Then I screamed for more
Oh make me feel sublime
Release me from my mind
Kill me one more time
And set me free
And all the high-born ladies so lovely and so true
Have been handed to the soldiers
When in Rome do as the Romans do . . .

The struggle for power—the conflict between black and white, the metaphorical duel between Phil Ochs and the shadow of his soul. In the final verse, death liberates:

> *Make me feel sublime.*
> *Release me from my mind.*
> *Kill me one more time*
> *And set me free . . .*

The day after the album was finished, Phil and Michael left for Europe. They toured the Continent for three weeks, greeted enthusiastically by the crowds and receiving a lot of good press. In Sweden, Phil visited with several radical and underground groups. One of his acquaintances gave him a lighter made of metal from American planes shot down over North Vietnam. Phil loved it, was fascinated by it, seeing it as a symbol for the bitter absurdity that was destroying America.

One evening, Phil came barging into the hotel room and told Michael the album hadn't been released yet in the States.

"How do you know?" Michael asked.

"I know. Call Jerry Moss right now and ask him why the album hasn't been released." Michael tried to reason with Phil.

"It's late in L.A. Why don't we wait until the morning."

"Now. And call collect." Michael got on the phone and called Moss. When he got through, he knew he'd aroused Moss from his sleep.

"Jerry, this is Michael Ochs. From Sweden."

"I know. You called collect."

"Phil wants to know why the album hasn't been released yet."

"Tell Phil not to panic. We had to rush like crazy, but it's out. How's the tour going?"

"Great."

"Goodnight." Moss hung up the phone. Michael relayed what Moss said. Phil nodded his head slowly, up and down.

When Phil returned from Europe he called Karen at the house from the airport. He was furious because she hadn't come to pick him up. "Listen, you bitch, you better get out of there before I get home or I'm going to kill you." He slammed the phone down. When he arrived at the house she was gone. He fell into a deep sleep for two days. When he finally awoke, it was to a breakfast in bed served by Karen. Phil rubbed his eyes, had a drink of wine, which he used to rinse his teeth before spitting it out over the side of the bed, and ate the bacon and eggs. He never looked at her, and first spoke after breakfast, to Wickham, in the living room. Wickham told him Rubin had been trying to get in touch. Phil fumbled through several notebooks until he found a number he could call in New York. Rubin answered and told Phil to meet him right away at the Newport '68 Festival.

"I wasn't invited this year."

"*I'm* inviting you. Nancy and I are going, and we want you to come along." An hour later, Phil left for the airport.

Phil, Jerry, and Nancy, Jerry's lady, were admitted to the festival wearing phony press passes Rubin had safety-pinned to their shirts. Rubin began passing out copies of *The Yipster Times* to everyone he saw. He spotted three nuns sitting together and couldn't resist going over and giving them copies of the yippie paper, which contained the following editorial:

> Who says that rich White America can tell the Chinese what is best? How dare you tell the poor that their poverty is deserved? Fuck nuns: laugh at professors: disobey your parents: burn your money: you know life is a dream and all of our institutions are man-made illusions effective because YOU take the dream for reality.

Someone recognized Rubin and he was immediately ejected from the festival grounds. That night, as Jerry, Nancy, and Phil were sitting in a local bar having a drink, William F. Buckley happened to walk in off the street to have a cocktail. Phil couldn't resist going up to him. A small group gathered to listen as Phil told Buckley about the McCarthy campaign. Ever since the death of Robert Kennedy, Phil had redoubled his efforts in supporting McCarthy, convinced now he was the sole hope for America. Buckley listened as Phil told him about playing a rally in Boston's Fenway Park with Pete Seeger. "You know, Mr. Buckley, it was the first time Seeger sang for a presidential candidate since Henry Wallace."

"You mean the first time since Moscow?" Buckley replied. "I

hope," he continued, "that Peter Seeger will be singing on the Czechoslovakian border to the Russian troops as they come marching through. When are you singing at the festival?"

"I'm not," Phil said. "I guess I don't fit into the folk music establishment at the moment."

"Oh, is there a folk music establishment too?"

As they spoke, George Wein, the director of the festival, walked up to Buckley. Buckley turned and asked Wein why Phil hadn't been invited to sing at the festival. The small gathering cheered his question, echoing, "Why didn't you invite him?" Wein quickly asked Buckley if he'd like to come to a party, and left. Rubin immediately suggested they all go to the party.

When they arrived, Phil was told at the door he could come in, but the others, meaning Jerry Rubin and Nancy, couldn't. All three left. "Don't worry, Phil," Rubin said. "The real party is just beginning."

Everyone assumed that Rubin and Phil were the best of friends. Actually, Phil's association with Rubin was almost exclusively in the realm of political protest. His alliance with Rubin was symbolic—Phil Ochs the Che Guevara to Rubin's Fidel Castro. If Phil needed Rubin to counter the distrust the radical Left had for the singer-protester bon vivant, Rubin, in turn, needed to validate his own poetic abilities through his association with Phil. Rubin made Phil politically acceptable with the radical fringe; Phil shared the literary stage with Rubin.

If Phil went out of his way to reinforce the public Rubin/Ochs bond in the media, he was as obsessed with keeping his friendship with Andy Wickham private. Rubin was an extension of the political, East Coast Ochs; Wickham, the private, West Coast Phil. He delighted in telling Wickham how much Rubin hated him, which he did, as much as he loved telling Rubin that the feeling from Wickham was mutual, which it was. Wickham taunted Phil about his association with Rubin, while Rubin was obsessed with wanting to be Phil's "best friend." He wanted to take acid with Phil, and tried to talk him into experimenting with it. Phil refused. He was petrified of psychedelics. Rubin longed for approval of his writing from Phil. After he'd finished "Do It," he showed Phil the manuscript, which he read with a shrug of indifference. Rubin was mortified; he rewrote the whole thing.

In the spring, Rubin challenged Phil to a rhetorical shoot-out, in print, in order to clear the upcoming Illinois air:

RUBIN: The battle in America is not between Democrats and Republicans, but between children and the machine . . . Johnson was just doing all he could in his own way to live up to Jack Kennedy's memory. I hate all rich bastards.

OCHS: You radicals are all alike, lashing out at the approaching tank with yo-yo's. But I also sense the machine is developing a rather apparent emotion, that of survival. Many people are very mad, many are in a drugged stupor, and being a semi-yippie, I'm hysterical.

RUBIN: Okay. That draws the issue clearly. I do not want this system to survive, you do. To me, the essence of America is viewing a man as a material, not a spiritual, object. In other words, the Death Society. America at her essence is irrational to man's freedom.

OCHS: Once again, I essentially agree with you. But I see a different pattern for the change. America must change the direction of its foreign policy and the character of its soul if it is to survive. And we're just a new generation of actor-comedian-revolutionaries who get to face the impossible but only worthwhile battle. I'm as unpatriotic as the next guy, but I realize the revolution requires timing as well as militancy. Look before you leap and consider who else might be dominating.

RUBIN: Fuck your timing. Johnson quit because, like you, he understands that the counterrevolution also requires timing as well as militancy. The yippies are a social movement, a dynamic energy force. International young people too alienated to become spare parts in somebody's junk car. I am part of that force; I celebrate life; I also have specific demands, like the legalization of marijuana, the curtailing of the police, the end of an imperialist foreign policy. I am not kneeling, but my feet are not completely off the ground either. America is the beautiful shipwreck; we are the orphans of technology and "Now" is an illusion. Just as sure as my name is Eugene McCarthy. Keep flippy for yippie; see you in Chicago!

Chicago. 1968. The scenario was simple. Permissiveness was permissible. In 1962 it had begun on campuses, specifically at UCLA; the issue free speech. In 1963 permissiveness meant civil rights, and marches on Washington. In 1964, the burgeoning protest against the war in Vietnam. In 1965, "soft" drugs like marijuana, and the revelation of acid. In 1966, the rise of the black militants and the coalescing forces against Johnson and the war in Vietnam. In 1967, flower power and the rejection on campus of American imperialism.

So they came to Chicago convinced they could do no wrong. The enemies were the politicians. Those who came to Chicago were sure it would be a demonstration benefiting America. There would be little, if any, violence; the media would protect them. Rubin, Hoffman, and the rest of the yippies had put out the call, and the young Americans of the sixties went off to fight in Alsace-Lorraine, Illinois. Blowing in the wind was the lusty perfume of the optimistic young.

Somehow the wind became a hurricane and the perfume turned to tear gas as, with the speed of insanity, the sixties died; assassinated by the Democratic Party and its chosen leader, Hubert Horatio Kerensky.

While Rubin was running around wearing Indian warpaint trying to gain support through aggressive street tactics, Phil was rushing up to his hotel suite to catch the replay of the day's action on the evening news. He sat and watched while the police machine of Chicago cracked the skulls of America's children as their parents applauded, relieved that the police could do what they couldn't.

The next day the gang broke into groups, their mission to find a suitable pig to nominate for President of the United States. Phil and Rubin rented a truck and drove until they found a farm and a pig. Once there, Phil bargained with the farmer, getting him down to twenty-five dollars cash, while Hoffman's team simply stole their pig.

A press conference was called but was held up due to a power struggle that developed over which pig was better. The larger, Phil Ochs-purchased pig was finally chosen, and its nomination for President formally announced. At that moment Phil, Abbie Hoffman, Stew Albert, Paul Krassner, Wolf Lowenthal, and Dennis Dalrymple, all principals of yippie, were arrested for violation of a city ordinance against bringing livestock into Chicago without a permit.

They were taken from the steps of the Civic Center Plaza to the county jail, where they spent the day behind bars. The mood in the cell was euphoric. There was singing, dancing, and the general feeling they'd indeed committed a revolutionary act. Outside, kids were gathering, as word spread that Rubin, Hoffman, and Phil were being held. By nightfall they were all released on bail and greeted on the steps of the courthouse with cheers and applause. They headed for the park.

The air sizzled toward its final charred climax. On one side stood the cops, white helmets glistening under the blue carbon arc lamps, black leather chin straps, clenched steel teeth. Their nightsticks slapped a cadence of fear into their gloved palms. Phil jumped on top of a car and began a rapid, stuttering, spontaneous speech, the consonants spraying tiny arcs of spit between his lips and teeth. He turned his head from right to left to right, talking through a bullhorn. Suddenly he turned to the line of police, asking them to put down their weapons and join the people. He begged them to understand what they were doing. It was as if everything rode on this one move; the trigger switch for the flow of power, out of the hands of Old America, into the hands of the New.

He jumped off the car and walked over to each cop, individually. He put the bullhorn down. "Will you put away your weapons and join us? . . . Will you put away your weapons and join us? . . ."

The soldiers stood, looking forward, tensed for action, ready to spring at any second. Finally, one broke formation and looked directly into Phil's eyes. "When I was in college I had a girlfriend who really liked your songs. One time she asked me to take her to one of your concerts and I did. The next day I went out and bought your album. After tonight, I'll never listen to your songs again."

Phil was devastated. He was so sure he'd be able to get them to put their guns away. He was so sure he was right, so sure he could convince them he was right, so sure.

He left Chicago the next day and went directly to Philadelphia, where he was scheduled to appear at the Philly Folk Festival. He was on stage soon after he arrived. He looked out over the audience and went into "I Ain't Marching Anymore." They started booing, waving their hands at Phil. The noise got so loud he had to leave the stage.

He was drinking boilermakers in a cheap bar somewhere in Philadelphia. Newfield had been right. Van Ronk too. They'd called it correctly. Chicago was a trap. While he'd been playing revolutionary, Van Ronk, Oscar Brand, Doc Watson, and Pete Seeger were playing the summer folk festivals. They weren't the fringe of folk music: they were its mainstay. They had a sphere of influence.

Phil began to seriously question his political affiliations: "At that point, having gone through almost nine years as a political singer, I had a kind of reaction to it. I had a reaction first of all against the counterculture. In order for there to be a real viable movement, the idea of a freak counterculture was disastrous. What was needed was an organic connection to the working class. That's what George Wallace meant; that's what Robert Kennedy meant. It had to be one country, and you shouldn't socially alienate the working class of America. At that point, I realized that Nixon was able to use all of this, maybe even form it, or the money behind him at least helping to form it, so that he could then say, 'It's them against us. No matter what you think of me, I'm a straight American guy. If you don't have me, you're going to have some hairy freak with dope in the streets and the destruction of the country. You have no choice.' That's the game he played, and played very effectively. So my feelings at the time were how to get some working-class base."

Phil returned to Los Angeles, extremely depressed. One night while having dinner with Andy Wickham, Phil started fantasizing about his own death. They'd just come from a screening of *Tunes of Glory,* Phil's favorite film. Over sweet and sour pork, he made Wickham promise to see to it that the arrangements for the funeral were handled correctly. Andy was to take Phil's body to Scotland, where he wanted to be buried. "Of course . . . of course," Wickham said. "What do you want for dessert?"

Phil was sure the rest of his friends were deserting him. Robert

Christgau, a friend who'd traveled with Phil earlier in the year to several political rallies, came out with a scathing attack on Phil's musical ability in *Esquire* magazine. Christgau wrote that Phil was "unquestionably a nice guy, he's so sincere, you know? . . . too bad his voice shows an effective range of about half an octave, almost no dramatic quality, and a built-in vibrato that makes it sound warped; too bad his guitar playing would not suffer much were his right hand webbed." The Christgau piece hurt Phil personally much more than the Reverend David A. Noebel's book *Rhythm, Riots and Revolution,* which characterized The Beatles as "dangerous" to Christianity, along with those "Marxist minstrels Bob Dylan, Joan Baez, and Phil Ochs." That one he loved.

Andy thought it would be good for Phil to get away for a while. He planned a trip for them to Mexico. They flew down first class, getting bombed on the way. Phil wanted to visit the Mexican whorehouses. He talked Wickham into going along; enticing his friend to take a look into the abyss; he might get to like it after a while. Phil told Andy that whores were the only honest women. "They don't play games, and I haven't got time to develop relationships." Phil was turned off by having to court and date and kiss and hug and wine and dine and maybe yes and maybe no. When he wanted sex he wanted it fast and dirty. His money's worth.

They came out of one brothel with Phil holding a pair of ladies' shoes in his hand. He'd gotten into an argument with a whore, claiming he'd been cheated. His sense of justice was constant, even if it meant having to steal a hooker's shoes to get even.

They had to run for their lives with half of Mexico chasing them, screaming for their blood.

It seemed the only good times now were with Andy. Being in the house was unbearable. Phil would speak little, preferring to rock back and forth on his rocking chair, puff his pipe, and stare into space. It was a time he wrote about in the strange musical chronicle "Bach, Beethoven, Mozart and Me":

> *Every morning at the dawn dust is in the air*
> *Karen rises early, runs brushes through her hair*
> *Then she buys the paper, I lay on my back*
> *Then she feeds the monkey, then she feeds the cat*

I'll talk, I'll talk they live by the sea
Surrounded by a cemetery
If you get tired come up for some tea
With Bach, Beethoven, Mozart and me

Frances is the next to rise powders up her nose
Working for the tailor makes the western clothes
Andy drives the sportscar to the Warner Brothers Ghost
Used to live in England, now he loves the Coast

Sometimes a friend comes by sings his latest song
But David fights with Susan, nobody gets along
Every other Sunday it's time to make the call
Judy has a barbeque, plays the volleyball

In the evening when the sun goes down streets are
     all aglow
We walk out on the hillside, city shines below
We sit down for our supper, the news begins to play
Walter he is speechless, Eric speaks for Che

Andy plays the Cricket game Frances holds the glass
Karen reads and darns her dress I dream of the past . . .

Ron Delsener got in touch with Michael to find out if it was possible to have Phil do another concert at Carnegie. Michael said he didn't think so, Phil wasn't doing much of anything these days. As a matter of fact, he and Phil had informally split. Phil just didn't seem to be interested in pursuing his career as intensely as before. Delsener pushed, and finally Michael agreed to ask, although he was sure it would do no good.

Michael went over to Jim and Jean's, where Phil was having dinner. They all sat around and talked, mostly about the old days.

The phone rang. Jim picked it up and, as he talked, began to wave the others quiet. He took the receiver away from his ear and said, softly, "It's the FBI. They're looking for somebody named Phil Ochs."

Phil smiled. "Tell them to meet me in Monument Valley at dawn."

"Don't tell them that," Michael said quickly, taking the phone from Jim. After he hung up, he told Phil it definitely was the FBI and they really did want to talk to him about certain "subversive elements" in connection with the events that had taken place in Chicago. Phil began stuttering, waving his hands in front of his face, tilting his head to one side. He was like a car which had run out of gas now sputtering on the first few drops of new ethyl poured into its carburetor. When he kicked over, he called the FBI back. Afterward, he turned to Michael and agreed to do the show for Delsener. "In fact," he added, "let's do another tour. And call Jerry Moss. I want to record a new album."

He wrote all the songs in two weeks. He called Larry Marks to set up a recording schedule for the new album. "Rehearsals for Retirement" was to be his swan song, the last, the greatest, Phil Ochs album.

Marks was reluctant to work with Phil again. The new songs offered little opportunity to expand Phil's music beyond what they'd been able to achieve with the first two albums. Besides, Marks was thinking about leaving the recording industry and moving into films. Finally, though, he agreed to return to the studio with Phil for one last time.

"Rehearsals for Retirement" completed the trilogy of Phil Ochs albums produced by Larry Marks. It served as Phil's *Grand Guignol,* his last creative breath, one final artistic gasp. It would be a glimpse into the abyss, a spotlight on the shadow.

> *I can see him coming*
> *He's a walkin' down the highway*
> *With his big boots on*
> *And his big thumb out*
> *He wants to get me, he wants to hurt me*
> *He wants to bring me down*
> *Ah, but some time later*
> *When I feel a little straighter*
> *I will come across the stranger*
> *Who'll remind me of the danger*
> *And then I'll run him over.*
> *Pretty smart on my part*
> *Find my way in the dark . . .*

The album was a two-act musical, dramatizing the transformation of democracy to dictatorship, and of Phil Ochs, troubadour, into the King of Cowboys. Chicago had been the final hope for America, and for Phil Ochs. He was now the King of Cowboys—reigning in the State of Darkness. The resurrection of Richard Nixon from the ashes of Chicago paralleled the emergence of the mad cowboy who *"wants to get me, wants to hurt me, wants to bring me down."* He'd always been there, coming closer, anticipated in the opening line of "Tape from California" (*who's that coming down the road, he looks a lot like me*). Act One climaxed with the final journey into darkness: "William Butler Yeats Visits Lincoln Park and Escapes Unscathed":

> *As I went out one evening to take the evening air*
> *I was blessed by a blood-red moon*
> *In Lincoln Park the dark was turning*
> *I spied a fair young maiden and a flame was in her eyes*
> *And on her face lay the steel blue skies*
> *Of Lincoln Park the dark was turning*
> *Turning*

But don't worry, folks. You ain't heard nothin' yet. Stepping in front of the curtain, during intermission, comes Phil Ochs, as in "greatest performer of all time." To prove it he's going to sing his heart out for you. A mike in one hand, a drink and a cigarette in the other. The song a platterish "My Prayer"-type ditty called "My Life." Good ole Phil's reflection on his career, his hopes, his dreams. Nothing serious here, folks.

> *My life*
> *Was once a joy to me*
> *Never knowing I was growing every day*
> *My life*
> *Was once a toy to me*
> *And I wound it*
> *And I found it ran away*
> *So I race through the night*
> *With a face at my feet*
> *Like a God I would write*
> *All the melodies were sweet*
> *And the women were in white*
> *It was easy to survive*
> *My life was so alive*

My life
Was once a flag to me
And I waved it
And behaved like I was told
My life
Was once a drag to me
And I loudly
And I proudly lost control
I was drawn by a dream
I was loved by a lie
Every serf on the scene
Begged me to fight
But I slipped through the scene
So lucky to fail
My life was not for sale

My life
Is now a myth to me
Like the drifter
With his laughter in the dawn
My life
Is now a death to me
So I'll mold it
And I'll hold it till I'm born
So I turn to the land where I'm so out of place
Throw a curse on the plan in exchange for the grace
To know where I stand
Take everything I own
Take your tap from my phone
And leave my life alone
My life alone

Thousands of strings were behind him. Lincoln Mayorga's wrenching piano accompaniment drove Phil to squeeze the song from the very depths of his despair. He left Side One with what was, simply, the greatest performance of his life.

If "My Life" was Phil's greatest performance, "The Scorpion Departs but Never Returns" was his greatest song. It began with a bit of musical journalism from the pen of the old Phil Ochs, the story of the disappearance of the nuclear submarine. It is this setting which serves as the final, perfect metaphor. Phil is the sailor once again. The King of Cowboys is gone, only a dream. The sailor is safe, aboard ship, away from the horror of the land, the terror of pursuit.

But wait. Something is wrong. The ship is sinking! The sailor has been caught by the cowboy, overtaken at the prime of life. His journey is over, he is dying. It is the creative death of Phil Ochs, the moment of realization preceding the moment of expiration. *I'm not dying, I'm not dying. Tell me I'm not dying.*

> *Sailors climb the tree, up the terrible tree*
> *Where are my shipmates have they sunk beneath the sea*
> *I do not know much but I know this cannot be*
> *It isn't really, it isn't really,*
> *Tell me it isn't really*
>
> *Sounding bell is diving down the water green*
> *Not a trace, not a toothbrush, not a cigarette was seen*
> *Bubble ball is rising from a whisper or a scream*
> *But I'm not screaming, no I'm not screaming,*
> *Tell me I'm not screaming*
>
> *Captain will not say how long must we make*
> *The fettered ship forever sail the sea*
> *It's all the same*
>
> *Captain my dear Captain we're staying down so long*
> *I have been a good man I've done nobody wrong*
> *Have we left our ladies for the lyrics of a song*
> *That I'm not singing, that I'm not singing,*
> *Tell me I'm not singing*
>
> *The schooner ship is sliding across the pitching sea*
> *My sons and my daughter they won't know what to think*
> *The crew has turned to boating and the officers to drink*
> *But I'm not drinking, but I'm not drinking,*
> *Tell me I'm not drinking*
>
> *The radio is begging them to come back to the shore*
> *All will be forgiven it'll be just like before*
> *All you've ever wanted will be waiting by the door*
> *We will forgive you, we will forgive you,*
> *Tell me we'll forgive you*

> *No one gives an answer not even one goodbye*
> *Oh, the silence of their sinking is all that they reply*
> *Some have chosen to decay and others chose to die*
> *But I'm not dying, no I'm not dying,*
> *Tell me I'm not dying*

Finally, the signature piece. "Rehearsals for Retirement," a tape left behind to be played in the event the body is never recovered; a chilling finale to the album and the trilogy. With Lincoln Mayorga's weeping piano underneath, Phil's voice sweetly wilted to a fragile moan, as he sang in memory of himself:

> *The days grow longer for smaller prizes*
> *I feel a stranger to all surprises*
> *You can have them I don't want them*
> *I wear a different kind of garment*
> *In my rehearsals for retirement . . .*
>
> *The lights are cold again they dance below me*
> *I turn to old friends they do not know me*
> *All but the beggar he remembers*
> *I put a penny down for payment*
> *In my rehearsals for retirement*
>
> *Had I known the end would end in laughter*
> *Still I tell my daughter it doesn't matter*
>
> *The stage is tainted with empty voices*
> *The lady's painted they have no choices*
> *I take my colors from the stable*
> *They lie in tatters by the tournament*
> *In my rehearsals for retirement*
>
> *Where are the armies who killed a country*
> *And turned a strong man into a baby*
> *Now comes the rebel they are welcome*
> *I wait in anger and amusement*
> *In my rehearsals for retirement*
>
> *Farewell my own true love, farewell my fancy*
> *Are you still owin' me love, though you failed me*
> *But one last gesture for her pleasure*
> *I'll paint your memories on the monument*
> *In my rehearsals for retirement.*

In L.A. Phil had a tombstone made for himself, which still stands in Topanga Canyon:

PHIL OCHS
(American)
Born: El Paso, Texas 1940
Died: Chicago, Illinois 1968
REHEARSALS
FOR
RETIREMENT

The tombstone was used as part of the album cover. On the back was a poem he'd written on a sheet of TWA stationery on the way to New York:

This then is the death of the American
Imprisoned by his paranoia
and all his diseases of his innocent inventions
he plunges to the drugs of the devil to find his gods
he employs the farce of force to crush his fantasies
he calls conventions of salesmen and savages
to reinforce his hopelessness
So the poet swordsmen and their beat generation
must divorce themselves from their very motherland
only for the beast sensation of life or love or pain
our deepest and most religious moments
were on elevators posing as planes.

Part two of this earnest epic
finds seaweed lapping against your eyes
the sailors have chosen the mystery surprise
to join the Flying Dutchman in his search for a
        green disguise
Still others invade the final colony
to present their tinted tributes to the millionaire
        assassin
While I stumble through this paradise
considering several suicides
for distant lavender lovers
or bless the violence of the ridiculous revolution
for self-bronzing brothers
and finally turn away from the turquoise towers
of this comic civilization

my responsibilities are done let them come let them come
and I realize these last days these trials and tragedies
were after all only
our rehearsals for retirement.

Carnegie Hall was sold out weeks in advance. New York eagerly awaited Phil's return to the concert stage. When he emerged from the wings he was greeted with waves of applause. He began with "The Rhythm of Revolution," explaining he'd changed the word "ringing" to "rhythm" because "it was better." He followed with "The Bells" and "I Ain't Marching Anymore." Then, without saying anything, he began singing the new songs.

"Pretty Smart on My Part" was met with cheers. Phil segued into "I Kill, Therefore I Am." Again the audience responded loudly. A piano was wheeled out. He sat and played the opening chords of "Rehearsals for Retirement," singing the song to his own accompaniment. Back to the guitar for "The War Is Over." A standing ovation. His first encore, "I'm Going to Say It Now."

He left the stage, brought back by the rhythmic clapping of the capacity crowd. He left them for the last time with a moving version of "Crucifixion." He walked off, whipping the guitar from his neck, and was met by Ron Delsener and Michael. Phil asked for a drink; someone handed him a beer. And a note, which remained, unread, in his pocket while he sat, exhausted, in his dressing room, ready to meet the fans coming backstage to see him, as they always did. It was part of a Phil Ochs concert; he'd instruct the ushers and security guards to let anyone backstage who wished to see him. He'd sit and listen as they'd tell him how great he was, how committed they were, how much they loved him.

Finally, after an hour of autographs and adulation, he went to the Carnegie Tavern to get something to eat and a couple of drinks. Reaching into his pocket for some money, he found the note. It was from William Kunstler. He wanted Phil to call him, to make arrangements for testifying at the trial of the "Chicago Eight."

The next afternoon, when Phil woke up in his room at the Fifth Avenue Hotel, the first thing he did was to reach for the phone.

VIII

Outside the cats are scratching
Inside the doors are latching
On the room, the greedy gloom
The trial is revealed.
Police are six feet deep
With switchblades in their teeth
So no one leaves and they all believe
This is absolutely real
Yes, it's real
And the Sergeant says, "Are you ready, boys?
Get ready, boys
Aim . . .
And fire . . ."

Phil Ochs, "The Trial"

"Rehearsals for Retirement" did poorly, barely reaching the thirty-thousand mark before being cut out by A&M.

Outside of New York the songs were received indifferently. Occasionally there would be shouts of other song titles during Phil's singing of "Rehearsals." He'd be competing with the audience. After playing a few dates, he canceled the remainder of the tour and returned to Hollywood.

He took the album over to Judy Henske's, to play it for her. He kept on telling Judy it was his best album, he'd really grown since "Tape." Afterward, they both went to Paul Rothchild's house, in the hills. Rothchild, the producer of Phil's three Elektra albums, hadn't seen Phil since he'd changed labels. Rothchild had company that afternoon, but Phil didn't care. He walked into the cocktail-saturated living room and told Rothchild to play the new album. No one said anything; the well-groomed crowd stared in amazement at the dusty, sloppy, stuttering guy in the middle of the room with the album under his arm. Phil went to the stereo and put on his record. Rothchild left the room. A few seconds later, all the power went off in the house. Rothchild returned and announced there'd been a power failure. "Phil," he said, turning toward his gate crasher, "I guess you can't play your album." Phil left without saying a word.

Phil and William Kunstler were speaking daily over the phone, formulating plans for Phil's appearance in defense of the "Chicago Eight." Kunstler felt Phil's testimony was crucial; he might even have Phil sing a song to demonstrate what he'd done in Chicago. The theme of Kunstler's defense was that people had the right to congregate; singing and dancing in the streets of America were not yet a crime. As the day of Phil's testimony approached, his nervousness grew worse. He made daily trips to the drugstore to refill his prescription for Valium, which he'd been taking to help settle his nerves, particularly when his stuttering became severe. Lately, he'd been chewing the tranquilizers as if they were M&M's. He had prescriptions in many drugstores, and whenever he felt an anxiety attack coming on, he would dash in to a druggist for a new supply. One time, during breakfast with David Blue, at Schwab's, Phil began to shake. The on-duty druggist wouldn't give Phil any pills, he couldn't find the reorder slip. Phil nearly went out of his mind. He began screaming and shouting at the druggist, demanding he call a doctor, any doctor, to pass those pills. David Blue took Phil outside and gave him a couple of his own Valiums, after which Phil calmly went back to finish his breakfast.

Phil arrived to testify in December, a year and a half after the events of Chicago. He took the witness stand following a screening, in the courtroom, of a film made at Grant Park by Sarah Daimant. While the pictures revealed the battle formations between the police and the demonstrators, the sound track offered a cacophony of street noise and political shouting: *"America,*

America, God shed his grace on thee. This is a free country. Jackson, Goodway, call Mayor Daley, pilot . . . I think it is a police night. America, America. Mace, Mace, Mace . . . walk, walk, walk . . . leave the area, get out of here . . . let's stay and see what happens here . . . hey, you, fucking, blow up the whole— come on, man, peace, peace, peace, America, America . . . get out of here . . . no, no, no, no, no we won't go. No, no we won't go . . . no no, we won't go . . . hell no, we won't go . . . hell no, we won't go . . . go to hell humor . . . go to hell humor . . . go to hell humor . . . walk, walk, walk, walk, walk . . . hey, we want to stay . . . hey, hey, we want to stay. . . ."

Phil Ochs was sworn in to testify for the defense. After a brief series of questions to establish that Phil was a singer by profession, Kunstler began to weave Phil into the pattern of the defense:

Q: Now, Mr. Ochs, can you indicate what kind of songs you sing?

A: I write all my own songs and they are just simple melodies with a lot of lyrics. They usually have to do with current events and what is going on in the news, which goes back to journalism, and you can call them topical songs, songs about the news, and then developing into more philosophical songs later.

Q: Now in your career did you ever write a song involving President John Kennedy?

A: Yes.

MR. FORAN (Prosecutor): Your Honor, I object to that.

THE COURT: I sustain the objection. If the witness made answer, I strike his answer and direct the jury to disregard it.

Judge Hoffman was against having Phil participate in the trial at all, and it was clear he was going to try to limit his contribution. Kunstler tried to indicate Phil's stature as a performer by asking him if he'd ever sung on television, and again there was a sustained objection. Kunstler turned to the bench and said, "Your Honor, we are trying to show the topical and political nature of his songs because they relate to the case and . . ."

THE COURT: Oh, he's given the details of his background, his profession. I think we have got that.

Sunset Boulevard, 1967 (*Ron Cobb*)

THE WHITE HOUSE

WASHINGTON

October 25, 1967

PERSONAL

Dear Mr. Taylor:

Thank you for sending the President a copy of
the recording, "The Pleasures of the Harbor,"
featuring Phil Ochs. Your thoughtful courtesy
is warmly appreciated.

With the President's every good wish,

Sincerely yours,

Juanita D. Roberts
Personal Secretary
to the President

Mr. Derek Taylor
1416 North La Brea Avenue
Hollywood, California 90028

Phil in New York at a press conference to announce the formation of Yippie (*Photo by Michael Ochs*)

Judy Sims, Phil, and John Carpent[er] in Los Angeles (*Courtesy of the Phil Ochs estate*)

Phil, at home in the Hollywood Hills (*Ron Cobb*)

(Ron Cobb)

(Ron Cobb)

THE SOURCE
OF OUR
LIBERTY

Meegan
(*Alice Ochs*)

Q: Now, Mr. Ochs, did there ever come a time when you met any of the defendants at this table?

A: Yes, I met Jerry Rubin in 1965 when he was organizing one of the first teach-ins against the war in Vietnam in Berkeley. I was living in New York City at the time.

Once again, a sustained objection. Kunstler attempted to show that Phil had sung on numerous occasions when Rubin had helped to organize political demonstrations no different from the one that took place in Chicago. At this point, Kunstler changed his line of questioning and began to ask Phil about the formation of Yippie:

Q: Now, Mr. Ochs, have you ever been associated with what is called the Youth International Party or, as we will say, the Yippies?

A: Yes. I was at many of the early meetings when . . .

THE COURT: You have answered the question. You said yes.

Q: Can you indicate what participation you had with the Yippies?

A: Yes. I helped design the party, formulate the idea of what Yippie was going to be.

Q: When was that?

A: In the early part of 1968.

Q: Can you indicate to the court and jury what Yippie was going to be, what its purpose was for its formation?

A: The idea of Yippie was to be a form of theater politics, a form of theatrically dealing with what seemed to be an increasingly absurd world and trying to deal with it in other than just on a straight moral level. They wanted to be able to set out fantasies in the street to communicate their feelings to the public and it stood for Youth International Party and was also conceived at the same time as the early discussions about Chicago coming up in the early part of 1968 in terms of what Yippie would do at the convention and what they wanted to do was to have a festival—

MR. FORAN: I object to that.

THE COURT: Sustained.

Q: Now, were any of the defendants at the table involved in the formation of the Yippies?

A: Yes, Jerry Rubin and Abbie Hoffman.

Q: Do you recognize those two men here?

A: Yes, I do. Jerry Rubin with the headband and Abbie Hoffman with the smile.

THE COURT: There was more than one person smiling at the table. He identified Mr. Hoffman as the one smiling, but there were others who were smiling, but I will accept the identification.

The cross-examination continued. Once again, Kunstler tried to get into the record that the event was planned as a festival, not as a conspiracy:

Q: Now, did there come a time when there was any discussion of Yippie plans with reference to the convention, the Democratic National Convention?

A: Yes, there were. I don't remember the exact date because there were several meetings, probably January or February of 1968, and that was . . . it was discussed immediately, discussed concurrently with forming the Yippies.

Q: Where did these discussions take place?

A: The Lower East Side, different apartments, sometimes Jerry's apartment and sometimes Abbie's apartment.

Q: Now, did there come a time, Mr. Ochs, when these plans reached a point where they were formulated and the plans were in existence?

A: Yes, it happened very quickly.

Q: Can you indicate in general to the court and jury what the plans were for Yippies in Chicago during the Democratic National Convention?

A: The plans were essentially—

MR. FORAN: I object.

THE COURT: I sustain the objection.

KUNSTLER: Your Honor, one of the central roles in this case is the Yippie participation around the Democratic National Convention.

THE COURT: I don't see that allegation in the indictment.

KUNSTLER: Well, the indictment charges these two men with certain acts in connection with the Democratic National Convention.

THE COURT: These two men.

KUNSTLER: I think I am entitled to show their intent.

THE COURT: These two men and others, but not as Yippies, so-called, but as individuals.

KUNSTLER: All right, Your Honor. I will rephrase the question.

Q: Did there come a time when Jerry and Abbie discussed their plans—

A: Yes.

Q: In coming to the Democratic National Convention?

A: Yes, they did.

Q: What did they say their plans were?

A: They said their plans were to have a festival of life.

MR. FORAN: Objection, Your Honor.

Phil went on to identify Paul Krassner, Ed Sanders (an original member of the Fugs), Bob Fass (a radio personality from New York's WBAI), and Tim Leary among those who had discussed participation in the festival. The questioning continued:

Q: Can you state to the jury what Abbie and Jerry said their plans were in coming to Chicago around the Democratic National Convention that evening?

MR. FORAN: Your Honor, I object to that unless they talked as a duet.

THE COURT: I sustain the objection.

Q: Well, we will start this way. Can you tell the conversation, indicating who spoke, from Jerry and Abbie, as to their plans in coming to Chicago around the Democratic National Convention?

MR. FORAN: Your Honor, may we refer to the defendants by their proper names so we will have a proper identification in the record?

THE COURT: Yes.

KUNSTLER: I think Mr. Hoffman has dropped his last name.

THE COURT: What did you say?

KUNSTLER: I think that Mr. Hoffman has dropped his last name as a protest against this court.

THE COURT: He will have to do that in law. Here he is indicted as Abbie Hoffman. I know that he said that in court,

Mr. Kunstler, but his mere saying of that doesn't deprive him of a last name.

KUNSTLER: I know, but legally, Your Honor, there is no requirement that you do have a formal change of name at all. A person can drop his last name.

THE COURT: That is not an issue here.

Finally, after more dialogue back and forth about how to refer to the defendants, Phil was able to relate to the court what Rubin had discussed with him about the festival:

A: Okay, so the question is—what Jerry Rubin said to me was that he planned to have a Festival of Life in Chicago during the Democratic Convention, basically representing an alternate culture on the assumption that they felt the Democratic Party did not represent them or a whole large mass of the American public. They wanted to have, therefore, an alternate convention. They would theatrically sort of spoof the Convention and show the public, the media, that the Convention was not to be taken seriously because it wasn't fair, and wasn't going to be honest, and wasn't going to be a Democratic Convention, and so they would have essentially events they hoped to do in Lincoln Park. They hoped to get permits. They discussed flying to Chicago to talk with Mayor Daley or people working with Mayor Daley. They several times mentioned they wanted to avoid any violence. They went way out of their way on many different occasions to talk with the mayor or anybody who could help them avoid violence.

The entire answer was stricken, because Phil had referred to Rubin as "they." Kunstler repeated the question, and Phil essentially repeated his answer. He then went on to discuss what specifically Abbie Hoffman had said, especially the part about having a "mock election."

This bit of information produced nearly ten minutes of discussion as to whether Document D–146, the official press release of the Festival of Life, could be admitted as evidence. Finally, it, too, was read into the transcript:

"YIPPIE ANNOUNCEMENT! YIPPIE!

> YIP is planning a 'Festival of Life,' an international youth festival from Sunday, August 25, to Friday, August 30, in Chicago, Illinois. This youth festival will take place at the same time as the National Death (Democratic) Convention in Chicago. It will be a contrast in lifestyles. Ours will be an affirmation of life; theirs is d-e-a-t-h."

The announcement went on to give details of how and when the festival would take place and some of the activities planned, including music and political consciousness-raising sessions, specifically about the war in Vietnam and the draft. The Yippie "calls" were cited:

> "Rise up and abandon the creeping meatball!"
> "We demand the politics of ecstasy!"

It ended with:

> "This will be the first national youth festival, the first coming together of all the people who have been involved in the youth revolution which has been taking place in America in the past decade. A lot will be concentrated in one time and place in August, and the result will be, we think, 'geometric' growth in the energy and spirit of our new culture. 'YIPPIE'"

Next came a series of questions about Phil's involvement in the planning of events for Chicago, including his mentioning it at all his concerts. Phil told the courtroom that when the negotiations for proper permits to demonstrate broke down, many show business and political personalities canceled their commitments to appear. He told how he came to Chicago early in August, as part of a rally held for Eugene McCarthy, and decided to stay through the festival. At this point, Kunstler asked Phil about the "mock" convention plans, particularly about a conversation with Rubin and Stew Albert:

Q: Can you relate to the court and jury what that conversation was?
A: We discussed the nomination of a pig for President.
Q: Would you state what Jerry said and what you said?
A: We discussed the details of—well, we had the idea, and where did we get the pig? We discussed going out to the

countryside around Chicago and buying the pig from a
farmer and bringing him into the city for the purposes of his
nominating speech.

Q: Did you have any role yourself in that?

A: Yes, I helped select the pig, and I paid for him.

Q: Where did you find the pig?

A: I don't remember the exact place.

Q: Mr. Ochs, can you describe the pig which you finally
bought?

MR. FORAN: Objection.

THE COURT: I sustain the objection.

Q: Was it a pig or a piglet?

MR. FORAN: Objection.

THE COURT: I sustain the objection.

Q: Did you buy the pig yourself or with other people?

A: I bought the pig with Jerry Rubin.

Q: And did anything happen in connection with that pig subsequently at a time when Jerry Rubin was present?

MR. FORAN: I object to the form of question, Your Honor. It
is leading and suggestive.

THE COURT: I sustain the objection.

Q: Would you state what, if anything, happened to the pig?

A: The pig was arrested with seven people.

The courtroom was filled with laughter, as Kunstler, around another series of objections and much gavel-rapping, once again
began to zero in on the nomination of the pig for President:

Q: What were you doing when you were arrested?

A: I was standing—I had driven the pig up to the Civic Center
and I was standing next to the pig and next to the seven
people who were arrested announcing the pig's candidacy
for President to a large number of people, probably—I am
not sure of the exact—over a thousand people, maybe two
thousand people, a lot of press people were there.

Q: And what was the purpose of being at the Civic Center?

MR. FORAN: Objection.

THE COURT: I sustain the objection.

Q: Did you speak at the Civic Center that day?

A: No.

Q: Did Jerry Rubin speak?

A: Yes.

Q: What did Jerry Rubin say?

A: Jerry Rubin was reading a prepared speech for the pig.

Q: To the best of your recollection, what did he say?

A: Something to the effect, "Why take half a hog when you can have the whole thing?" He announced the pig's name, Pigasus. He said—the opening sentence was something like, "I, Pigasus, hereby announce my candidacy for the presidency of the United States." He was interrupted in his talk by the police who arrested us.

Q: What did the pig do during this announcement?

A: The pig was peeing.

Phil said he was arrested with the others for violating an obscure livestock ordinance and disturbing the peace. Kunstler, aided quite skillfully by the blustering prosecution, had managed to reduce Phil's testimony to a study in absurdity. Court was recessed until Thursday morning, December 11.

Phil returned to the stand. Kunstler took him through a lengthy recapitulation of his meetings just prior to the convention with Rennie Davis and Tom Hayden, in connection with attempting to secure permits once again, this time by approaching John Bailey of the Democratic Platform Committee. They hoped Bailey would go directly to Mayor Daley and get the required documents. Then Kunstler asked Phil about a particular Sunday evening when he went to pick up Rubin, on the way to Lincoln Park:

Q: When you arrived at the apartment was Jerry Rubin present?

A: Yes, he was.

Q: And did you have a conversation with him?

A: Yes, I did.

Q: Can you indicate to the jury what he said to you and what you said to him?

A: He said—well, first of all, he was laying in bed. He said he was very ill. He looked very ill. He was very pale. I said, you know, the last time I saw him was when we were arrested, and I had to leave town and come back, and I said we had agreed to go to Lincoln Park that night, and so I

said, "I hope you are still going to Lincoln Park." He said,
"I don't know if I can make it. I seem to be very ill." I
cajoled him, and I said, I said, "Come on, you're one of the
Yippies. You can't not go to Lincoln Park." He said,
"Okay," and got up, and he went to Lincoln Park with me,
and I believe Nancy, his girlfriend, and my girlfriend,
Karen, and the four of us walked from his apartment to
Lincoln Park.

Q: And did you enter the park?

A: Just the outskirts, I mean we basically stood in front of the
Lincoln Hotel, and walked across the street from the Lincoln Hotel and stood in the outskirts of the park. All of a
sudden there was like a burst of people racing, running out
of the park in large scattered numbers, and there was—I
mean, we smelled some tear gas. We continued standing
there. We stood and watched them run right at us, as a matter of fact. Finally, we walked through the streets around
that area, essentially following the crowd. They were just
chaotic and sort of unformed, and people just continued
away from the park and just seemed to move, I think toward the commercial area of Old Town where the clubs are,
and the nightclubs, and then police clubs were there, too,
and I don't—I just, I mean, it is sort of hazy in my mind—it
was just, it was a flurry of movement of people all kinds of
ways, and it just, it seemed to go on for about—I think we
stayed there for an hour or two hours among the flowing
crowds through the streets. I mean, I just remember crowds
moving. I don't remember the crowd and the police ever—

MR. SCHULTZ (Prosecution): If the court please, the witness
was asked what he observed and spent a couple of minutes
telling us what he didn't observe.

KUNSTLER: I asked him to describe what he saw, Your
Honor, and I think he described it.

MR. SCHULTZ: Instead of going through the whole explanation again, if you would simply tell the witness to listen
carefully to the question so he can answer the question, so
we can move on to something else.

THE COURT: I did that this morning. You are a singer but
you are a smart fellow, I'm sure.

At which point Phil turned to Judge Hoffman, looked him straight in the eye and replied:

A: Thank you very much. You are a judge, and you are a smart fellow.

Finally, Kunstler turned to Phil's music. He attempted to have Phil sing for the court.

KUNSTLER: Now I want to show you an exhibit. One moment, Your Honor. I am showing you what has been marked as D–147 for identification and I ask you if you can identify that exhibit.

A: This is the guitar and—this is the guitar I played "I Ain't Marching Anymore" on.

THE COURT: How can you tell? You haven't even looked at it.

PHIL OCHS: It is my case.

THE COURT: Are you sure your guitar is in there?

PHIL OCHS: I'm checking.

KUNSTLER: Open it up, Mr. Ochs, and see whether that is your guitar.

PHIL OCHS: That is it, that is it.

Q: Was that the guitar you used that day?

A: Yes, it is.

Q: How many verses did the song "I Ain't Marching Anymore" have that you sang that day?

A: Six and two bridges.

Q: Who wrote that song?

A: I did.

Q: When you sang it, were you seated or standing?

A: Standing.

Q: Would you stand and sing that song so the jury can hear the song that the audience heard that day?

MR. SCHULTZ: If the court please, this is a trial in the Federal District Court. It is not a theater. The jury is sequestered. We don't want to take too much time. We don't have to sit and listen to the witness sing a song. Let's get on with the trial.

KUNSTLER: Your Honor, this is definitely an issue in the case. Jerry Rubin has asked for a particular song to be sung.

THE COURT: And the witness has testified that he sang it.

KUNSTLER: Right. But the point is that there has been testimony in this court that Jerry Rubin gave an inflammatory speech that day and this is one of the acts which the Government has laid before this jury. What he asked the witness to sing and what he sang to the audience reflects both on his intent and on the mood of the crowd, and I think since we have had a right to play into the record here speeches from a bandshell, even from people who are not on the witness stand and are not present here as defendants or as witnesses, and to give the crowd noises in exhibits and to indicate what levels were—

THE COURT: If you have, sir, a recording of this witness' singing, on the occasion in question, of the song "I Ain't Marching Anymore," I would agree with you, you could offer that record and probably it would be admissible if it is a record of what was done on that occasion. I sustain the objection.

KUNSTLER: Your Honor, he is prepared to sing it exactly as he sang it on that day.

THE COURT: I am not prepared to listen, Mr. Kunstler.

KUNSTLER: Your Honor, I think—

THE COURT: And I sustain the objection.

Q: Mr. Ochs, I would then ask you to recite to the jury the words which you sang on that day to the audience.

A: The words? Okay.

"I marched to the battle of New Orleans
At the end of the early British wars
The young man started growing;
The young blood started flowing,
But I ain't marching anymore.
For I killed my share of Indians in a thousand
        different fights.
I was there at the Little Big Horn.
I saw men lying, I saw many more dying,
But I ain't marching anymore.
It is always the old to lead us to the wars;
Always the young to fall.

> Now look at all we've won with the saber and a gun
> Tell me, Is it worth it all?
> For I marched to the battles of the German Trench
> In a war that was bound to end all wars."

At this point Phil, true to form, forgot the words, saying he was used to singing them. He quickly hummed the verse to himself, and continued reciting:

> A: "Oh, I must have killed a million men;
> And now they want me back again,
> But I ain't marching anymore."

Kunstler once again requested Phil be allowed to sing the remainder of the song, and once again the request was denied. Actually, Kunstler was stalling to give Phil enough time to recall the rest of the words:

> A: The verse I am beginning is about the Civil War, which says:
> "Yes I even killed my brothers
> And so many others, but I ain't marching anymore.
> For I flew the final mission in the Japanese skies
> Set off the mighty mushroom roar
> When I saw the cities burning,
> I knew that I was learning
> That I ain't marching anymore.
> Now the labor leaders screaming
> When they close a missile plant
> United Fruit screams at the Cuban shore.
> Call it peace or call it treason
> Call it love or call it reason
> But I ain't marching anymore.
> No, I ain't marching anymore."

The courtroom was silent when he finished. Kunstler said softly, "Thank you, Mr. Ochs."

As soon as he left the courtroom he was mobbed by network reporters and asked to sing the song he wasn't allowed to perform on the stand. At a hastily called press conference, he sang two choruses of "I Ain't Marching Anymore," his suede jacket wrapped around his shoulders, his greasy hair flopping in his eyes.

He raced to his room at the Hilton to watch, transfixed, as the "CBS Evening News" with Walter Cronkite presented Phil Ochs performing "I Ain't Marching Anymore." He cracked up laughing, falling on the bed, a bottle of half-drunk wine in his hand.

Phil couldn't wait to get back to Los Angeles. Wickham picked him up at the airport. The two of them spent that night getting drunk and going to the fights. The next morning was 1970.

IX

Seems like only yesterday
I climbed aboard a plane
Raping distance in the air
While diving in Champagne
I would be in exile now
But everywhere's the same
Ticket home
I want a ticket home
Phil Ochs,
"One-Way Ticket Home"

Andy Wickham couldn't have cared less about Phil's theatrics in Chicago. He dismissed Rubin as "rubbish." He wanted nothing to do with Phil's political activities. He couldn't even sustain any enthusiasm for the new album, because he didn't agree with Phil's point of view about Chicago. As far as Wickham was concerned, the police hadn't gone far enough.

Before recording the album, Phil had tried out a few songs for Andy and Judy Henske. Phil sang "Lincoln Park, the Park of Lincoln." Henske told him the title was ridiculous. "You might as well call it 'Pismo Beach, the Beach of Pismo.' What does it mean, Phil?" He changed the title to "William Butler Yeats Visits Lincoln Park and Escapes Unscathed." Wickham rejected the songs with an academic flick of his wrist. "Dark doesn't turn," he said to Phil. "It falls." He told Phil the reason his albums didn't sell well was because he still didn't know who his fans were.

"Look, Phil, you know you don't represent the Left any more than Hubert Humphrey. You're just a closet right-winger."

Michael got four tickets to Elvis Presley's opening-night comeback performance in Las Vegas and he gave them to Phil, Karen, Andy, and Frances. Phil was fibrillating with excitement. He tried to brace himself as they flew to Vegas, hoping he wouldn't be let down, hoping Presley wouldn't embarrass himself after being away from performing for so long.

The orchestra began a long, amplified "Thus Spake Zarathustra," as Elvis emerged in white satin, sequins, and gold cape, to the ecstatic frenzy of the audience. Phil sat, stunned, unable to swallow. Presley was fantastic that night. He sneered his way across the stage, belting out song after song; moving, dipping, gyrating, pumping, throwing scarves to the yellow-haired ladies, going down on one knee, flipping his blue hair away from his eyes. At one point he came over to Phil's table and sang directly to him. By the end of the show the Vegas audience was on its feet, and Phil led the applause.

On the flight back to L.A., all Phil could talk about was Elvis. Elvis was great, Elvis was the greatest. If only he could come back like Elvis had. If only he could be Elvis. If only . . .

Phil did nothing for weeks except think about Elvis Presley. Anyone who called him on the phone or came by the house had to hear Phil's recapitulation of that night.

Phil and Andy were playing pool one night on the east end of Santa Monica Boulevard, a neighborhood Phil loved to frequent, with its stucco shack bars and neon strip joints, when they started to "what if." What if Nixon died of a suntan? Each time Phil came up with a new one, they'd laugh louder than before. What if Che Guevara and Elvis Presley teamed up to form a nightclub act? And what if, instead of being managed by Colonel Parker, they were managed by Colonel Sanders? Wickham brought it home. What if Phil became the Elvis Presley on the Left? What if Phil became the combination of Elvis Presley and Che Guevara? Wickham was laughing so hard tears rolled down his cheeks. Phil wasn't laughing at all.

Phil went to Nudie Cohen, the Los Angeles tailor who'd made Elvis' gold suit, to have one made exactly like it for himself.

He wanted to do a concert in the gold suit, backed by a rock-and-roll band, singing Presley songs. Michael was totally against it. First, Phil looked fairly ridiculous in the suit. He was terribly out of shape, getting no physical exercise, eating huge amounts of junk food, or expensive, thick blood-rare steaks with mounds of french fries, drinking wine and rum and beer throughout the days and nights. His face, once so tight, was now puffy, his cheeks round as a squirrel's. He still had the large, deep-brown eyes, and the soft, curled lips, but his stomach was a globe. He looked nothing like Elvis Presley.

Phil went to Doug Weston and asked him to produce the show. Weston sat back, lit a yellow Russian cigarette, and, as the acrid smoke filled his office, began to get off on Phil's latest inspiration. "I like it," he said, and set the show for a weekend in February.

As if to celebrate his return to performing, Phil decided to throw a thirtieth birthday party for himself in the big house. He invited everyone who was in town, and all of his friends from New York. It was a Sunday-afternoon black-tie affair. By ten o'clock in the morning the house was filled with people. It was the only time in his life he had ever worn a tuxedo. For the occasion, Karen washed and combed out his hair.

They arrived in droves. Andy Warhol and his entourage, Mickey Dolenz and Davy Jones, neighbors from the hills, David Blue, Van Dyke Parks, Peter Asher and Betsy, now living in Beverly Hills, Doug Weston, Jerry Moss, Elliot Mintz, dozens of other friends, and dozens more he had never met. Phil also invited Alice. She couldn't make it, so she sent Meegan instead. They'd kept in touch regularly over the years, Meegan moving easily between them, each letting the other have the child when any one of them, including Meegan, felt like a change. At the party, Meegan calmly walked around emptying ashtrays.

The cigarette smoke was thick and blue-gray in the house when, late in the afternoon, someone asked where Phil was. Judy Henske started a search for him, Betsy helped out.

They found him at the bottom of the hill in front of his house, where he'd eventually come to rest after stumbling drunkenly out the front door and rolling down the slope—his skid halted by a huge tree at the base of which he now lay unconscious.

He was on stage with his new group, Lincoln Mayorga on piano, Bob Rafkin on guitar, Kenny Kaufman on bass, Kevin Kelly on drums. The Troubadour was jammed. Elvis Presley sung by Phil Ochs.

Phil was convinced the concert was a breakthrough. Wickham told him he ought to do the show all over the country. How funny it would be at Carnegie Hall, where he'd sung all those ponderous songs so many times.

Phil wanted to record again, to release an album in conjunction with a projected gold-suit tour. He booked a string of dates, starting with Carnegie Hall, winding through Nashville, Memphis, and ending in Berkeley, California.

The album was in trouble from the start. Phil called Larry Marks and asked him to come back into the studio with him one more time. Marks declined politely. He was no longer producing records.

Phil looked for a new producer. He chose Van Dyke Parks, an eclectic, classically trained musician, and his next-door neighbor in the hills. Van Dyke had just produced a successful Arlo Guthrie album. He'd always wanted to work with Phil because he loved Phil's sense of humor, and thought his music was great.

Van Dyke felt Phil needed a new sound. The first cut on the album, and the single from it, was "One-Way Ticket Home." Van Dyke went wild with the song. He began with a roll of timpani drums. He put a black female rhythm chorus behind Phil, as he sang about how he would "be in exile now, but everywhere's the same, ticket home (la, la, la la), I want a ticket hime."

> *Elvis Presley is the king*
> *I was at his crowning*
> *My life just passed before my eyes*
> *I must be drowning*
> *Seems like only yesterday*
> *I climbed aboard a plane*
> *Raping distance in the air*
> *While diving in Champagne*
> *I would be in exile now*
> *But everywhere's the same*
> *Ticket home*
> *I want a ticket home*

Once again, the metaphor of drowning. Whereas the old Phil Ochs had been politically assassinated in Chicago (*I'm not dying, I'm not dying, Tell me I'm not dying*), the new one was drinking himself to death. The new songs were a recapitulation of everything that had come and gone. In "One-Way Ticket Home" Phil saw his life pass before him as he drowned, and realized he experienced a thousand "little deaths." "Boy in Ohio" reflected the death of innocence; "Basket in the Pool," the decline of glamor; "Ten Cents a Coup" (*It was a used-car dealer's election* . . .), the end of democracy; "Chords of Fame," a lament for those he left behind, on the other side of fame; "No More Songs," the recognition of his own creative death. If "Rehearsals for Retirement" was about the act of dying, "Phil Ochs' Greatest Hits" was about a living hell.

The entire album was recorded in two days. The second side contained only three new songs, the previously unrecorded "Bach, Beethoven, Mozart and Me" and a monologue by Phil put together from tapes made at a fall 1969 moratorium rally.

In terms of sales, the album was an out-and-out embarrassment, failing to make back its production costs. What had started as a joke—"PHIL OCHS' GREATEST HITS. *50 Phil Ochs fans can't be wrong*"—became a reality. The picture of Phil on the cover in the gold suit, overweight and uncomfortably posed, didn't help any. Michael told Phil people would think it was a collection of his old songs, they could confuse it with the upcoming concert, and they would accuse him of jumping on the "oldies" bandwagon. Phil was sure his fans would buy it, no matter what he put on the cover, because it was a Phil Ochs album.

Ads placed in *The Village Voice* and the New York *Times* for the Carnegie Hall "Gold Suit" concert produced by Ron Delsener showed Phil with one leg raised in the air and bent at the knee, shoulders stooped and mouth wide open, dressed in the gold suit, playing an electric guitar. And he insisted Jerry Moss come to the show.

The band's instruments were already on stage, as the audience filed in. Phil walked on and the audience cheered. All right, he was dressed in a funny suit, but it was still Phil. Maybe a bit paunchier than last time, but it was *still Phil*. After he did "I Ain't Marching

Anymore," which he dedicated to Jerry Rubin, who was backstage ("This is the number they didn't let me sing at the trial for the 'Chicago Eight,' but I'm going to sing it now!"), he signaled for the members of the band to join him. Was this still Phil? They went into a version of an old Conway Twitty hit, "Mona Lisa," and the boos began. Someone in the balcony screamed, "Where's Phil Ochs?" and the audience applauded. "Send that band back to California," someone else shouted. His voice cracked, his hand motored through his hair, as he wanted to explain his new act. But there was no way he could talk to this tough New York crowd about Elvis Presley being Che Guevara. Damn it, they wanted Phil Ochs!

His stage smarts told him to cut the fifteen-minute intermission, knowing if he took a break there'd be no audience left to sing to when he returned. The show lasted for less than an hour, ending early because of a bomb threat someone had phoned to the theater. Phil left the stage under a shower of programs thrown by the angry audience.

Phil was embarrassed. His mother was in the audience. Sonny had come and Jerry Rubin had flown in for the occasion. Andy Wickham was there. Jack Newfield, and even Arthur Gorson showed up. They all huddled around Phil's table at the Russian Tea Room as he drank himself further into a sweaty, stuttering state of confusion. How could this have happened? How could New York miss the point? Rubin said that he loved the show, that it made important points, while Newfield just shook his head and told Phil it was all over, he should forget the second show and throw the suit away. At that point, a group of ticket holders from the first show approached Phil at the table. A spokesman said his group felt it hadn't gotten its money's worth. Phil asked for a list of their names. He assured them tickets would be left for them at the box office for the second show.

Phil went to arrange for the free tickets. He handed the list over to the house manager and went back to the Tea Room. About five minutes later the kids were back, telling him the list had been torn up. The second show was sold out. Phil became enraged. He flew out of the restaurant, bounded up the stairs of Carnegie Hall, and began banging on the box-office window. No one answered.

He continued to bang until his fist went through the glass. Blood gushed from his thumb. Ron Delsener grabbed Phil, taking him back into the dressing room. He tried to fix Phil's thumb, but it wouldn't stop bleeding. All the while Phil, his eyes unfocused, continued to mumble about "liberating those tickets." Delsener promised the tickets would be taken care of. He got on the phone to get the name of a doctor who could see them immediately. Dr. Benjamin Gilbert, on Forty-fifth Street. Delsener wrapped Phil's hand in a towel and took him outside to grab a taxi.

By the time Phil got to the doctor's office he'd become petulant, not wanting any "doctor" to touch him. He refused to show his thumb to anybody, and wouldn't give his name or address. Delsener, meanwhile, was trying his best to cool the situation. Phil kept on talking about how he didn't trust doctors, how doctors wanted to hurt him. Finally, he let Gilbert's associate, Dr. Priest, dress the wound and administer a tetanus shot. Phil pushed the door of the office open and walked out in a huff, Delsener chasing behind.

They got back in time for the eleven o'clock show, Phil having a few more drinks and a handful of amphetamines in order to face another audience.

He went directly into "Mona Lisa." Then:

"Thank you very much. That was a song made famous in the 1950s, and what we propose to do here tonight is a combination of songs of mine from the sixties and songs of other people's from the fifties."

He introduced Rubin once again, and this time dedicated "I Ain't Marching Anymore" to the "Chicago Eight." "Now the trick is, with wearing a suit like this, is the same trick as living in America today, which is how to come to terms with wealth."

"Strip," shouted a girl from down front. The audience went wild.

"No, no, I could never do that, for it would be cheap. I prefer to maintain my dignity as an American citizen. I will never strip! So I will now try to wear this gold suit and sing a song of significance. I'll try to have wealth come to terms with responsibility.

"It used to be that all the songwriters were left-wing types. And now, as we get toward a fascist America, which is coming in the seventies in a big way, we start to see a change in the right wing. The right wing usually does without artists. They usually have to rely on William Buckley and his good looks and a lot of television time. To present the facade that the right wing has a mind or a sense of art, which Buckley has, which the right wing doesn't have. Just lately, though, they've come up with an artist who is a genuine songwriter who's as good as anybody around. His name is Merle Haggard, and he has the possibility of being today's Hank Williams, who is still the foremost songwriter, and so I've been accused many times in my career of being a radical, and troublemaker, which is not true, it's just not true, I'm just a regular American guy like anybody else in the gas station. So I'm going to sing a Merle Haggard song tonight, which I think shows the other side of America. To answer all those critics. It's a song called, 'Okie from Muskogee.' "

The audience enjoyed the song and its blatant attack on hippies.

"I've been living in Hollywood, California, for two years. I don't think it's had any effect on me." This produced the biggest laugh of the night. "The Chords of Fame" was all he said to introduce the next song.

> *Found him by the stage last night*
> *He was breathin' his last breath*
> *A bottle of gin and a cigarette*
> *Was all that he had left*
> *I can see you make the music, cause you carry your guitar*
> *But God help the troubadour who tries to be a star . . .*
>
> *So play the chords of love my friend*
> *Play the chords of fame*
> *If you want to keep your song*
> *Don't, don't, don't*
> *Don't play the chords of fame . . .*
>
> *They will rob you of your innocence*
> *They will put you up for sale*
> *The more that you will find success*
> *The more that you will fail*
> *I've been around and I've had my share*
> *And I really can't complain*
> *But I wonder who I left behind on the other side of fame . . .*

"Bring back Phil Ochs," someone shouted from the balcony. The audience supported the demand with more applause.

"Hi, I'm Phil Ochs," Phil shot back. "I'd like to sing some songs that are just as much Phil Ochs as anything else. I'm going to do a group of songs here, now, first recorded by somebody I hold very dear to my heart, from the 1950s, who formed part of my musical mind."

More boos from the audience. "Could this be a generation gap?" he quipped, but there were no laughs. "He formed a part of my musical mind which wrote anything like 'I Ain't Marching Anymore' and 'Changes.' That kind of thought process came from certain people. And this is one of them. His name is Buddy Holly. He died at an early age in a plane crash; these are a collection of songs I memorized when I was a kid and re-memorized here. I'd like to do some of them for you. Take it away. One, two, one, two, three, four . . ." He did a medley of Holly hits.

There was a good five minutes of solid booing, stopping only when Phil grabbed the mike with one hand and said, "Now, look, let's not be like Spiro Agnew," for which he got an enthusiastic round of applause. "Let's not be narrow-minded Americans. You can be a bigot from all sides. You can be a bigot against blacks, you can be a bigot against music. I think what we're doing up here is music, and I think it should be heard. Here's a song called, 'Pleasures of the Harbor.' "

By now, Phil was slurring his words, his eyes wet and blurred. "I am America . . . I am gold . . . I am money . . . I am hip . . . I am moral . . . I am everything, I am America . . . I own the world . . ." It was his introduction to "Tape from California," which he performed incredibly fast, as if he couldn't wait to finish it.

"As you know, I died in Chicago, I lost my life and I went to Heaven because I was very good and I sang very lyrical songs. I got to talk to God, who said, 'Well, it's all over here on earth, there's only a couple of days left. What do you want to do? You can go back and be anybody you want.' So I thought, Who do I want to be? I came up with the answer. The guy I wanted to be most was the king of pop, the king of music, the king of show business, Elvis Presley. And if there's any hope for America, it lies in a revolution, and if there's any hope for a revolution in

America, it lies in getting Elvis Presley to become Che Guevara. If you don't do that you're just beating your head against the wall, or the cop down the street will be beating your head against the wall. And that's Elvis Presley. The thing is, we've got to discover where he is. He is the ultimate American artist, he was the root of American music. I've lost my voice now, but I'm going to try and sing him anyway. Here comes Elvis Presley." Phil launched a medley of Presley hits, "My Baby Left Me," "I'm Ready," "Heartbreak Hotel," "All Shook Up," and "Are You Lonesome Tonight?" Throughout, there were cheers, applause, and dancing in the aisles.

It was three in the morning, and the Carnegie Hall management had seen and heard enough. They cut the electricity off to the microphones on stage. "Who's in charge of power?" Phil asked. "I want to do more; give me the guitar, please," he shouted, once he realized he'd been cut off by management. "Hey, Carnegie Hall, give me the power and the guitar, please, all right?" The audience cheered him on, pushing him further. "Look, this is such bullshit," he shouted. "Can you hear me?" The audience whistled and stomped. "Look, I'm telling you . . ." Fists were in the air. The crowd was shouting, egging Phil on. "Carnegie Hall, give me the guitar and the power." *"We want power, we want power, we want power, we want power . . . ,"* the drum keeping the cadence. When the first electrified notes came out of Phil's guitar, Carnegie Hall erupted into madness. Phil did an encore of "My Baby Left Me," followed by a fabulous version of "A Fool Such as I."

As the audience finally began to leave Carnegie Hall, someone shouted toward the stage, "Phil Ochs is dead."

Jerry Moss hadn't stayed for the second show, going instead to see Joe Cocker, A&M's hottest act, at Madison Square Garden.

The next day, Phil went to see Moss at A&M's New York offices to ask him for the tapes of the gold suit concert. Moss sat Phil down and offered him a drink. He poured two scotches.

"Phil," he began, "I'm not going to release a live album of that show. It just isn't there."

Phil reminded Moss of his contractual agreement not to censor any of Phil's material.

"I'm not interfering," Moss insisted. "Sit down and write some new songs, I don't care what the topic is, and I'll record them for you. You know that. But I won't embarrass the label, and you, by releasing that album. Why don't you forget it, Phil?"

There was no way he would forget it. The next day, "The David Frost Show" called him. Frost had read a lengthy review of the concert in the New York *Times,* and was interested in having Phil do his gold suit number on the show. Phil was elated.

It was the first time he'd been invited on a major TV show. Frost, although syndicated, was on more than a hundred stations across the country. It would mean more exposure at one time than he'd ever had before. The next day, Phil appeared in gold to tape the segment. Frost interviewed him about the gold suit concert. Phil explained the Elvis/Che theory, after which he performed his Presley medley. Even though the studio audience reaction was lukewarm, Phil was sure he'd won them over. After the taping he thanked Frost profusely, shaking his hand, telling him how grateful he was for the chance to be seen on American television. Frost smiled, then hastily excused himself.

The gold suit tour lasted only a few more performances, including one in Memphis, before Phil disbanded it. He returned quietly to Los Angeles, disappointed with his apparent failure at "going rock and roll" and making a comeback.

A few days later, back at the house, things got worse. On his living-room floor were Jerry Rubin, his girlfriend Nancy, Stew Albert, and Judy, Stew's lady. Karen was in the kitchen fixing drinks. Wickham was sitting nearby, drumming his fingers slowly on the arm of his stuffed chair. Phil sat in his rocking chair and said nothing. When he could stand it no longer, Wickham decided to throw the whole bunch out. He stood and announced that the "meeting" was adjourned. Rubin stood up to him, saying, "You know, Wickham, you've been a thorn in my side for a long time. I want you to know that I have a list of people I'm going to get, and you're number three on that list."

"Number three on the Jerry Rubin hit parade. I suppose I should be flattered," Wickham replied.

After the others left, Andy announced he was moving out. He just couldn't stand the thought of those "thugs" ever stepping foot into his house again. The next day Wickham and Frances were gone. That night, Karen and Phil had a terrible fight, ending in a flurry of punches and blood. The following morning, while Karen went into downtown Los Angeles, Phil removed every item of hers from the house and dumped it all in front of the garbage, before getting into his Minx and driving away. While he was gone, everything Karen owned was stolen. She returned to a house that no longer had anything in it that belonged to her. She left without once looking back.

When Phil finally returned, he went to bed, where he lay, with his hands behind his head, staring up at the ceiling. He stayed like that for the rest of the day. And part of the next one too.

X

And the crabs are crazy, they scuttle back and forth
The sand is burning,
And the fish take flight and scatter from the sight;
Their course is turning,
As the seagulls rest on the cold cannon nest,
The sea is churning,
The marines have landed on the shores of
Santo Domingo.
Phil Ochs, "The Marines Have Landed on the Shores of Santo Domingo"

Carnegie Hall banned Phil Ochs from ever performing there again. It hardly seemed to matter to him. He was sure his career was over, this time, for good. The gold suit fiasco, A&M's refusal to release the live album of it, Andy's moving out, and the break-up with Karen threw Phil into a major, extended depression. His friends thought Phil was depressed because he couldn't write. In fact, he couldn't write because he was depressed.

During Michael's tenure, Phil had made more money than he ever had before. Between 1967 and 1969, he grossed over a half million dollars. Michael had skillfully balanced Phil's political commitments and professional goals. Once Phil stopped touring, his income dropped considerably. He soon gave up the big empty house in the hills, having tried unsuccessfully to find a new roommate to share the four-hundred-dollars-plus monthly rent. He moved to a small furnished apartment on Rangeley Avenue, not far from The Troubadour. Newspapers soon piled up next to the dirty clothes and empty gin bottles.

One of the things Michael had arranged for was a professional accounting firm in New York to receive all the money Phil earned, pay Phil a weekly allowance, arrange for the issuance of an American Express card in his name, and pay all his bills. Phil assumed he would never have to perform again for money if he didn't want to. His goal now was to visit every country in the world before dying.

He flew to London with Jerry Rubin and Stew Albert, and decided to look up Tina Date once more. He found her easily and invited her to lunch with him at one of London's finer hotels. When Tina saw him, she was shocked. Gone was the lean, intense image of a Parisian poet. Coming at her now was a bloated, greasy figure with puffy features and dirty clothes. He smiled broadly as he sat down next to her and lit up a fat cigar. He ordered rum and orange juice for himself, a glass of wine for Tina. They spoke for a long while before Tina told Phil how "different" he looked to her. "I've mellowed a lot since the last time you saw me," he said. He told her about his adventures in Hollywood.

They talked for hours. Tina looked at her watch; it was time for her to go. Phil walked out with her, watching as she disappeared down the cobbled street. He pushed his fists into his peacoat and walked slowly back to the hotel.

Rubin had arranged a guest appearance for himself, Stew Albert, Brian Flanagan (a friend they'd met in London), and Phil on "The David Frost Show." Rubin had planned an "overthrow" of Frost's program, which was broadcast live. Phil rejected the idea. He refused to participate in anything that might embarrass Frost.

Rubin, Albert, and Flanagan were on stage being interviewed. Phil was in the audience, watching. Suddenly a group of British and Australian hippies rushed the stage. Frost was petrified; his producer kept the cameras running. The police were brought in and, with nightsticks swinging, chased the instigators out of the studio. But not before a stream of obscenities and shouts of "up the IRA" had gone out over the airwaves, and a gay hippie had kissed David Frost full on the mouth.

It made the front pages of the British newspapers, something Rubin said proved it had been a success.

The four of them, Flanagan included, decided to head for Belfast, where they were promptly deported. They flew to Holland, where they met up with the *Kraubauterzen,* the Dutch version of yippies. Phil was impressed with the *Kraubauterzen* because they'd managed to get someone from their group elected to the city council.

Everywhere they traveled they met with the underground and/or yippie communities. Phil was constantly asked to help raise money by performing, which he steadfastly refused to do. Even in Paris, where he was most tempted, he turned down an offer to sing for the students. Instead, he went to the movies.

Phil returned to Los Angeles early in 1971. Michael filled him in on the financial facts of life. Phil's savings were in danger of running out. Michael suggested a tour to earn some money. Talking about money depressed Phil, as did the thought of returning to the stage. It would mean singing the same old songs. He told Michael a Phil Ochs concert would be "a tired replay of a good thing."

He began hanging around The Troubadour, hardly ever bothering to see the show, preferring to stay by the bar and rap with Weston. He wanted Doug to take a trip with him into the desert. The next day they climbed into Doug's car and headed toward Death Valley.

While Doug drove, Phil talked constantly about how it was all over—his creative years, democracy in America, the sixties. Phil drove for a while, and was like a madman behind the wheel. Sudden accelerations, short chirping stops, wavering from side to side. Suddenly, Phil pulled into a motel. He was going to try to write a song! He sat by the desk in their room with sharpened yellow number-two pencils with erasers, and a fresh yellow legal-sized pad of paper. Over and over he would sing the new lines he'd come up with for Doug. He worked on the song all night before giving up on it in the morning.

That evening they reached the desert and laid out their camping gear. Phil began to talk about how eerie it was to be alone in the desert. He started rambling about getting lost in the desert, what if the car broke down, and both of them suffered wretched, parched deaths? There wasn't much chance of any of this happening. Although Doug didn't bother to remind Phil, they had set up camp a quarter of a mile from the highway.

Later that night, after a couple of bottles of wine, Phil talked about his breaking up with Karen, equating it with the split between Howard Hughes and Jean Peters.

When Phil returned to Los Angeles, he called Jerry Rubin and Stew Albert, both of whom were now in New York, to ask if they'd like to meet him in Chile.

Phil's newest hero was Salvador Allende, his seventies version of Fidel Castro. Allende's victory had been the first peaceful Marxist revolution in the world. To the government of the United States, it was the first major outbreak of Commycancer since the inoperable malignancy in Cuba. The CIA had done everything wrong in Cuba, culminating in the Bay of Pigs invasion. Cuba became the CIA's concession to the enemy. The Pentagon resolved never to make the same mistakes again, hence "Project Camelot," run by the Pentagon and sanctioned by the CIA; its mission to refurbish, re-educate, retrain, and modernize the armies of South America—in effect, to take control of the military power in one of the most transient and unstable countries of Latin America.

Allende's ascent was therefore all the more extraordinary, and at the same time doomed to almost certain failure. Later on, when all economic assistance to Chile would be cut off, including the International Monetary Fund, U.S. aid to Chile's military would continue uninterrupted. The Chilean Army became in effect an arm of the CIA. As long as Allende survived, Chile would be an embarrassment to the United States, a kick in its Nixonian balls.

Allende had risen to power peacefully, by the use of democratic tactics and free elections rather than force. He insisted the Chilean Left couldn't turn its back on electoral politics. Allende knew his enemy in Chile was the military. He apparently trusted a number of Chilean generals, including General Augusto Pinochet. He believed these military leaders would remain loyal to the constitution and continue to support him. He unleashed a torrent of social reforms, including the nationalization of many of the American-controlled copper mines. Chile was being closely watched by the rest of the world. And Phil wanted to be there.

Jerry Rubin, Stew Albert, and Phil were walking along a street in Santiago when they first noticed the young fellow with a guitar slung over his shoulder coming the other way. Phil asked if he was a singer. It was Victor Jara, the most famous folk singer in Chile. He introduced himself to Phil, in somewhat limited English, and they shook hands. Phil told him he was also a folk singer, from the United States. They smiled at each other, Jara having never heard of Phil, Phil having never heard of Jara. Jara was on his way to the copper mines, high in the Andes, to join a college basketball team which was going to play a team of miners. He invited Phil and his friends to come with him and meet the students and workers.

They arrived in the newly nationalized mining camp by dusk. At half-time, Jara introduced Phil to the crowd in the stands, and then reached for his guitar. He sang "Little Boxes," after which he handed his guitar to Phil, who did "I Ain't Marching Anymore," with a line-by-line translation by Jara.

After the game, Phil and the others were invited to spend the night deep in a vein of the copper mine. They traveled down the long, dark shaft, and spent the rest of that night talking with the revolutionary students and miners.

The Communists resisted Jara because of his criticisms of Allende. The right wing hated him and began a campaign to discredit him by spreading rumors that he was a homosexual, which put a further strain on his acceptance by the Left. Jara remained popular only with the people, something Phil understood completely.

The next morning, they arose early and ate fresh hot bread before starting the long journey back to Santiago. Jara arranged for a Chilean network television special starring himself and Phil Ochs. Phil had never entertained on network TV in the United States during his ten-year career; now, in a matter of days, he had done it in Chile!

Phil, Rubin, and Albert met Jara several times at the University, where he would conduct informal political discussions with the students. Phil was delirious, likening Chile to Paradise on Earth.

Rubin and Albert decided to split to Peru, while Phil chose to stay in Chile, anxious to visit the whorehouses and to eat more of the good food. He ran into Dave Ifshkin, former president of the National Student Association, who also happened to be in Chile. Ifshkin talked Phil into going to Uruguay, where they were promptly arrested.

Phil and Ifshkin had been at the University of Montevideo, talking and mixing with the students, when the Army attacked the campus. The students, all armed, ducked behind barricades and started shooting back at the soldiers. Phil and Ifshkin had no idea what was going on. They were instructed to stay behind a barricade and not move, or even breathe heavily, if they wanted to stay alive. Phil had been carrying around a box of Cuban cigars with him for days, his only piece of luggage. In the confusion, he'd dropped the box between two barricades. He turned to Ifshkin.

"I don't want to lose those cigars."

"What about your life?"

"I'm getting those cigars," Phil said, crawling on his belly, under fire, to them. When the shooting finally stopped, he was detained by the police, branded a troublemaker, and expelled from the country.

They tried Bolivia next, but were stopped at the border. They wanted to return to Chile, but were denied access through the neighboring countries. Finally, they were allowed into Peru, with the proviso they leave quickly and quietly for the United States. Which they did.

THE RETURN OF THE ORIGINAL PHIL OCHS
Live . . . In Person . . . Himself . . . Guaranteed . . .

Year after year, Phil Ochs played Carnegie Hall to sold-out houses and standing ovations. Then, last March, he was billed to appear again, but instead a strange apparition materialized on the stage. He looked like Phil, but he was wearing a gold lamé suit. And carrying an electric guitar. And there was a rock band behind him. Needless to say, that Phil Ochs is no more.

He walked out onto the stage at Hunter College strumming his acoustic guitar. The audience cheered an old friend.

"You know," Phil began, "leaving America is like losing twenty pounds and finding a new girlfriend." The crowd roared.

Phil began a song, then stopped. "I can't believe I'm here. I should be in South America, and I would be if they hadn't thrown me out. So I guess I'll sing because I need the money." He went into a rousing version of "The Marines Have Landed on the Shores of Santo Domingo." The audience loved it. "I can't believe it," he said into the mike. "I'm a nostalgia item."

He returned to Los Angeles in May. Doug Weston asked him to do a two-week stint at The Troubadour. His fans and friends filled the club, as he delivered what one reviewer in L.A. described as a performance "with an acoustic guitar and a strong, straightforward voice. It was the best thing that happened to Ochs since he took off his gold lamé suit. It was a wonderful set— special, authoritative, and truly exciting."

Phil continued to go to the movies. Through a friend he acquired a pass to the American Film Institute's daily program of screenings, which were held in walking distance from the Rangeley Street apartment. He followed a daily routine: breakfast at Schwab's, usually with David Blue or Andy Wickham, a morning screening, lunch at Schwab's, an afternoon single or double feature, dinner with Andy Wickham at a dingy sparerib house on Santa Monica Boulevard, another film at night, followed by a couple of drinks at The Troubadour.

Wickham suggested they fly to Italy for "Midem," the annual music convention, and to have some fun on the Riviera. Andy in his immaculate Panama suit, sitting in the private section of the beach, drinking juleps with the elite; Phil, fully clothed, standing on the public beach holding a bottle of wine, staring into the Mediterranean.

He returned to Los Angeles drunk and dirty, and immediately returned to the movies, taking time away from them only when he needed to make money. With a few phone calls he'd set up a concert. He did Yale one weekend, flying in for the concert and returning the next day so as not to miss any screenings.

Summer became fall; fall became winter. The only thing he kept up as faithfully as going to the movies was drinking. His friends hardly ever saw him sober, if they saw him at all. When they did manage to catch up with him, usually late at night at The Troubadour, they'd ask him what was on his mind.

"Suicide."

Late one April evening, he nearly killed himself in a brutal car accident on Sunset Boulevard. He left The Troubadour drunk and, while driving down Sunset, crossed over the double white line, smashing head-on into a car driven by an elderly gentleman. They were both rushed to the hospital, where Phil was subsequently arrested by the police for driving while intoxicated, a felony in Los Angeles. The next morning he was transferred from the hospital to the county jail, where Michael came to bail him out. Phil greeted him with a toothless grin.

"Guess what, Michael? Every one of my teeth was knocked out."

They drove directly from the jail to a lawyer's office. Even before a date for the trial was set, the other driver filed a suit against Phil for a staggering amount. He was sure he was going to lose whatever money he had left. He called Alice to tell her there would be no more child support coming; soon he would be completely broke.

Meanwhile, Phil's lawyer had discovered, going over the police records of the accident, that both drivers had taken breath tests for drinking and both had failed. This resulted in the suit being dropped. A few days later, all criminal charges were dismissed.

Phil was fitted for a set of false teeth. When they were ready, he drove over to Henske's to flash his new smile at her. Henske told him they were the worst false teeth she'd ever seen. Phil grinned, and continued to smile all day.

He kept the tooth-marked steering wheel on his mantle in the apartment.

By 1972, Phil's career was lost in limbo. He would visit A&M Records occasionally, and Jerry Moss never refused to see him. They would talk about the Carnegie tapes, and Phil would never fail to ask about the live album. Moss continued to refuse to release it. Phil would ask for money against royalties, and Moss, without hesitation, would give him whatever amount he wanted, even though Phil was already far behind.

Phil began hanging out with Lee Housekeeper, whom he'd first met the night of the Carnegie Gold Suit concert. Housekeeper, a record producer at the time, had been invited to see the show by Doug Weston. They'd both hopped on a plane and come to New York for the evening.

Back in L.A., Phil got to know Housekeeper better. Phil was surprised to learn that Housekeeper was a committed right-winger, who'd actively campaigned for Barry Goldwater in 1964, and for

Ronald Reagan's drive for the governorship of California. Before long, he found himself embroiled in political debates, sometimes lasting several days, broken only by temporary shifts in location, or time out for Phil to replenish at the liquor store. Phil was fascinated by Housekeeper, the trim, short-haired, gung-ho Californian who looked like Steve McQueen.

One time Phil challenged him to a game of chess, and when it looked as if Housekeeper had him mated, Phil looked up from the board and asked if he could remove one of his own men, a novel form of defense. "If that's your idea of a revolution," Housekeeper replied before mating Phil, "I want no part of it."

Housekeeper was a neighbor of Phil's, and every day they would meet for breakfast, before Phil went to the movies, either to play a game of chess, or talk about what was happening in the music industry. Phil began to depend upon Housekeeper for companionship, inviting him to join the regular Friday-night poker games held in Phil's apartment, whose regular players included Michael, actor Burt Ward, Alan Garfield, David Blue, Peter Asher, and Scott Wilson (one of the stars of *In Cold Blood*).

Housekeeper participated in one of Phil's favorite L.A. pastimes—the search for the Great American Hamburger. Every day for lunch, Phil would meet Housekeeper at a different place for burgers. For six months Phil was occupied with charting, comparing, and evaluating the hamburgers of Los Angeles, all the while explaining to Housekeeper how what they were doing was evidence of the overall deterioration of life in America.

In the early spring of 1972, Housekeeper, working with Raquel Welch's manager, became involved with the production of the film *Kansas City Bomber*. Parts of the musical score were being recorded at his studio. Housekeeper suggested that Phil write a theme song for the picture. Phil was scared at first, having written nothing he considered any good for years, and not having a clue as to how to go about writing "on assignment." He worked on the song for days, writing a line, ripping up the paper, throwing it away, starting over again. He tried to write around a melody, playing the chords on his guitar. He tried to write a chord progression to words he'd scratched out on a pad. His idea was to write a Roy Orbison-type song about the popularity of the roller derby. Finally, he cut a demo, with background harmony sung by Mickey

Dolenz. Phil gave the demo to Housekeeper to pass along to the producers of the film. Before any decisions could be made, Phil decided to go to Australia.

In 1971, Ron Cobb's cartoons started appearing frequently in the Australian underground press. This was due in part to the resurrection of the Labor Party in Australia, a remarkable comeback for the leftist faction, which had been out of power for nearly twenty-five years and was now threatening to gain a majority in the government. The climate was becoming increasingly permissive, and the underground Left was slowly coming up for air. Cobb was invited to Australia by the Cultural Foundation, a student-run organization, to give a series of lectures. He'd never lectured before and wondered if a tour could be successful on the strength of his name and cartoons. He asked Phil to join him on the tour. It meant a plane ticket to Australia and all expenses paid, and Phil never turned down a free trip.

The tour was almost canceled before it began. Phil and Ron had problems acquiring visas from the still officially conservative government. There was a week's delay before they were able to enter Australia, during which time they visited Tahiti, where Phil stayed drunk right up until Monday afternoon, just hours before they were to make their first scheduled appearance. Word arrived by telegram from the Cultural Foundation that they had been cleared for entry into Australia.

Robin Love was in charge of all the concert and tour arrangements made by the Cultural Foundation, including meeting Ron and Phil at the airport. Part of the job was to find out what their personal preferences were: drug, type of sex, etc. Because Phil was a musician, she'd arranged to have Australia's most prominent groupie meet him at the plane. Neither Robin nor the groupie had any idea what Phil looked like.

The two women sat for hours in their car waiting for the 707 to arrive. The first to deplane were Ron and Phil, both drunk. Phil was wearing a snap-brim cap, his hair hanging out on all sides like wet straw. His shirt was filthy, the tails hanging down to his knees. His pants were belted just above his groin, where the swell of his stomach began. He walked on his cuffs.

"Forget it," the groupie said, and left.

Robin wanted to cancel the first concert when she saw the boys were exhausted and drunk. Phil insisted he wasn't going to miss a single performance. They arrived an hour late for the concert at Sydney University. Just before going on, Phil turned to Robin and told her he didn't think he was going to be able to remember the words to any of his songs. The blood evacuated Robin's face. "Look," he told her, "you sit in the front row with this songbook. If I go blank I'll yell out to you, and you feed me the words."

Robin was horrified, imagining herself standing up to tell Phil the words to a song, and being stoned to death because of her proximity to the target of the students' anger. When Phil introduced "Crucifixion," he looked at Robin for an extra second and she skimmed down the page, counting the endless verses. She promised herself she was going to quit the tour first thing in the morning.

Phil wouldn't hear of Robin leaving, saying he would quit too, if she did. The next day the three of them were off to Norwood, Phil drinking and singing, telling Ron and Robin about his new song, "Kansas City Bomber," and how he was going to have a whole new career writing music for movies. He was in constant touch by telephone with Housekeeper. Lee told Phil his song was well-liked, but the version he'd cut with Dolenz wasn't quite what the producers were looking for. "No problem," said Phil. He'd re-record it in Australia and send the master back to L.A.

Phil spent the next several days flying back and forth across the country, cutting the record in the day, using "Daddy Cool," a fifties doo-wop group for backup, and giving a concert at night.

Once the record was completed, Phil announced his desire to finish the tour by car, not realizing that Australia was as big as the United States.

They would start driving early in the morning, around nine. By ten the pubs opened, and Phil would be desperate for a drink. He would insist they pull over for a few quick ones. Ron and Robin would order coffee, Phil would have beer. Invariably, he would get into long, spirited conversations with the bartenders, the morning drinkers, and the hired help. Torrents of questions would pour from him while he drank. He would leave with a six-pack under his arm. Soon the floor of the car would be a shallow pool of foam.

Robin, a sexy, wild-eyed Australian girl, found herself attracted
to Ron, and it wasn't long before they were sharing a bed. The
morning after they slept together for the first time, Phil took a
walk with Ron and asked, "Why'd she pick you?" Ron had no answer for Phil.

For the rest of the journey, Phil was eager to stop at every
whorehouse he could. He was content with prostitute pit stops,
although occasionally women would pursue him after seeing him
perform. One time it became a bit ticklish when the wife of a very
prominent Australian politician started following Phil from town
to town, giving Robin a full-time job keeping Phil and the lady
discreet.

> Hi Judy,
>   It's so good to get away from the cheap vulgarity of Hollywood
> into the rugged bush country of down under. I've been to Sydney,
> Melbourne, Perth, Tasmania, New Zealand. In a couple of weeks
> I'm off to Indonesia, Hong Kong, etc. —Life is so boring now,
> now that I've seen it all. Perhaps someday I'll return to Ohio and
> write about all this.
>   I swam naked in the Indian Ocean, I boxed a kangaroo, I even
> got some Australian women.
>   Regards to Tom Eagleton,
>
>   Your Pal,
>   P. Ochs

Eventually, the tour took them through the small town where
Tina Date was now living. Phil insisted they stop off to see if she
were there. He called her and invited himself over for a few days.
Although it would mean the cancellation of several concerts, there
was no way they were going to talk Phil into giving up this opportunity to see Tina. He just got into a car and drove to her house.
The servants took his suitcase, and for three days he hung around
the house with Tina, the two children, and her husband, who didn't
seem to mind at all that Phil was in a state of protracted lust for
his wife. Eventually, Phil got the message. During a very long and
dramatic farewell, he told Tina she would never see him again.
Tina was tempted to ask Phil to make that a promise, but let it
go. When Phil rejoined Ron and Robin, who'd locked themselves
in a hotel room enjoying the extra free time, he was sullen, answer-

ing questions in monosyllabic grunts, staring out the window of the back seat, getting drunk on Aussie brew. After a while, he sang a verse of his newest song.

> *I'm gonna marry an Australian lassy*
> *And settle down and live in old Sydney*
> *It'll be good for my pain*
> *It'll be good for my brain*
> *But it sure will be hell on my kidneys*

There was only one more series of concerts left. They headed for Kings Town. When they arrived, Phil wanted them to stay in the best hotel. After checking in, Phil asked the management for an electric blanket. That night, he slept like a baby.

Whenever Phil was behind the wheel, Robin feared for her life. He was always drunk. Ron and Robin devised games to get the wheel away from Phil, who didn't want to hear about giving it up. Robin made believe she really liked driving, and would beg Phil to let her "have some fun too." Often they would stop for supplies they didn't need so there could be a driving switch, and Phil would have to surrender his seat.

One afternoon, to break the monotony of driving, Robin and Ron decided to take some "magic mushrooms." After much persuasion they got Phil to try some. A half hour later, Phil clutched his throat. He desperately needed a drink of water. Ron floored the accelerator, trying to find a place where the flipping-out Phil could get a drink. He began to itch terribly. As soon as the car stopped, Phil dove out the door and ran for a nearby water hose. He lay on his back with the hose plugged into his mouth. When he felt better, they were off again.

The next day, they passed through a town where prostitution was tolerated by the law. Phil took one of his infrequent showers and went about getting himself a woman for the night. The next morning he was convinced he had VD, and instructed Robin to find the woman. Robin protested at first, but seeing that Phil had no intention of trying to locate the hooker, thought it best if she did it herself. Robin and Phil got into a long argument, which continued for the rest of the trip, about feminism. Phil labeled women's lib a CIA plot, designed to undermine the radical Left. He went on a final extended drunk, and for the last concert of the tour, was so bombed he started repeating verses, sometimes three and four times in a row.

After the long, grueling tour, Ron and Phil decided to travel north through Singapore and the Philippines, eventually to Asia. Phil wanted to visit Vietnam, but wasn't able to make it. His money ran out in Hong Kong, when his hotel room was broken into and all his cash was stolen. All he had left was his American Express card, which he'd taken with him to buy dinner. He was sure he'd been robbed by the CIA in an attempt to keep him from entering Vietnam. He had no choice but to buy a plane ticket for home.

The first thing he did when he got back was to call Lee House-keeper, to find out about *Kansas City Bomber*. Lee told him the studio had decided to go with another concept for the sound track, and wouldn't be using his song. No matter, Phil thought; he called Jerry Moss to ask him to release it as a single. Moss, convinced the record didn't stand a chance, nevertheless stood by his agreement and released it. The record received no air-play and sold so few copies that only Phil's most faithful fans were even aware a new song had been recorded. The failure of the single threw him into a new depression.

The only time he left his apartment now was to go to the movies. Doug Weston tried to get him to play the club, telling him how great it would be for him to do a couple of shows. Phil simply told him he was tired of singing the same songs and didn't want to perform again until he had new material.

Doug kept at him until Phil offered a compromise. "Look, I'll perform under one condition. If you'll get on the stage with me. You're always trying to get me up there. I want to see you do it for once." Doug agreed. Soon, Phil was on the phone, arranging for his friends to come by and join the program. He tried to call Bob Dylan, now living in L.A., but couldn't get through and soon gave up. The rumor spread that Dylan might appear. Suddenly The Troubadour was a hot ticket, a fact not overlooked by Weston, who was having difficulties with the club. The "in" spot in L.A. was now The Roxy, on Sunset Boulevard, offering the caliber of act The Troubadour once did. When Phil agreed to do the gig, it was like the old days in more ways than one.

Phil was drunk, but not out of control. He started off the evening with "The Bells," Doug Weston sitting next to him on stage with a little triangle, playing along for effect. Phil introduced Weston, who read T. S. Eliot's "The Love Song of J. Alfred Prufrock" to a most enthusiastic audience, noting it was his first time ever on his own stage. Loudon Wainwright followed with an up ditty, "Rufus Is a Tit Man," which the audience enjoyed. Roger Miller did a set of his hobo hits. ("No matter how big you are, the size of your funeral depends on the weather.") David Blue, whom Phil spotted outside the club and dragged in, performed a song. Phil introduced him as "Stuart David Cohen," to which Blue replied, "If you ever referred to Dylan as Zimmerman, he'd kill you . . ." Bob Rafkin accompanied Blue on the guitar, and the elusive Bob Lind joined in for a number or two. Ed Begley, Jr., the son of the famous actor, tried out his new comedy act for the now well-lit crowd. Even Peter Asher got up and performed the old Peter and Gordon hit "World Without Love." A newcomer to the scene, Jackson Browne, was also invited to sing.

It was all good-time until Phil introduced Jerry Moss from the audience. Moss stood and took a bow. Phil asked him to come up on stage. Phil told everyone the reason they hadn't seen a new Phil Ochs album in a while was because Moss refused to release the live album of the Carnegie Hall Gold Suit concert. Moss stared at Phil.

"Jerry Moss," Phil said, "I'll make a deal with you. If you'll release the album in a test market, and it does well, will you then release it nationally? And if it does poorly, I'll never bring it up again. I choose the test market."

The audience urged Moss to go along with Phil, and he finally did, asking where the test market should be.

"Canada."

He'd caught Moss off guard, but a deal was a deal. Work began the next day on the packaging of "Gunfight at Carnegie Hall."

> *Who pulled the trigger at Attica*
> *It's the same one who did at Kent State*
> *Who's the biggest dope dealer in the world*
> *Ladies and gentlemen, the President of the United States . . .*

Richard Nixon's rise to the presidency and his demolition of

George McGovern was the beginning of a very slow resurrection of Phil's active interest in politics. As Watergate began to take over the headlines, Phil rewrote "Here's to the State of Mississippi":

Here's to the state of Richard Nixon
And Billy Graham
Where the Sunday morning sermon
Panders to their lust
And the fallen face of Jesus is chokin' in the dust
And God alone can know in which God they can trust

And here's to the government of Richard Nixon
In the swamp of their bureaucracy they're always
    bogging down
And criminals are posing as advisors to the crown
And they hope that no one sees the sights and no one
    hears the sounds
And the speeches of a Spiro are the ravings of a clown

Here's to the land you've torn out the heart of
Richard Nixon, find yourself another country to be part of.

Early in 1973, Michael formed Michael Ochs Management, MOM, signing Phil as his first act. Before he would let Michael book a tour, Phil wanted to test his abilities in front of a live audience. He hadn't performed on stage in a long time except the "Phil Ochs and Friends" show at The Troubadour, and even there he'd had to sing very little, serving mainly as an emcee. Michael booked him into The Lion's Share, in San Anselmo, outside San Francisco. He played there for two nights, for six hundred and fifty dollars, well below his usual fee. He performed adequately, and allowed Michael to take the next step, setting up a cross-country tour, to begin in New York and end in California. The New York show was to be done at Gerde's Folk City. It would be the first time Phil would perform at Gerde's new location, just off Sixth Avenue on Third Street, across from where The Third Side had once been. Porco had been forced to move when his lease expired. Business had fallen off at Gerde's ever since rock had reduced folk to a footnote in the history of pop music. Porco hadn't been able to break a new performer in years. Phil heard about the lean times the club was experiencing, and insisted the first annual "Phil Ochs Returns to New York Spring Concert" be held there, to officially launch the tour.

They lined up around the block to get into Gerde's, on the strength of a single blurb in *The Village Voice*. The first show was scheduled for eight o'clock, and by six o'clock the lines were already past McDonald's, heading south down the Avenue of the Americas. Word was out that it was going to be like the "old days," with friends of Phil dropping by to sing a few songs. Maybe even Dylan, dot, dot, dot.

Phil was across the street in Emilio's having a few beers, stepping outside every few minutes to see if the line was still there. After a while, he went to the club and asked Porco to put a TV set on stage. Nixon was scheduled to broadcast a speech about Watergate. As the audience was let in, Phil, guitar slung over his shoulder, sat on the stage, watching the speech. He raised his middle finger and stuck it up Nixon's electronic nose. He turned the sound off, leaving the picture on, stood next to the set and sang, "Here's to the State of Richard Nixon." The audience loved it. Smiling, Phil ceremoniously turned off the tube.

Both shows sold out, with people stuffed into Gerde's for a glimpse of Phil. Stopping by that evening, at one time or another, to sing a few songs and to wish Phil well on his return, were: Carolyn Hester, John Hammond, Jr., Ed McCurdy, David Blue, Harry Chapin, Bob Cohen and Allen Corby, Anita Scher, Dave Van Ronk, and Jean Ray, who was in New York trying to start a solo career after receiving her final divorce papers from Jim. It wasn't until four in the morning that the last of the audience stumbled out of the club. Porco laughed; it was like old times.

Phil spent the next couple of nights drinking with Van Ronk, as they celebrated this brief renaissance of folk music in the Village. Van Ronk was scheduled to perform with Pat Sky at a WBAI "Free Store" radio concert, held in the church location of the listener-sponsored New York radio station. He insisted that Phil come along.

Three stools were set up, Phil at one end sharing a mike with Van Ronk. The live audience cheered enthusiastically when he was introduced. Pat Sky sang a song, Dave Van Ronk did one, then it was Phil's turn. Van Ronk turned to him and said, "Hey, Phil, why don't you play something. And take off your coat, it's hot in here." The audience laughed. Phil unleashed a rock-and-roll "Flower Lady," written about the woman who appeared every night in the Village selling her flowers from table to table in the restaurants and bars. It was a New York song, one Phil thought appropriate for the occasion. When he finished, Van Ronk ribbed Phil about it. "There was a Cadillac parked over on Houston Street, waiting for her every night after she'd sold her flowers. Far enough away so nobody would see, you know. She would hobble out of the restaurants, and by the time she was south of Bleecker, her walk would improve considerably. I bought a flower from her once myself."

"You bought that one from me," Phil shot back. The audience loved it. After a couple of songs by Van Ronk and Sky, Phil slowly took his coat off, to a burst of applause. "Okay, I'll stay for a while."

"I thought this was going to be an interview show," Van Ronk said, at which point Phil turned to him and asked, "How did you get started in folk music?" More laughter.

"Remind us of our social responsibility," Van Ronk replied to Phil.

"Well . . . social responsibility . . . we'll do a song about American sexual paranoia." He did a rousing version of "Pretty Smart on My Part," which received the longest ovation of the night. Van Ronk turned to Sky and said, "Okay, Patrick, top that!"

Awhile later, still on the air, Phil and Van Ronk discussed a bet they'd made at dinner. Phil took out his pipe and started to light it. Van Ronk commented that Phil was now smoking a pipe to look intellectual.

"No," Phil said. "It's from hanging out at the Playboy mansion. Over dinner tonight we were having a little discussion about the impeachment of Nixon. In this corner," gesturing to Van Ronk, "we have the protagonist against and I'm the protagonist for. It's a debating technique I learned in college."

"I don't think it's going to happen," said Van Ronk. "You underestimate the cowardice of the United States Senate." He called them all pigs, and said they "wouldn't stand up against Warren Harding."

"Well," Phil replied, "maybe there's nothing more courageous than frightened pigs. On the possibility that their power has been steadily eroding, they're all basically greedy people as you know, I think if two or three people, whether Martha Mitchell or Dean, point the finger, Nixon might get impeached here . . . The point is I want to make a public bet here so you can't cop out. What is it, ten dollars to eight dollars, even though it might be illegal over the air, so New York knows, the bet is this. At least three people, whomever, accuse Richard Nixon of being involved in the Watergate incident, then I bet he's going to be impeached, and you bet he isn't going to be impeached. Impeached means charges are brought against the President. The other point is, nobody seems to have said it but it's so obvious, I for one believe that Nixon obviously was the man behind Watergate, he planned the whole thing with the boys, so I accuse." Van Ronk and Pat Sky joined, "J'AC-CUSE!" Phil continued. "I hereby accuse Richard Nixon as being the man behind Watergate. I believe this is the first time over the mass media that this has been said. Richard Nixon was the guy who planned Watergate. I hereby would like to start a little movement here in New York City to impeach Richard Nixon. Spread the word around, tell everybody you know, call up your pals on the West Coast and let's get the word out, because the straight media is too chicken."

"I suspect you're just trying to protect your bet," said Van Ronk.

"Exactly. I don't want to lose a bet." Laughter. "And the mere act of impeaching President Nixon is far more important than whether or not Spiro Agnew becomes the President. They're both the same person anyway." It was the spring of 1973, before anyone knew of the existence of Nixon's tapes.

He played New England, Canada, Philadelphia, Washington, D.C., Michigan, Chicago, and finally Los Angeles, where he closed out the tour at The Ash Grove. The next day, Phil was interviewed by *The Berkeley Barb*. He talked about the possibility of becoming a professional pool player. When asked about his next album, he said, "It will come out as soon as I write it. Right now, for some reason, I feel blocked." This prompted the newspaper to begin an "Inspire Phil Ochs" campaign. A&M Records picked up the idea, and "Inspire Phil Ochs" buttons were distributed. They came and went with no new album from Phil.

Instead, he turned to writing for various newspapers. Chris Van Ness, the editor of the Los Angeles *Free Press,* asked Phil if he'd like to write some articles for the FREEP. That summer, Phil published two interviews he'd done—one with Tom Reddin, chief of the Los Angeles Police Department, and one with Mike Mazurkey, the actor/restaurateur. During the Reddin interview, Phil suffered an anxiety attack and had to excuse himself, telling the chief of police that he, Phil, couldn't go on. The published interview re-created this moment. The Mazurkey piece was filled with fascinating stories of early Hollywood, Mazurkey telling Phil how he'd broken into the movies because Cecil B. DeMille thought he looked like a wrestler.

By August, Phil was totally engrossed in the Watergate hearings and wrote an article for the Los Angeles *Weekly News,* "Will Elliot Richardson Be Our Next President?":

> It is becoming increasingly obvious that there is no possible way for Nixon to continue his charade as "The President." Slowly but surely the immensity of the corruption of Watergate, the illegal campaign "dirty tricks," the misuse of Federal power (political use of the IRS), the deals with ITT and the large wheat handlers, the enemies list, the failure to release tapes, and the pure greed of ten million dollars spent on home improvements (bulletproof swimming pools!) is seeping into the middle-American mentality like a huge turd into a steamy swamp.
>
> McCord was the left jab and John Dean the right cross. Nixon is dead. He is no longer President. If the Japanese attacked Pearl Harbor again, he would go on TV and call for support; the general reaction could well be, "So what—it's been done before."
> . . . The most likely way out is resignation—either voluntary or forced. I believe the decision that Nixon has to resign was made at least three months ago. I assume that, as usual, it was a matter of capital and finance. America is in desperate trouble. The dollar is in grave danger, inflation is rampant, the scars of Indochina will take a long time to heal, and the government stands there paralyzed like (excuse the expression) a pitiful, helpless giant. . . .
>
> I suppose the final lesson of all this is that your character is your fate. Here is Nixon on election eve, licking his chops at the

point of his greatest victory. He believes he is loved. He believes
he has finally beaten John Kennedy. And then, twenty-five years
of lies, deceit, and hypocrisy come whipping around like a giant
cosmic pie and flies splat! into his jowly and corpse-like face.
Maybe there is a God.

In September, Phil decided to take a trip to Africa. He was convinced that Africa, rather than Southeast Asia, held the most revolutionary potential in the world. Idi Amin fascinated him. One of
his goals while in Africa would be to try to meet the Ugandan
ruler.

He set up several concerts in African cities to coincide with a
month-long safari he planned to take. Phil was fascinated by the
sound of the African languages, and decided, while in Kenya, to
record a single, in Lingala. He wrote a tune entitled "Bwatue" and
recorded it with the Pan African Ngembo Rumba Band, backed
with a song he wrote called "Niko Mchumba Engombe." This one
he sang in Swahili. One of the reasons Phil was so anxious to record while in Africa was so that he could deduct the trip from his
income tax. He still thought he was making enough for this to
matter, which he wasn't and which it didn't. He even called Jerry
Moss collect and told him about his plans. He asked Moss to set
up all the recording dates, which Moss did. The record failed to
go African top ten.

He told everyone—tour guides, fellow travelers, shopkeepers—he
intended to go to Uganda to meet Idi Amin. The first evening he
was in Tanzania, he took a long walk, alone, on the beach at Dar
es Salaam, as the ocean glowed gelatinous white. Suddenly, without provocation, he was jumped from behind by three black men.
One held him around the neck, while the other two went through
his pockets. Phil tried to scream as the arm tightened around his
neck, rupturing the vocal cords. He couldn't breathe, he tore
frantically at the steel-like arm with his hands. His knees began to
buckle, he felt himself starting to fall, blacking out on the way
down. The men beat him savagely before taking off with his cash.
He lay sprawled on the beach.

They found him early the next morning and rushed him to a
hospital. His wounds were mostly superficial, except for his throat.
The upper register was gone. He had no high notes. He panicked in
the hospital room, trying to scream away the nightmare, but only

wind came out. My voice, oh God, where is my voice? . . . who were those guys? . . . why did they do this to me? . . . why did they do this to me? . . .

He was in the hospital for several days. When he was discharged, the doctors warned him not to try to sing. He insisted his voice was all right, and was adamant about fulfilling his commitment to do a concert in Johannesburg.

During that show, which lasted all of forty minutes, Phil drank beer continuously on stage, the icy brew helping to cool his burning throat. He put it down next to him at one point and kicked it over. He stopped singing until the bottle of beer was replaced. Then, while slurring something about his voice not being in the best condition, he fell completely off the stage, headfirst, into the orchestra pit. The next day, the front page of the Johannesburg *Star* headlined the story.

"Yeah, man, I was pretty crazy," he told a reporter. "Getting all that beer down was not a normal part of my act. I've been in a dilemma for days, as I can't decide whether to stay in South Africa or go back to America. I've got trouble with my voice. In Dar es Salaam three guys jumped me and strangled me as they robbed me. My voice is not right yet. I'm seeing a doctor."

A few days later, he flew home to America.

He arrived in New York, the middle of December, and immediately tried to find a doctor who could restore his voice. He'd contracted with Max's Kansas City to do a Christmas concert before he'd gone to Africa, and now it looked as though he would have to cancel out. He called Sam Hood, who had recently taken over management of the popular downtown club, to give him the bad news.

It had been a rough couple of years for Hood. The Gaslight had died its natural death, he'd divorced his wife, and had only recently become involved with Max's when it seemed it too might shutter. One of the first things he did when he took over was to contact Phil and book him into the club. Phil had resisted but finally agreed to do it, with conditions, as a personal favor to Hood. He wanted to be paid more than anyone else who had ever played Max's. He also wanted a huge guarantee. This put the burden on Hood, because if Phil bombed, it would probably hasten the end of Max's. He'd agreed to guarantee Phil five thousand dollars a week for two weeks.

Hood booked Patti Smith as Phil's opening act, seeing it as a perfect combination of the poetess of the seventies with the troubadour of the sixties. Only she was against it, and so was Phil. Neither had heard of the other. She asked a few of her friends who Phil Ochs was, and afterward told Hood she wasn't going to share the stage with any "folkie." Hood was able to cool them both out to the point where they agreed to honor their commitments. Until Phil returned from Africa and called Hood to say the concert was off—he'd lost his voice. Hood was sure Phil was just being dramatic, and reminded him if he failed to make the date, the club would probably close. Reluctantly, Phil promised to make it.

It was the first time tickets were put on sale in advance at Max's. The fourteen shows were sold out in three days. Even so, hundreds of people lined up each night, only to be turned away. Sam Hood was relieved. But no one was more surprised than Phil. He couldn't believe anyone still wanted to see him perform. At the beginning of every show Phil explained to the audience he'd had an "accident" in Africa, and as a result his voice was not in great shape.

Phil wanted to do material from the "Greatest Hits" album, maybe some Ewan MacColl. However, each time he went away from his familiar sixties political songs, the audience became hostile and shouted its disapproval. One night Phil left the stage, and returned with the gold suit jacket on, threatening to do Elvis if they didn't behave.

Hood watched every night, and it made him angry to see Phil unable to control the show, always giving the audience what it wanted, not knowing how to bring them around. Phil and Sam were relieved when the two weeks at Max's ended.

Phil wanted to be paid in cash. He didn't want to have to turn the money over to his accountants. He didn't want to tell anyone about the money. Hood explained to Phil he had to be paid by certified check, that was the way the club did business. Phil asked him to cash it. Hood told him to come by the apartment the next day; they would go to the bank together. At five-thirty in the morning, Hood's doorbell rang. It was Phil. He'd lost the check. They tried to retrace Phil's steps, but it was no use. Sam had to have it stopped, and have another issued, not an easy thing to do with a certified check. This time, Hood had it issued directly to Phil's accountant. Disgusted, Phil returned to his apartment on Prince Street where he'd been staying, curled up on one of the large pillows in the living room, and fell asleep.

The cold New York winter drove Phil back to Los Angeles. He went to Frank Sinatra's throat doctor, and after a series of examinations was told that if he stopped drinking completely, and did special vocal exercises for several hours a day, every day, he might get his voice back in two, maybe three years.

It wasn't until he'd been in Los Angeles for several days that he first heard about the military coup in Chile. Incredibly, he'd missed the news of Allende's overthrow and murder. When he finally did hear about it, he was astonished. His first reaction was disbelief, then furious anger. He took it personally, as if *he'd* been overthrown. He thought back to the days in Chile with Stew and Jerry and Victor Jara. He remembered the beautiful drawings and writings by the people on the sides of the buildings in the heart of Santiago. He could see the faces of the Chileans, the spark of pride flashing in their eyes. Allende, the gentle doctor, the man of peaceful changes, had been slaughtered in his palace, Victor Jara tortured to death in the Santiago Stadium. Phil got into his car and drove aimlessly around Los Angeles. By nightfall he was on a plane back to New York.

Nudie the tailor and an
unidentified model (*Courtesy
of Nudie the Tailor*)

Custom-made charisma,
also by Nudie (*Courtesy
of A&M Records*)

Performing in the gold suit at The Troubadour (*Photo by Michael Ochs*)

Later, with Doug Weston (*Courtesy of the Phil Ochs estate*)

Phil and Meegan, 1971
(*Courtesy of the Phil
Ochs estate*)

Jerry Rubin and Phil in Chile (*Photo by Stew Albert*)

Phil in Australia (*Ron Cobb*)

1973

IS THIS MAN A PATRIOT? TRAITOR?

Oh her power shall rest
On the strength of her freedom,
Her glory shall rest
On us all.

Here's to the land
You've torn out the heart of,
Richard Nixon find yourself
Another country to be a part of.

FIND OUT!
ON THE NEW PHIL OCHS SINGLE.
"POWER AND GLORY"
b/w
"HERE'S TO THE STATE OF RICHARD NIXON"
(AM 1509)
ON A&M RECORDS

"We have nothing to fear
but fear itself."
—Franklin Delano Roosevelt
(1933)

Phil and Meegan
(*Alice Ochs*)

Phil and Andy at a trucker's
party, Los Angeles, 1974
(*Courtesy of A&M Records*)

XI

Time must have her victory
It's that I've always known
But I won or lost alone
And then a voice calls out "There's someone you
    must meet."
With every strength remaining
I will suffer one more scene
I'll gather all my dreams
And with my final breath
I'll lay them at your feet.
Yes I'll be back again no matter where I roam
For it's only love that frees the fire for burning,
Then I'll take you in my arms and tell you all I know
As I sing the final song of my returning . . .

            Phil Ochs, "Song of My Returning"

       The plane went into its final descent as Phil was just taking
off.

He went back to Prince Street. He started making phone calls,
setting up small engagements nearby; a couple of nights in Philadelphia, a concert at Bryn Mawr, anything to generate immediate
income. He had a plan. It was going to be a massive concert, a
happening, a show unlike any ever seen before. It was going to be
called "An Evening with Salvador Allende." Or, fuck death.

He was sitting with Sam Hood at a table in Max's when Arthur
walked in. Gorson was there to catch J. F. Murphy and Salt, a

new act performing at the club. Phil was invited up to do a song after the regular show. He sang "Here's to the State of Richard Nixon." After the song, Arthur walked over to Phil and hugged him. It had been a long time. They talked for hours. There were good feelings now between them, time allowing them to recall the great moments and forget the bad ones. Arthur told Phil how much he loved the new version of "Mississippi."

"Why don't you produce it as a single?" Phil said. "I'm sure A&M would release it."

They made the record, and Phil started hanging out at Arthur's place. He told him about his idea for the Chile benefit. He needed a good producer, someone to help him pull the whole thing together. He knew no better organizer than Arthur. It had to be an evening of rage, nothing less.

Arthur was into it immediately. It would be tremendous if it could be pulled off. They worked long hours into the night, planning the event, making lists of performers they wanted.

"We'll get John Denver and Bob Dylan," Phil said, "we'll get Joan Baez and Shirley MacLaine, we'll get . . ."

"Let's get organized first," Arthur said.

Later that week, Phil was put in touch with several Chilean exiles, key members of an underground organization dedicated to the overthrow of the government of General Pinochet. Arthur called a friend of his he'd worked with before, a young lady by the name of Deni Frand. Many things had to be done. Was she interested in helping? Yes. "Fine, I'll have Phil call you."

Phil arranged to meet her at The Lion's Head, a bar in the West Village.

Deni arrived early, hoping to be able to pick him out of the crowd. She'd asked Arthur what Phil looked like. "Just watch out for a Ralph Nader type." She sat at the bar having a glass of red wine, the only other customer in the room a fat guy in a blue-and-white checked shirt, drinking rum and orange juice. After a few minutes, Deni went outside, preferring to wait for Phil in the fresh night air. A couple of seconds later, he emerged and asked if she were waiting for him. She tried to conceal her surprise when she realized he'd been Phil Ochs all the time. She followed him back into The Lion's Head, over to the table where he'd been sitting. He interviewed her about her abilities as an organizer, and about her allegiance to "the cause." It was all very Casablanca. Deni, with her huge black eyes wide for adventure, her thick black hair cut short and pulled away from her face, looked every bit the eager would-be revolutionary. Phil liked her right away and offered her the job. He would pay her fifty dollars a week. She would help Arthur with the organization of the benefit and be Phil's personal assistant. She accepted.

Claudio Bedal, a Chilean refugee in New York, was trying to raise money to help finance the overthrow of Pinochet. He was working with various Latin-American left-wing organizations. Word reached Claudio about the benefit Phil was putting together. He got in touch and offered to do whatever he could to help. He became Phil's errand boy. He was an airy, flamboyant soul who loved to be entertained. He found it amusing that Phil Ochs, a sixties leftover, was trying to organize a massive benefit for Chile, and that Deni Frand, a political neophyte, was his assistant.

Claudio was a friend of Francois De Menil's, the millionaire Texan into making movies and hanging out with rock stars. Claudio recruited Francois to help with the concert.

The final member of the initial group was Cora Weiss. Cora first met Phil in 1969, in Washington, during a major anti-war demonstration organized by the Mobilization Against the War Committee. When Cora received a phone call from Deni Frand asking her to help organize the benefit for Chile, she immediately agreed because, she said, "something had to be done."

They took a one-room office in the Methodist Center building across from the United Nations. The first meeting took place early in March. Deni, Phil, Claudio, Cora. They sent out for Chinese food. Soon white cartons filled with steamed rice, egg foo yung, and spareribs were being passed out. Cases of beer lined the floor. Phil explained his plan to the group. All he needed, he said, was a few thousand dollars to get started. "You're crazy," Cora told him. "You can't just pick up the phone and say to somebody, 'Give me ten thousand dollars.' " Yet, that was exactly what he had in mind. He started calling everyone he knew, everyone he'd ever done a favor for, putting together promises for money. If he had to borrow, he'd promise to pay the money back in two days, figuring he'd borrow from somewhere else if he really had to make good. Claudio persuaded Francois to start the group off with a loan of three thousand dollars.

Phil booked a mini-tour for March and April, to raise more money for the benefit. At the end of every concert he would ask the audience for donations. Each time he'd return from the road, he'd deliver paper bags filled with money to Deni. He would then take her for Chinese food, and while they were eating he would get into long raps with her about books, movies, politicians. He would stare away from her eyes and just talk as he ate and drank. He started calling her Tanya. Every time he'd take off for another concert, she'd rush to read the books he referred to, to see the movies he described. It was her first dose of radical politics. By the end of the winter, she was a committed supporter of the "cause," totally committed to the unification of the radical Left. At fund-raising parties, she would filter through the crowd, telling the Trotskyite in the corner to be careful not to talk to that one over there, he's a Marxist.

Phil was booked into Avery Fisher Hall for April 17, 1974. He was on fire when he took the stage. So what if his voice was sandy? For this one show he'd drop his voice a couple of octaves and talk the lyrics. The real point was to reach the New York fans, to tell them about the Chile concert.

He strode onto the stage, met by a whistling, throbbing ovation —his head down, tilted to one side, waiting for the applause to stop.

"Thank you very much. Here's a medley of three songs about prison written by three guys who spent some time there." It began with "There but for Fortune." "Then there was Johnny Cash, who used to write a lot of good songs before he started hanging out with the wrong company there at the White House . . . He was once one of the greatest living Americans. He now stands as living proof that television can kill . . . Here's a song he wrote back in 1954, 'Give My Love to Rose.'" Finally, a Merle Haggard tune, qualifying by Haggard's having done time for armed robbery. "While a prisoner . . . he wrote this tune . . . 'Sing Me Back Home Before I Die.'"

It was classic Phil Ochs, a medley of songs about the absence of freedom. From Haggard back to the wistful "There but for Fortune." It brought a standing ovation from the audience.

Someone shouted, "Small Circle of Friends." It seemed to startle Phil. The titles started coming from all over the hall. After a
few moments, he regained his composure and started joking with
the audience. "What kind of crowd do we have here tonight? Now
me, I'm an old-timer and I go way back." Applause and cheers. "I
go back to the time of the students, when students, instead of
streaking, were striking . . ." Wild applause. ". . . Over, pardon
the expression, political issues." More applause, a guitar strum
underneath. "You can be sure all the assholes like Jerry Ford,
they're all publicizing this streaking thing, they love streaking, 'It's
as funny as hell, it sort of reminds me of my goldfish days.' All of
these guys have the same writer. The purpose is to ignore the sixties, because the sixties were, in my opinion, the most important
years of the century . . . The reason they were, the reason you
can't believe what *Life, Time,* the newspapers say and the propaganda they're putting out that this is the sleeping generation, the
reason it's the sleeping generation is because of the input of drugs
and a number of other factors. Back in the fifties things were
different, on the weakest level, people really didn't know what was
going on. The purpose of the sixties was to educate, not only
America but the rest of the world. That succeeded. They came in
with their drugs about seven years too late. The word got out. The
people sitting up in Vermont growing vegetables, at least they
know what's going on. They're not the same crew they were in the
fifties." Blasting applause. "They're on the way, they're going to
make a comeback, at the right moment." Stomping and shouting.
"If you've ever been known to misjudge the right moment, we'll
all be dead. Seems bitter, but true. Anyway, for old times' sake,
here's an old-time protest . . . song . . . *Oh, I am just a student,
sir, and I only want to learn . . . But it's hard to read through the
risin' smoke of the books that you like to burn . . .*" When he
came to the last verse, his guitar quieted to a two-chord alternating
vamp, and his mouth came close to the microphone, so close he
had to turn his head to one side.

> *So I am just a trucker, sir, and I only want to learn*
> *But it's hard to read through the rise of the smoke*
> *From the fuel that you like to burn*

So I'd like to make a promise and I'd like to make a vow
That when I've got something to say, sir, I'm gonna
  say it now.

"There've been a lot of comeback stories this year, so I think I'll name some . . . Janis Ian's coming back . . . Bob Dylan and his contract furor . . . new stories of The Beatles' reunion . . . certainly a lot of comeback trails there . . . but I think the biggest comeback story of the seventies is that of Jesus Christ . . . back on the charts . . . I've always tried to be a crowd pleaser so I figured I'd have to do a song about Jesus . . . I went through my repertoire and discovered a few tunes . . . one was written by Ewan MacColl . . ." Phil did MacColl's haunting "Jesus Was a Working Man."

As the audience burst into applause, he segued into "Small Circle of Friends," adding a new final verse.

Down in Santiago where they took away our mines
We cut off all their money so they robbed the storehouse
  blind
Now maybe we should ask some questions, maybe shed a tear
But I bet you a copper penny, it cannot happen here
And I'm sure it wouldn't interest anybody
Outside of a small circle of friends . . .

It was the first direct reference he'd made to Chile. "Small Circle of Friends," originally about a murder allowed to be committed because nobody would come to the victim's aid, now took on a new meaning. Americans had allowed Allende to be murdered by America. To Phil, tenement crime and international assassination were the same thing.

"Uh, the New York *Times* claims they run all the news that's fit to print. The fact is they don't. In fact, they print the facts which are sometimes misleading. Somehow they failed to run the story of the semi-military coup that happened in 1963 in America when a right-wing paramilitary squad killed John Kennedy . . . the New York *Times* failed to carry this bit of information, and has failed to carry it yet." He played the opening notes of "Crucifixion" softly, below his patter. "Here's a song that was written in England after that assassination . . . the people in charge then are the people in charge now, and I guess they're just going to keep on killing everybody . . . *And the night comes again to the circle studded sky . . ."*

When he finished, the audience again started shouting names of songs at him. He surprised them with a new one:

> *How high is the watergate, Mama, She said it's one foot high*
> *and risin'*
> *How high is the watergate, Papa, He said it's two feet high*
> *and risin'*
> *There's a flood around the poker game*
> *Jerry Ford must be insane*
> *Oh my God, it's Mickey Spillane, the tides are risin'*
> *How high is the watergate, Mama, three feet high and risin'*
> *How high is the watergate, Papa, three feet high and risin'*
> *Nixon's gone and taught you lies*
> *A face that screams out for replies*
> *And the only one workin' is David Frye, oh the tides*
> *are risin'*
> *How high is the watergate, Mama, four feet high and risin'*
> *How high is the watergate, Papa, four feet high and risin'*
> *If there ever was a crook, he's it*
> *Perversion is the soul of wit*
> *Pack your shovel, he's full of shit, the tides are risin'*

"Here's to the State of Richard Nixon." The applause came again in waves. It was the final song. He waved once to the audience before disappearing behind the curtain. They kept up the applause. He returned to the stage and stood in front of the microphone, waiting for the cheers to die down. Before he could speak, a woman stood up in the audience and shouted, "Phil Ochs is dead!" Phil just stared blindly into the light. He didn't know what to say. He apologized for not being able to do an encore, explaining his voice was gone. Then he invited everyone backstage to talk about Chile. He left the stage once again, this time to a standing ovation. They began heading for his dressing room before the house lights came up.

He arrived at the office the next day with bags full of money for Deni. He also gave her a handful of tickets for the Chile benefit. She was to go out and not return until they were sold. He was supervising all aspects of the production, even the program book, which he wanted filled with the lyrics of Victor Jara and the poetry of Pablo Neruda. He wanted Isabel Allende, daughter of the murdered president, to come to the United States to attend the concert. She accepted the invitation immediately, but was prevented from entering the country until the last minute when the government finally granted her a conditional visa. She could come to the United States, but was not to make any public statements.

Phil was invited to sing at a rally for Puerto Rican independence in Riverside Church. He agreed to play, figuring it would be a good place to promote the Chile concert. He hailed a cab across the street from the United Nations and told the driver where he wanted to go. On the way up, Phil practiced a few songs on the guitar. At a red light, the driver turned and said to him, "You know, you're pretty good. You ought to do that for a living."

Arthur was trying to get the Madison Square Garden Felt Forum. Ron Delsener lent his name for credibility, and they were able to reserve the evening of May 9 for the event. Press releases were issued. Every day new performers were committing themselves to appear. Already set were Arlo Guthrie, Pete Seeger, Melvin Van Peebles, Gato Barbieri, The Living Theatre, Dennis Hopper, and Dennis Wilson. Phil wanted Joan Baez. When she turned down Phil's invitation, he was furious. He told everybody she was a no-class bitch. Dammit, she owed him this for "There but for Fortune!" All her bullshit about the problems of the world didn't mean anything if she wasn't going to show.

By the first week in May, less than a quarter of the house was sold. Phil tried desperately to come up with some kind of angle to sell more tickets. He sat in a corner of the office, head down, arms folded, legs crossed. Suddenly he jumped out of his seat and started dancing. "We'll get Frank Sinatra! We'll get Sinatra to sing at the benefit! That'll sell tickets." He went to work, and about an hour later had Sinatra's lawyer on the phone. He explained who he was and what he was doing. The lawyer told Phil that Sinatra would be "unavailable."

Time was running out.

A week before the show, Delsener was advised by the Felt Forum management to pull out; there was no possible way they could break even based on how tickets were selling. They already owed the Forum eighteen thousand dollars, which had to be paid, no matter what. Delsener suggested to Phil it might be a good idea to call it quits, but Phil was more convinced than ever that he could, somehow, pull it off. He left the office waving his arms, telling the others—Deni, Cora, and Claudio—not to worry, he would come through.

The weekend before the show, Phil appeared at several functions to try to raise money and sell tickets. He showed up at a "Samuels for Governor" affair, where he gave out his autograph to anybody who bought a ticket for the concert. Later that night at a party at Michael Harrington's apartment, during pâté and white wine, he insisted everyone listen to the Victor Jara record he put on the turntable. He played one song twenty times. Someone asked him what the song meant; he made up translations on the spot, improvising lyrics, the more outrageous the better. He then made a speech declaring that one of the reasons he was doing this concert was to avenge Jara's death, for the sake of his poor widow.

Phil was drunk by the time he and Deni left there. They got into a cab and headed uptown to Columbia University, where Phil was scheduled to make an appeal for people to buy tickets over the campus-based FM radio station, WKCR. In the cab, he kept mumbling they had to meet Claudio. "I know, Phil, I know," Deni said as she held his hand. He'd been taking Valium steadily throughout the day. By the time they arrived at 116th Street, he couldn't stand up. Deni paid the driver, and when she turned around to get Phil, she couldn't find him anywhere. She went to the front of the wrought-iron-gate entrance to the university and started calling his name. She walked up and down Broadway several times before finally entering the campus. There, just behind a stone bench on the grass, was Phil, curled up, mouth open, unconscious. Deni panicked; she thought he was dead. She pounded on his chest to try to revive him. He didn't move. Out of the darkness, like a ghost, emerged Claudio. He began to laugh. "Help me," Deni screamed. Claudio stood there while she gave Phil mouth-to-mouth resuscitation. He awoke, pushed her away, and threw up on himself. Claudio laughed harder. By now, a few students had gathered around to see what was going on. One of them said, "Hey, you're Phil Ochs, I'm a great fan of yours."

Somehow, Claudio and Deni were able to get Phil to the radio station. By the time they arrived, WKCR had shut down for the night.

A couple of days before the concert, Phil ran into Bob Dylan in front of the Chelsea Hotel and threw his arms around him. It was the first time they'd seen each other in years. Phil insisted they have a drink together. Over a bottle of wine, he told Dylan about the Chile concert, how great it was going to be, how everybody was going to be there. Dylan said nothing.

The next night, in the Prince Street apartment, Phil stood up and recited, word for word, Allende's Inaugural Address for Dylan. It was a performance worthy of an Academy Award. A close friend of Phil's who was there that night remembers: "Dylan had no inkling or knowledge as to what had happened in Chile. There was a natural warmth between the two of them, contrary to what everybody thought. Phil was brilliant when he was talking about Chile, and Bob totally agreed with everything. Bob wasn't as verbal as Phil. Phil was sitting there trying to convince him of the necessity of doing the concert. There was really never any doubt that Dylan was going to do it. When Phil finished reciting Allende's speech, we all sat there in silence. I think Bob, from the very moment that Phil asked him to do it, was going to. He was baiting Phil. He didn't tell Phil until twenty-four hours before, if he gave them that much time. Everyone else knew, of course, that the Chile concert was the reason Dylan was in New York. He'd heard Phil was in trouble and he'd come in to help."

The day before the concert, Phil went on WBAI to announce that Dylan was going to appear. Within hours, every ticket was sold.

Phil had all the performers come out on stage at the beginning of the concert. The crowd saw Dylan and erupted. Phil, drink in hand, came to the mike to try and quiet them down. "Okay . . . now listen, listen . . . listen to me, please . . . please . . . okay, can you keep quiet . . . hold it down, everybody relax . . . now listen . . . will everybody keep quiet now because the show is beginning . . . we . . . all right . . . now we got over the star-fucking excitement . . . now we can get on with the show . . . we're here for a political purpose . . . we're here for a political purpose, you're not here to see Bob Dylan, you're here to see Salvador Allende . . . okay . . . so relax, relax . . . relax and calm down, the program changes by the minute . . . the first suggestion is Pete Seeger has to sing someplace else tonight so he'll now do his set . . . please listen to Pete Seeger . . ."

It was a powerful evening. Phil would introduce each act and then run backstage to sit with Dylan. They drank a lot of wine, Phil never letting Dylan out of sight, fearing he might somehow disappear, or change his mind and not go on.

Film clips of Allende were screened. Dennis Hopper read Allende's final speech and cried. The Living Theatre did a piece dramatizing the torture of political prisoners in Chile. Melvin Van Peebles sang one of his own songs about repression. Dave Van Ronk dedicated "He Was a Friend of Mine" to Allende. Gato Barbieri and his group performed a Latin jazz set. Fernando Navarro, Isabel Allende's aide, read a poem written by Pablo Neruda. The final performance of the evening belonged to Dylan, who sang "Blowin' in the Wind," with Phil Ochs standing on one side of him and Dave Van Ronk on the other.

Recalls Ron Delsener: "A couple of days after the concert, Phil called me up and says, 'Let's meet in the Carnegie Hall Tavern, I want to talk to you, Bob wants to talk to you.' So I went over to the Carnegie Tavern, and I'm waiting." Phil and Dylan arrived together an hour late.

"Okay, what are we doing here?" Delsener asked.

Dylan told him he and Phil wanted to tour together. Delsener: "Bob was really hot for the idea. Phil had gotten him excited about playing small places, little clubs, and giving the money away. To charities. So I say, 'Okay, Bob, what charities do you like?' and he was mentioning, off the wall, countries and causes. Phil is saying, 'Well, I want this for the Indians, and some for a river, and some for pollution, and some for other radical causes.' Anyway, we kind of agree to narrow it down to two or three charities, and they tell me to fix it up, small halls, two and three hundred seaters . . . This, of course, was the seed that started Dylan, two years later, on 'The Rolling Thunder Review.' Only by then it had gotten out of hand, ball parks, arenas, everyone wanted to be in on it. Bob would say, 'Yeah, yeah, come along.' "

After the meeting, Phil took Dylan to a party to meet Cuba's delegate to the U.N. "Go ahead, Bobby, ask him anything about Cuba. Anything at all." Dylan couldn't think of a single question. He shrugged his shoulders, excused himself, and went into the kitchen for something to eat.

Phil paced back and forth at the Prince Street apartment for hours, in a diagonal, across the living room, saying, half to himself and half to Larry Sloman, the current subleasee, "Geez, geez . . . geez . . . what am I going to do? . . . what am I going to do? . . . I can't write . . . I can't write . . . I can see it now. Folk singer found dead. Phil Ochs was found hanged today in his apartment on Prince Street." Phil had a strange look on his face. The staircase banister was broken in one section. "It really got bad, and I tried to kill myself," Phil said. He explained how he'd looped one end of his belt around his neck and the other around the banister. "I'm too fat, and the old wood snapped." Phil was grinning.

Sharing the Prince Street apartment with Sloman was Jay Levin, a reporter for the New York *Post*. Phil started hanging around with him in the city room of the *Post,* eagerly awaiting the next installment of Watergate to come over the news wires. Phil was fascinated by the process of Nixon's downfall, and would spend hours with Jay talking about its implications. Phil was convinced that Nixon was a victim of the CIA, and that Colby was really emperor of the United States. For a while, Watergate became his only obsession, getting him out of bed in the morning and giving him something to do. He would stand in alleys of the Village in the middle of the night, shouting at the top of his lungs to Richard Nixon, warning him his days were numbered.

After a while, Phil stopped coming home. Deni asked him to stay at her place in Queens for a few nights, and he said okay. She would become nervous when he came home late. He was always drunk. Many times she would remove pills from his clothes while he was sleeping. He was filthy, his clothes smelled of vomit and urine. Deni would wash them for him.

He would sit around her apartment, saying over and over, "What am I going to do? What am I going to do? . . ." He was convinced he had stomach cancer and was going to die. He complained of severe constipation while continuing to eat enormous amounts of food.

She thought it would be good for him to sing before an audience again. She convinced him to do a benefit performance at The Village Gate for Ramsey Clark, then campaigning for Senator.

The Gate was nearly empty. Clark was sitting at a table, a look of defeat on his face. Phil told him not to worry. He went outside and stopped people as they passed the club. "Hi, I'm Phil Ochs. I'm playing for Ramsey Clark tonight, and I'd like you to see the show." A few people went in.

When it was Phil's turn to perform, he went up on stage and said, "Hi, I'm Phil Ochs. I've never campaigned for anybody but Gene McCarthy and George McGovern. I never should have done it for McCarthy because he was no good. I never should have done it for McGovern. And I never should do it for Ramsey Clark." Deni covered her mouth with her hand. "I shouldn't do it for Ramsey Clark because he shouldn't be Senator from New York. He should be President of the United States." He began to sing. At one point, two of the people he'd brought in got up and left. In the middle of his song, Phil jumped off the stage and ran after them. "You said you were going to stay for the show." They went back inside and took their seats, waiting politely until Phil finished his set. Then they left.

Later that night, Phil went with Deni to The Bottom Line to see Pete Seeger's show. Between sets, Seeger came over to Phil and told him he should try to take care of himself, reminding him how politically unwise it was not to keep himself in better shape. Phil said nothing. Seeger took Deni aside. "Watch him. He's very sick."

XII

Hello, hello, hello
Is there anybody home?
I only called to say I'm sorry
The drums are in the dawn
And all the voices gone
And it seems that there are
No more songs.

Phil Ochs, "No More Songs"

Phil wanted to go home. He couldn't take another New York winter. Deni drove him to La Guardia. They had a drink in the terminal before he boarded the plane. She hugged him tightly when it was time for him to go. "Take care of yourself," she told him.

She went to the observation deck to watch the 747 as it disappeared into the sky. How wonderful it could have been, she thought.

At first L.A. seemed to bring Phil up. He called Michael, saw Andy a few times, even talked about putting a tour together. Soon, though, he began to spend more and more time alone, in his apartment, seeing no one, calling no one, not even Andy. He just wanted to be left alone. He would go for the newspapers every morning and spend the rest of the day reading, sleeping, or watching television. On his way to the paper stand one day, he happened to run into Lee Housekeeper, and they began to talk. Housekeeper had moved to a larger house, with a swimming pool. He invited Phil to come by sometime for a swim. The next day, at nine o'clock in the morning, Phil showed up, knocking on House-keeper's front door.

Housekeeper was smart enough to know he shouldn't say any-thing to Phil about the way he looked. There was no use trying to "help" Phil, he could see that. Instead, he suggested they get a couple of bikes and do some riding. Phil said he didn't want to, that he'd rather sit by the pool and read the New York *Times*. Housekeeper said fine, and started riding his own bike around the pool.

Soon they were both doing a couple of miles every morning. Phil huffed and puffed to keep up with the speedy Housekeeper. He soon began to drop some of his weight. Color came back to his face. He stopped drinking.

Housekeeper started bringing a portable TV to the pool, and together they watched the final days of Watergate unfold. The day Nixon resigned, Housekeeper threw a huge party. He invited lots of friends, and called up a local TV news program to come and interview his guests to get some reactions. A reporter asked Phil how he felt about Nixon's leaving office.

Well, first of all, I think, uh, the, the resignation speech was terri-ble . . . irresponsible. He's leaving open a very big legal question, the way he left it was so general, so cliché, a lot of supporters could take it to mean that he's innocent, and so I would say that it's now necessary for him to be impeached anyway. I think it's necessary. He's left us this cloud of P.R. that he always had be-fore. When he was innocent, when in fact he was guilty . . . I'm very happy that he's gone. I think he's been a very evil man his entire career, and I think he's totally supported the forces of reac-tion. I think he's responsible for prolonging the war in Vietnam rather than claiming credit for ending it, when it's still going on anyway with our support even now as we're talking. What I'm afraid of is that there's been a steady policy ever since the assassi-nation of John Kennedy. With Johnson, Nixon, and Ford's voting record, it might continue through television, through public rela-tions. I don't think there'll be any basic change with Ford. Just personal gratification. The one guy particularly known for his tac-tics has fallen. People in general seem happy to see him go.

Michael got in touch with Phil. There was a possibility of getting on "The Midnight Special," NBC's rock-and-roll program aired 1 A.M. Saturday morning.

At first, Phil didn't want to do it. His voice was in bad shape, and he didn't have any new material to sing. Michael suggested he do "Here's to the State of Richard Nixon." Phil thought that was a great idea and got in touch with Jim Glover to ask if he'd sing backup.

The dress rehearsal went smoothly. Phil was nervous, pacing backstage. After all these years, he was getting his first network shot.

The taping of the show lasted for hours, with long breaks between the recording of the musical numbers. They'd begun at eight o'clock; it was now after two. Phil peeked out from behind the curtain. He was scheduled to go on next. The problem was, the audience had long gone. He asked Michael to get some people into the front rows.

"How am I going to do that, Phil?"

"Ask Gladys Knight and the Pips to take the first row. They're still here."

"Phil, I can't ask them to do that. I'll think of something." Michael got some of the crew members to come out to watch his brother.

At the last possible moment, one of the executives from the station decided Phil's song was unacceptable. Michael was furious. Why had they waited so long? What was Phil supposed to do now? Jim suggested they try another song. Backstage, Phil and Jim ran through "Chords of Fame." It was the song they finally sang over the air when the show was broadcast.

By the pool, Housekeeper taught Phil how to play backgammon. Each day at nine they would go to the pool and play. Phil became obsessed with the game. After a few weeks, he declared himself among the world's greatest players. As they played, Phil began to confide in Housekeeper. He said he was embarrassed about being overweight, he felt ugly, he was sure none of his friends liked him any more.

"Fuck 'em," Housekeeper said. "Do whatever you want to do, Phil. It's your move."

"I don't know what I want to do."

"What do you like to do?"

"Nothing."

"Look, Phil, you're a writer. Why don't you write some new songs. What's happening at the *Free Press?* Didn't you do a couple of pieces for them?"

Phil decided to drop into the offices of the FREEP, visit Chris Van Ness and see what was happening.

Van Ness was working on a story about the possible CIA link to the Symbionese Liberation Army's kidnaping of Patricia Hearst. Van Ness was sure it was part of a plot to discredit the Left. He was holding editorial meetings in his house, to make sure the information didn't leak. He invited Phil to come to the next meeting.

Phil sat on the sofa puffing his pipe, while the others talked. Someone asked Phil what he thought. He just shook his head slowly, having nothing to say.

Within days, and without warning, Van Ness and the entire staff were fired from the paper, replaced by the editor of the porno insert section. It marked the end of Phil's involvement with the FREEP.

He decided to call Andy Wickham. They met for dinner before catching Rod McKuen's show at The Troubadour. McKuen was talking a lot during the show about "Jacques Brel," how wonderful his lyrics were. Phil turned to Andy. "That's McKuen. Always Jacquing off."

Phil called Elliott Mintz, a Los Angeles FM radio host who was a friend and admirer. They talked for a while, and Mintz invited Phil to a birthday party. Phil hesitated until Mintz told him Sal Mineo was going to be there. Phil said he would definitely attend the black-tie affair. He'd even rent a tuxedo. Mineo had appeared in two films with James Dean: *Rebel Without a Cause* and *Giant*.

Mineo showed up at the party wearing a black leather jacket and black pants with a white ruffled shirt. Mintz introduced Phil to Mineo, and they talked for hours, Phil asking the movie star a million questions about Dean. Later, Mintz gently put his arm around Phil's shoulder, and thanked him for coming.

The next day Phil got a call from Jerry Rubin. He was coming to L.A. for a few days. He wanted to get together if possible.

They met for dinner. Rubin had just come from a celebrity est training program in San Francisco. He told Phil it was something he should definitely do.

"I don't know . . ." Phil said. Finally, Rubin convinced Phil to try it.

As Phil was leaving his apartment the next night, he got a phone call from the People's Bicentennial Celebration Committee, also in San Francisco, inviting him to attend the opening festivities. He said he would try to be there.

Later, he met Lee Housekeeper for dinner at Dan Tana's. It was Phil's last night in Los Angeles before heading north. Phil had his first drink in weeks. By the time he left the restaurant he was drunk.

Phil actually came to the door of the est meeting before he decided to go instead to the People's Bicentennial. And from there he flew to New York.

Phil's stomach problems returned. Once again, he was convinced he had cancer. He would get drunk, take a couple of Valium, and sit for hours with Larry Sloman, asking him what to do. Maybe he should check into Memorial Sloan-Kettering and begin radiation therapy. Sloman told Phil his problems might be cured if he went to visit a certain witch doctor up on 116th Street.

Phil went with Sloman to find the witch doctor. After several incantations, she gave Phil a special concoction of herbs to take which, she assured him, would restore his health. For days Phil forced himself to drink the foul-smelling sludge, giving it up only when his stomach problems got worse.

In April, the end finally came to the war in Vietnam. The boys were coming home. The news cut through the alcohol, the pills, and the imagined diseases. Phil Ochs wanted to celebrate. It would be his third, and greatest, "War Is Over" rally.

Cora Weiss heard the news of the end of the war on television. She telephoned Phil, who suggested they work together to organize a giant rally, to be held in Central Park. At a meeting the next day, Cora suggested the perfect time to hold the celebration. Mother's Day. It gave them eleven days.

Phil worked like a madman. David Livingston, a local union representative, donated office space for them to work out of. They got a number of people to commit themselves to appear, including Dr. Howard Levy, Jim Daly (a former POW), Pete Seeger, Odetta, Harry Belafonte, various Indian organizations, and Joan Baez, who had gained respect for Phil's organizational abilities after the Chile benefit and committed herself immediately.

A number of volunteers helped to put the show together. Phil pushed everyone to work a little harder than they thought they could. He would go for two, three days without sleeping.

He designed a poster like the one he'd used in 1967, with the sailor kissing the nurse on V.E. day. At a meeting, the poster was rejected because some of the women considered it "chauvinistic." Phil was lost. He couldn't understand what they were talking about; it was a famous World War II poster. Still, he was overruled, and for the new poster they used a photograph of a Vietnamese woman, her arms extended, with doves landing on them. It had been taken by Don Luce and Cora Weiss when they'd gone to Vietnam in 1973 at the invitation of Madame Binh.

It was magnificent. Over one hundred thousand people showed up on that sunny spring day, turning Sheep Meadow into a huge carnival of joy, welcoming the return of peace to America. Phil sang "The War Is Over," Joan Baez joined him and together they sang "There but for Fortune," after which Baez kissed Phil softly on the cheek.

Phil was overjoyed. Once again, he felt rejuvenated, he wanted to do things, to see people. He talked about writing new songs, maybe even cutting an album.

Then Dylan's "Blood on the Tracks" was released. Recalls a friend: "Phil was destroyed by that album. He loved it, thought it was Dylan's greatest work of the past ten years. But he also realized how far away Phil Ochs had gotten from writing songs."

A few days later, Phil went to a bar near the Chelsea Hotel and got smashed. It was the beginning of the terrible summer of John Butler Train.

XIII

Phil Ochs checked in to the Chelsea Hotel,
There was blood on his clothes, they were dirty.
I could see by his face he was not feeling well,
He'd been to one too many parties.
He walked in the lobby a picture of doom,
It was plain to see he'd been a-drinkin'.
I had to follow him up to his room,
To find out what he was thinkin'.
"Train, Train, Train,"
From the outlaw in his brain.
But he's still the same refrain

> Phil Ochs, "The Ballad of John Train"

It got worse after Phil Ochs lost a backgammon match to Mike Halverian, the owner of Knickers restaurant. Phil had challenged Paul Colby, owner of The Other End, to a game of backgammon, betting three days at the Plaza Hotel with three hookers to be supplied by Colby against three days at the club for no pay. Colby insisted he be allowed to name anybody he wanted to play the games for him. Phil agreed. Colby called Halverian, an expert player who'd learned the game as a child in Armenia. The match was set.

The rules were simple. Phil had to win one game out of the three they would play. He called Lee Housekeeper in Los Angeles and asked him to fly in for "The world's greatest backgammon tournament." He told Housekeeper he was responsible for changing everything. "You did it with backgammon therapy, and I want

you to be there. It's very important that you be there." Housekeeper booked a seat on the next flight to New York.

The evening of the match, Phil came prepared. He'd invited a
lot of people to watch the games, including several attractive
women dressed, according to his instructions, in "provocative
outfits." After he lost the first game, he excused himself and
stepped outside. The women followed. He told them he wanted
them to take their shirts off and during the game stand behind him
with their breasts exposed. They refused. He tried to convince them
it was for the sake of art, but they wouldn't do it. Shrugging his
shoulders, he returned to the match and lost the second game. On
his way to losing the third, he tipped the board over in anger and
stormed out.

Early the next morning, Housekeeper picked Phil up in his limousine. He wanted company for the ride to the airport. It was obvious Phil was drunk. "How are you feeling?"

"Look, man," Phil said, "things are happening. I'm changing
my name and forming a new, important organization. It's called
'Barricade.' I want you to run it for me."

"You really can't do it, Phil, unless you make a commitment to
health."

Phil shook his head. "This is really important."

"Is it important enough to stop drinking?"

"Yes."

"Will you?"

"Yes."

When they got to the airport they shook hands. Housekeeper
told Phil to call him when he was ready to talk business. He then
told the driver to take Phil wherever he wanted to go. Phil got
back in the car. "Where to, sir?"

"The nearest bar."

The Prince Street apartment had too many people in it. He preferred to stay at Arthur's place to play the piano and sleep on the
couch. He was producing a new act and needed a name for the
singer. He asked Phil. "John Train." Arthur loved it.

A couple of days later, Arthur and Phil were walking on Fourteenth Street, when Phil turned and said, "Don't use that name I
gave you. I want it for myself."

His voice was shot. There was no way he could fulfill his commitment to Colby. He went to the club to explain why he had to cancel out. Colby was angry. He'd advertised the show and tickets had been selling well. The following night Phil returned to The Other End and started banging on the bar with his fists, demanding something to drink. Colby had him thrown out, telling him he could always come back for something to eat but could never drink in the club again.

Phil wanted Colonel Parker to manage him. He'd gotten in touch with the Colonel's office and they told him Parker wasn't interested. So Phil chose Colonel Sanders, of fried-chicken fame, instead. Sanders was actually a figurehead of the Heublein Corporation, which had bought him out and retained his image for advertising purposes. Phil wrote a letter to the Heublein Corporation's headquarters in Kentucky, outlining his concept for Barricade Inc., a huge multimedia corporation producing movies, record albums, and new acts, as well as taking over the management of the careers of Bob Dylan and John Train. He invited them to check out his credibility with A&M Records, and to contact him when they were ready to begin serious negotiations. Phil told Arthur he was confident Heublein and the Colonel would be more than eager to get involved with Barricade. Arthur said nothing, convinced Phil was just playing out one more fantasy.

Around this time, Arthur was contacted by Peter Kun, a Peruvian music promoter, who was in the United States looking for an enterprise which would focus the eyes of the world on the mountains of his homeland. He'd heard about the benefit for Chile that Arthur had helped to produce, and was anxious to talk with those who'd made it happen. As they talked, Phil dropped by. Arthur introduced Kun, and immediately Phil took over. He thought it was a great idea to do a concert in Peru like the one he'd done at the Felt Forum for Chile.

In a couple of hours Phil had the whole thing mapped out. It would be a statement to all artists in the Americas, in the world, for unity over and above government policy. It would be a free concert. There would be a film made of it, a record album, and various other related enterprises, with all proceeds going into a fund, in Lima, to create an international art center.

The more Phil learned about Peru, the more excited he became. The government there was unique, the antithesis to Chile's. Whereas General Pinochet had led a right-wing military coup, General Velasco of Peru had led a military uprising which had replaced the existing "democratic" government with a left-wing military dictatorship. The military had immediately moved to create a socialist society by expropriating large international land holdings. Sugar and mining co-operatives were set up. Velasco wanted to incorporate Peru's Indian population into the mainstream of political and social life. Lima, the urban center of Peru, was much like any other large Latin-American city. Yet the Indians who lived in the nearby mountains were totally removed from the twentieth century, isolated from the rest of Peru by their language. Quechua hadn't been recognized by the government for hundreds of years. Among the first official acts of the Velasco government was its legalization. Phil saw Peru as being on the verge of what Chile might have been had Allende survived. It seemed the perfect place to revive the spirit of the Chile concert.

Phil told Arthur and Kun there would be no problem getting Bob Dylan for the show, that he could also get Jane Fonda and Joan Baez.

Kun went back to Lima. Arthur was in touch with him on a regular basis, and, in July, flew to Peru to meet with the Intellectual Committee, including General Segura, the Minister of Culture. Segura loved Arthur's idea of tying the concert in with the anniversary of the birth of Tupac Amaru, a descendant of the last of the Incas, who'd led a rebellion in 1780 that had begun the move toward the liberation of Peru from Spanish rule. The goals of his revolution had been freedom from imperialist rule, and equality among the Indians.

Arthur was taken to the mountains and shown the proposed concert site—a natural Inca fortress 11,000 feet above sea level, a giant amphitheater able to hold 200,000 people. The Intellectual Committee agreed to underwrite the cost of producing the concert by providing approximately a quarter of a million dollars in local currency, two DC-10s, and a cargo plane. All those connected with the concert would fly into the country enjoying total diplomatic immunity. No one would be searched. Special trains and planes would be provided to get the people up the mountain for

the concert. Arthur couldn't wait to get back to Phil, to let him
know all that was happening.

When Arthur returned to New York, the last week in July, Phil
was all but unrecognizable. He'd become completely undone. At
first he'd tried to stay in the Prince Street apartment, not talking
to anybody, not doing anything except drinking and listening to
the radio. One night, while listening to WBAI, he heard what
sounded to him like a young Bobby Dylan. Only it wasn't Dylan
at all, but somebody by the name of Sammy Walker. Phil threw
on his peacoat and hopped into a cab.

Bob Fass, a friend of Phil's from the old days, and host of the
all-night WBAI radio show, introduced him to Walker. Phil was
astonished. Walker not only sounded like Bob Dylan, he looked
like him—his face young and sweet, his eyes deep-set and fragile.
"You're Barricade's first new act," Train said to Walker.

The next day Train called Sis Cunningham at Broadside Records offices. He told her he wanted to produce an album.

"Great," Sis said. "How many songs have you written for it?"

"None," Train said. "But Sammy Walker has dozens."

"Who?"

"Sammy Walker, who's young and shy and greater than Phil
Ochs, greater even than Bobby Dylan. Will you let me produce
the album?"

"If he's as good as you say he is, Phil."

"Train, not Phil."

The album was recorded the third week of June at The Basement Recording Studio. Walker was nervous, chain-smoking.
Train was drunk and raving, telling everybody what to do, where
to sit, how to act. Each time Walker began a song, Train stopped
him, telling him he was singing too fast, or too slow. Or he
was standing too far from the microphone, or too close. He became unbearable. In order to salvage the recording session, Train
had to be thrown out.

There were very few clubs left in the Village where Phil's be-
havior was tolerated. One place he was always welcome, no matter what, was Gerde's. He'd arrive early in the afternoon while
Mike was mopping the floor or maybe stocking the bar. He'd sit in

the corner, drinking. Mike Porco would ask him how he felt, if there was anything he needed. "You name it, Phil."

"Train. How about a gig?"

"I thought you were going to do a week at The Other End," Porco said.

"I changed my mind. I've decided to give up performing. In fact, my next performance will be my last." Train stood and waved his right hand, as if gesturing toward a great expanse. "The Farewell Performance of Phil Ochs. We'll hold it right here at Gerde's, where it all began."

Walker was Barricade's first step; Che its second. Train had been searching for the right location to open a bar when he heard the Soho Darts Bar on Broome Street was for sale. He made the owner an offer. Bob Bonick was actually looking for someone to invest in the place, to buy a piece of it, help fix it up and make a go of it with him.

"How much do you want?" Train asked.

"Thirty thousand," Bonick answered. "Seven thousand up front, the balance by August first. No matter what, the seven thousand is nonrefundable."

"It's a deal," Train said. "Here's my brother Michael's telephone number in California. Call him and tell him I said to send you the seven grand."

That night Bonick called Michael.

"Okay," Michael said. "I'm going to tell you up front. In Phil's current financial state he can't come up with that amount of cash. He doesn't have it. The most he can come up with is maybe twenty thousand. Maybe. As it stands now, he probably won't be able to make that."

The next day, Bonick told Phil what Michael said. Train was furious. "I'll kill him. I'll blow his brains out with a magnum .45 like the one Clint Eastwood uses." He was desperate to raise the first seven thousand to cement the deal. He would get the rest from Michael later. He went to everybody he knew to raise the money. One friend, who'd bailed him out with money in the past, wrote a check for the entire seven thousand.

Then Arthur returned. Train filled him in on Sammy Walker, the Farewell Concert, and the new bar.

"I'm going to call it 'Che.' It's going to be a place where artists can hang out. It's going to open the morning after The Farewell Performance of Phil Ochs. After that, anyone who calls me Phil Ochs will get his head smashed in."

Arthur was very worried about Phil. He knew his friend needed help. He had to make sure Phil kept away from Peter Kun, due back in New York the following week. Phil was talking about challenging Pinochet to a duel, the kind of lunacy that could blow the whole Peru deal.

Train now insisted that Arthur arrange for Barricade, and not the government of Peru, to retain the rights to the record and film deals that were sure to be made from the concert. Arthur told Phil not to worry about the subsidiary deals, just to concentrate on getting himself together.

Train was having lunch at O'Henry's, with Claudio, telling about his latest Barricade project. He was going to produce a movie version of *Billy the Kid* better than all the other versions combined. Elvis Presley was set to play Pat Garrett; Bobby Dylan, Billy the Kid. "Now get this. The final scene has Presley gunning down Dylan in a fantastic shoot-out." With that, he ordered drinks for the table.

At the same time, Arthur was entertaining the independent committee which had formed, and was at the apartment to hand over a check for five thousand dollars—seed money for operating expenses. As they sipped drinks, the phone rang. Someone was calling to tell Arthur the government of Peru had just been overthrown.

Train's plans for the bar were extensive. The first thing he did was have the name changed officially to "Che." Train would be the bartender and the host. He had the jukebox filled with Frank Sinatra and Tony Bennett records. He planned a huge masquerade party for the opening night, inviting everyone to come as his favorite revolutionary. Food was to be free. Members of the Mafia would be allowed to drink on the house. A small stage was set up for anyone who wanted to get up and perform.

There was only one problem. Train hadn't paid Bonick the balance of the money.

"Don't worry," Train kept telling Bonick. "I'll get it." Before he did, they had a falling out over the jukebox. Train insisted it be played full-blast at all times. Bonick wanted it kept at a reasonable volume. They argued about it, and when Bonick refused to turn the volume up, Train, enraged, hurled a stool through the front window, sending glass flying everywhere.

The next day, Train called Michael and told him to hurry up and send Bonick the rest of the money.

"I told you," Michael said, "you haven't got that kind of money."

"Yes I do," Train said. "I did some checking on my own. Either you arrange to have the money sent to Bonick or I'll kidnap Sonny's children and hold them for ransom."

Michael hung up. He knew it was no use. There was no legal way he could prevent his brother from getting the money. He called Phil's accountants in New York and had them make out a check for the twenty-three thousand dollars, to be delivered to Bonick. It was nearly every cent Phil had left.

But it wasn't enough. Business had fallen way off. The next weekend the lights went out: there hadn't been enough money to pay the gas and electric bill. Everywhere he turned there were new problems. He either had to put more money into the failing business, or get out. He had to face it. Che was over.

In September a letter arrived for Phil at Arthur's apartment. Heublein was interested in Barricade. Arrangements were being made for a representative to fly to New York to inspect Barricade's physical setup, the one Phil had described in his letter. "No problem," Train told Arthur. "We'll just get a building for Barricade." Arthur pleaded with Phil to let the Heublein people come to the apartment. "Not only will we get a building, but we'll have the meeting filmed for posterity by Francois De Menil. In front of the future sight of the corporate headquarters of Barricade Inc."

He found a building on Sixth Avenue which he felt was perfect. It was an empty warehouse with enough space to build recording studios, movie theaters, and hold live concerts. He called the owner of the building and arranged for access the day the Heublein people would be in the city.

Train arrived drunk for the meeting, his greasy hair down in front of his shaded eyes, the tails of his filthy shirt hanging below his black leather motorcycle jacket. He wore shoes with no socks.

Already there were Francois and his film crew, Sammy Walker, a reporter and photographer from *People* magazine, friends Train had called to witness what he assured them would be an "historic" occasion, and Arthur, who stood nearby, arms folded, a grim look on his face.

Tony, the Heublein representative, pulled up in front of the building in a limousine. He'd come directly from the airport. Train introduced himself as Phil Ochs, for practical purposes, and welcomed Tony to New York. Tony didn't know what to make of Phil, or the film crew that was shooting him.

"Can you play basketball at all?" Train asked.

"I can't. I don't have my sneakers," Tony replied, chuckling corporately. Train was pointing to the courtyard across the street where a pick-up game was in progress. No one understood what he was talking about, why the sudden interest in basketball. Train had arrived earlier that day to make sure the building was open. The custodian told him no one was going to get inside while he was on duty; he wasn't going to be responsible. That is, unless fifty dollars was produced for "insurance against damages."

Train didn't have the fifty dollars. He'd walked the streets asking people for money. Desperate, he'd devised a fantastic scheme. He'd form a team, challenge the players across the street, win the game, pay off the janitor, and gain access.

"Play barefoot," Train suggested to Tony.

"What if we lose?" Tony asked, still trying to sound jovial.

"We can't lose," Train said.

"Look, I've got to make a couple of phone calls, Phil. I'll be right back." It was the last anyone ever saw of Tony.

It started to rain. Train stood, alone, in the downpour, as Francois packed his equipment and left with the others.

A few nights later, Train sat in a friend's room at the Chelsea Hotel. They'd both been drinking, when Train started talking about the death of Phil Ochs. His friend wanted to get it down on tape.

"Train does nothing for free. How much will you pay me?" He was offered a box of Cuban cigars. "Where's the microphone?" Train asked.

"On the first day of summer, 1975, Phil Ochs was murdered in the Chelsea Hotel by John Train, who is now speaking. I killed Phil Ochs. The reason I killed him was, he was some kind of genius but he drank too much and was a boring old fart. For the good of societies, public and secret, he needed to be gotten rid of. Although he had brilliant ideas, i.e. an evening with Salvador Allende and a couple of good songs like 'Crucifixion' and 'Changes,' he was no longer needed and useful. He was too embarrassing at parties . . .

"Everyone respects Phil Ochs no matter what he does, his name was valuable. He never once told a lie, always sang for free.

"So Train decided to kill Ochs, and he decided to kill him mercifully. He liked Phil Ochs. Everybody liked Phil Ochs, he was the most likable guy who ever lived. He never wanted to offend anybody, he wanted to attack society, he was so nice that nobody would want to kill him, which is how he survived the sixties. The crucial, specific songs were 'I Ain't Marching Anymore,' 'White Boots Marching in a Yellow Land,' 'The Marines Have Landed on the Shores of Santo Domingo'—all those songs that totally attacked 'truth' while Dylan in cowardly fashion hid behind images —after his third album.

"Okay. But Phil Ochs was an amateur, he never made a good record, so he could be safe to criticize for making bad records, so therefore don't play them on the radio. Phil Ochs was also smart, to make bad records purposefully so they could have their excuse and they wouldn't kill him. He knew if he ever became The Beatles they would kill him. Colby and company would be more than happy to put a slug through his head at that point. But they held off because he wasn't that dangerous. Now the war is over, so the real Phil Ochs can emerge safely without being killed. His name is Train. Train kills Ochs in the Chelsea Hotel. Coincidentally, there stands Bob Dylan. Ochs's enemy. Jealousy figure. Rival in poetry. Train was laying for Ochs in the bar, watching him come home every night. The second night, when Ochs was passed out in his living room, with a Bruce Lee shot, Train killed him, painlessly, one split second he was dead. Goodbye, Phil Ochs, and good riddance. Still around, though, for sale, from Train, if they want him. He can still appear in public and sing 'I Ain't Marching Anymore' and get paid for it. He will probably make fifty thousand dollars in the next couple of weeks just doing that. For cash value. Strictly. Train does nothing for nothing . . .

"The company is called Barricade. Barricade means protection against the bullshit world. Anybody who's got real talent is given all the money, girls, boys, and tools to work, so he won't be bored. Suicide pills are available also. And Bruce Lee is available. It's the best way to die. You go out in bliss and that's it.

"Train became Ochs's manager the last couple of weeks of his life. He set up a couple of deals. One was with Hassan the Assassin, who was the best backgammon player in the world, supposedly. So in comes Paul Colby and asks the dying Phil Ochs, 'Will you play my club?' Ochs, who didn't want to sing any more, who has no voice any more, says, 'Well, I'll play your club under one condition. If you can find anybody to beat me in backgammon three times in a row, I'll play your club for three days for free. However, if I win, I want three nights with women for free. And *you* pay for it.' Colby says, 'All right, you got a deal.' He goes to the phone and calls Hassan. Hassan agrees and sends Phil Ochs a message. 'I know your game. I understand your soul. I will destroy you.' The contract was signed, and we agreed to meet. At his place, his board, his dice. Phil Ochs and John Train playing the great strategy, bringing forty people in, Melvin Van Peebles, and beautiful women in costumes. At the stroke of midnight, forty people stormed into his place. Hassan was undisturbed, unimpressed. Three girls started to seduce him, showed their nipples while he was playing; it didn't mean a thing. The first game, Hassan beats him by one point. Nobody could have beat him, but Hassan beats him. At this point Ochs decides he's a real artist and it would be wrong to beat him. He eventually turns the board over and says, 'All right, you won. Now give me ten minutes.' During which he goes outside and starts to work on three girls he wants to fuck. He tells them to start taking their clothes off for the purpose of distracting Hassan. All three refuse. Ochs says his dying words: 'Women are full of shit. You say you're artists but you won't even show your nipples, even though you've shown them at parties I've seen you at. Here you are at this crucial moment in time and you're afraid to let Hassan see your nipples. So fuck you. You're still my girlfriends, but you're businesswomen, you're not artists.'

They all fluttered like butterflies. 'Oh, no, we're artists.' 'Well, if you're artists, take off your clothes. If you're not, shut up.'

"Ochs is now bored with the evening and wants Hassan to win. He turns the board over and says, 'You won again. Goodbye.' He goes downtown and gets drunk. He returns to the Chelsea. Train is watching, and waiting for the moment. Two days later, Train kills him.

"Two days later, Dylan arrives in the Chelsea Hotel unexpectedly. Just at the point where he's walking down the hall, Train opens the door and says, 'I just killed Ochs.' Train grabs Dylan by the collar and says, 'Listen, asshole, I can kill you as soon as look at you. You're the most boring man in the world, because you were Shakespeare at twenty-five, and now you're dogshit.' 'What about "Blood on the Tracks"?' 'Well, yes, that was very good, but you're still full of shit, plus I can beat you at backgammon.' At which point Dylan says, 'No, you can't. I'm the best in the world.' Train says, 'All right, let's make a deal. We'll go to a private room and make the following deal. The rematch. Hassan and Ochs, the same trip. This time Train will figure it out and destroy Hassan.' He calls Hassan and says he wants a rematch, only Hassan has to play Dylan. Hassan hesitates, and at that point Ochs knows he has him. Hassan wants to play Dylan three out of five. Hassan was through, for good. Hassan was not impressed by forty people, by the women, by Phil Ochs, but he was impressed by Bob Dylan, which means he's through.

"Now, Victor Jara was a friend of mine. He was twenty-seven years old and a friend of mine. He was the Pete Seeger of Chile. He was a Communist, he made a lot of records. He wrote songs and plays, and his wife was an English ballerina. He had a couple of kids. When I was in Chile he came up to me and said, 'Hey, you, you're the North American protest singer, right? Phil Ochs.' I said, 'Yeah. You're a Communist and I'm a socialist.' He said, 'Well, why don't you come with me and sing to the workers up in the copper mines?'

"Anyway, he's twenty-seven years old and looks like Victor Mature, and doesn't give a shit. The coup happens, and everyone expects Allende to be sent to the Bronx; no one expects it to be bloody. But Victor says, 'Wait a minute. I'm a Communist, I'm for the workers, I'm going to sing for them, and that's it.' He says,

'No safety, no wife, no children. Where's the action?' The action is the university, the most Communist place in Santiago. So he zooms right over there. His friends are saying, 'Victor, asshole, get out of here or they'll kill you, man.' He's a known Communist. Victor says, 'You don't understand. My role is to be here, so shut up. I'll sing.'

"So he sang, and inevitably the Army arrives. They drag him away after asking who he is, and he telling them he's Victor Jara. Jara. Hara. Horror . . . 'Come with us to the stadium.' Victor says, 'All right. Can I bring my guitar?' 'Sure, bring your guitar. We don't give a shit, man.'

"So he's there in the Santiago Stadium filled with thirty thousand people, and Colby, Kissinger, and Rockefeller had given orders to kill every Communist, like in Indonesia. In one week. Quick. The only one in town who's not afraid is Victor Jara. He believes in his music, he believes in the worker. Once in a while Pete Seeger accepts money. Once in a while Phil Ochs accepts money. Jara never accepts money. So there is the prison, at the stadium, Jara is singing this dumb song about boxes, and a general recognizes him, saying, 'You're the singer.' Victor Jara sunk. He knew at that point he was dead. And painfully dead. But he said, 'Yeah, I'm the singer, shaking with fear.' 'All right, go sing in the stadium, Victor, and we'll talk about it. Bring your guitar, Victor.' So he goes to sing in front of thirty thousand people, mostly soldiers and prisoners. Victor now knows he's going to die. So he prepares himself to die. The general is neurotic and crazy and he likes Victor, he even likes some of the songs, but he's going to kill him. It's 'The Outcasts of Poker Flat.' Trapped in the Santiago Stadium. So the general says, 'All right, Victor, sing a song.' Victor grabs the guitar and starts to sing a song. 'Victor, put your hands on the table.' I heard two stories, I don't know which one is true. One story I heard was, they took an axe and cut off both his hands; another was, they grabbed his fingers and broke them. I hope they took an axe because it was quicker. Harry's cringing a little bit in the background. At this point Victor fell to the floor of the stadium. They picked him up and said, 'Sing, Victor, sing.' With the blood pouring out of his hands, Victor chose to stand up, wobbly, and sang. The other prisoners cheered. At this point they sprayed the stands with machine-gun fire to kill off a few. Who knows? So the general says, 'All right, let's cut off his tongue, knock out his teeth, and cut off his balls and see what he sounds like.' The details keep getting mixed up. 'Now, asshole, now you sing.' He was really dying, or he was dead. At the point of death, he stood up. He was serious, he stood up and said nothing, but sang again, with no tongue and no teeth, just noises. At which point they took out a .45 and killed him. They threw his body with the other corpses. Just another dead body. His wife found him a week later. When that happened I said, 'All right, that's the end of Phil Ochs.' "

Train was having trouble with the law. He was driving a car one night without a license or registration. It was four in the morning. He'd been drinking heavily when he lost control of the wheel and smashed into several parked cars, coming to a bloody halt on Houston Street. He was immediately picked up by a couple of officers from New York's tough ninth precinct.

Train's face was covered with blood. The police took him to a hospital, where he became violent and tried to punch a few of them out.

Six o'clock the next morning he was allowed to make a phone call. He dialed Deni's number. She picked up the receiver while still in a sleepy fog and at first didn't recognize the voice on the other end shouting, "Police brutality . . . police brutality . . ."

Deni arrived at the hospital while Train was in the process of being booked for assaulting an officer, several doctors, and a couple of nurses. He was due in court later that day. Deni called Michael in Los Angeles to ask what she should do.

"Don't do anything," Michael said. "If they keep him locked up they might be able to get him the help he needs."

Train appeared and managed to get released. He'd sobered up while awaiting his hearing. He told the judge he'd been having personal problems and would arrange to pay all damages. After a severe lecture, the case was dismissed.

Deni was waiting for him outside the courtroom. "Boy, Deni, I had the best damn time in my life. I met the greatest bunch of people. I also hired a couple of new guys to be my bodyguards."

Train hired a limousine to get around. The judge had warned
him never to drive a car in New York again without a license,
proper registration, and insurance. After several days, the driver
demanded that, before he took Phil another block, the bill be
paid. Train was insulted and refused, saying the bill would be paid
by Barricade. The driver called the police over his CB. A patrol
car pulled up alongside the limo. The officer and the driver talked
things over. The policeman then asked Phil to get out of the car.
"Look, pal, why don't you just pay the bill?" Train became abu-
sive and the cop threatened to arrest him. "Call my lawyer, call
my lawyer," Train began shouting. The cop asked Phil who his
lawyer was. "Ramsey Clark."

"Okay, come on, let's go . . ."

"Here's his telephone number. Call him." The cop went to a
phone booth and dialed the number.

Ramsey Clark was entertaining guests in his apartment when
the phone rang. He picked it up and listened as the policeman
asked about his "client," Phil Ochs. Clark advised the officer that
it was against the law to arrest Phil, because there was no longer
a debtor's prison in the state of New York. "Have the driver bring
him to my apartment and I'll pay the bill," Clark said.

Michael contacted all of Phil's friends. Something had to be
done before Phil got into really serious trouble. Michael had
looked into the possibility of having Phil committed, but unless he
was arrested for a serious criminal offense, it was almost impossible. Michael asked everyone he spoke to not to bail Phil out of jail
the next time he was arrested.

Phil had no place to stay. He couldn't go to Arthur's any more,
there were too many distractions. He called Jean Ray in Los Angeles to ask if he could use her old apartment on Thompson Street.
She couldn't say no to him.

There were problems right away. Train would come home late
at night, drunk, unable to open the locked vestibule door. At first
he began to ring some bells, but after the neighbors complained,
he simply broke the door down whenever he wanted to get in. If
he didn't have the key to the apartment, he would bust that one
open also.

Newspapers, dirty clothes, and garbage piled up. The only thing of value Train owned was a Sony Portapak videotape machine, which he'd bought for cash the day after The Farewell Performance of Phil Ochs. Video was his new passion. The Portapak replaced the guitar someone had stolen. He didn't care about that any more. All that he had in the world that mattered was that Sony. He loved it so much he put it next to him in bed at night.

Sleeping was out of the question. As soon as he'd hit the pillow the itching would begin. He would scratch himself to a bloody pulp, tossing and turning until dawn, sometimes getting so frustrated he'd get up and destroy the room—throwing chairs, kicking the kitchen table, smashing his fists against the wall.

The neighbors asked the landlord to have him removed from the premises. Jean was contacted and warned that unless Phil left she would be evicted. Jean called Phil and asked him to please leave the apartment before she lost it. This went on for several weeks, Train always having some excuse why he couldn't leave that day, but promising to leave the next.

Finally, Jean contacted Wendy Winsted, a girlfriend living in New York, and asked her to have the locks changed. Wendy called the apartment and, when she got no answer, went over to see what was going on.

Wendy was nauseated by the place. It was filthy, crawling with roaches. She decided to do Phil a favor and clean the place up. She noticed the Portapak in the corner and, afraid it would be stolen from the apartment (the door had no lock at all since Phil had broken it), took it to her apartment for safekeeping.

When Phil came home later, he panicked. He was sure someone had stolen his Sony. He started banging on the doors of his neighbors, trying to find out if anyone had seen the thief. He vowed to kill him.

He went back to the apartment. While he was having a drink, the phone rang. It was Wendy. She explained she had his machine. Train told her she'd better get the Portapak in the apartment in twenty minutes or she was a dead woman.

A few minutes later, Wendy knocked on the door. Train let her in. She handed him his machine, which he carefully put on his bed. Wendy explained she was a friend of Jean's, and was supposed to change the locks. He then turned to her and said, "Don't take

care of me, bitch. I'll take care of myself. Don't try to take care
of me, or I'll knock your teeth down your throat."

Wendy was scared. When she got home she called Jean, who
begged her to see to it that the locks were changed. Jean then
called Michael, who repeated his instructions. If Phil is arrested,
don't bail him out.

The next day, after calling to make sure Phil was out, Wendy
came over to wait for the locksmith. He came, and she paid him
for his work. She was about to leave when there was a knock on
the door. "If you don't open up by the time I count to three, I'm
going to bust it down. One . . . two . . . three . . ." Train broke
in, John Wayne style. Wendy reached for the phone to call the
police, but Train pulled it from her, ripping it out of the wall.
There was fire in his eyes. He started hitting Wendy with the
receiver. She tried to escape but she couldn't get by him. He picked
her up and threw her against the refrigerator. She finally made
it to the door, screaming as she fled down the stairs and into the
street, Train in hot pursuit. She finally lost him after ducking
into an alley.

Train gave up looking for her and headed back to the apartment. He was still there when she returned with the police. As they
put handcuffs on him he kept asking them to call his lawyer, Ramsey Clark.

Wendy called Jean to tell her what had happened. Jean called
Michael.

A hearing was set. Phil appeared before the judge and seemed
perfectly normal. He was sober, clean, soft-spoken. Once again he
was set free.

Jean lost the apartment.

Train decided he needed weapons to protect himself. He began
carrying hammers, lead pipes, knives. He went to Sam Hood's
house to challenge him to a fight to the death. Hood tried to reason
with him, but when Train wouldn't back down and went for
Hood, Sam threw him out of the house. It was the last time he
ever saw Phil Ochs.

Van Ronk barred him from his apartment, telling him he wasn't
welcome there any more. He was afraid of this Phil Ochs.

Train went to Arthur's apartment carrying a Bowie knife with a blade a foot long. Arthur was one of the few people Train felt he could still trust. He relaxed a bit and began playing records. The knife slipped out of his belt onto the sofa. Arthur hid it. When it was time for Train to leave, he turned and asked where his knife was. Arthur said he didn't remember seeing it. Train went into a rage, running out of the house, desperately retracing his steps. He called Arthur the next day to see if he'd found the knife. He was in tears over having lost it.

Train was sitting at Gerde's bar. He asked Porco for a drink. Orange juice with rum. Porco was used to pouring with a light hand for Phil. This time Train watched closely as Mike made the drink. When Porco put it in front of him, Train threw it over on its side. He threatened Porco and started banging the hammer on the bar. Porco came around and took Phil by the arm and threw him out. Train stood outside by the window looking menacingly in at Porco. Then, after disappearing for a few moments, Phil popped his head through the front door, smiling softly. Porco smiled back. Phil stepped inside. He stood, his arms at his sides, his shirt hanging out of his pants, his face very tired. Porco threw his arms around him, patting him on the head. Phil wept gently on his shoulder.

A close friend: "He was experiencing a kind of terror. He was acting the way he'd learned to react against fear, to push against it. When you lose control you try to associate with control forms, which is why Phil talked about the Mafia so much. When you think you're crazy you go into a real panic state, you make associations which seem crazy to others. John Train was an invented shield of armor, a character necessary to prevent the panicking Phil Ochs from danger. Of course, all the time he was doing it he knew he wasn't Train, which was part of the real fear."

Train would do anything to keep from being alone. Even sing. Phil went back to the Prince Street apartment to see Larry Sloman. While there, Phil started complaining again about not being able to write in his present state of mind. "Write about that," Sloman suggested.

Somewhere in Train's head the connection was made. All those years he was Phil Ochs writing about the King of Cowboys. Now it would be John Train's turn to write about Phil Ochs. At Sloman's one evening, the shadow of Phil's soul performed the new songs. They were episodic tunes linked by the imposing identity of the cosmic anti-hero "John Butler Train."

"The Ballad of John Train":

> *Phil Ochs checked in to the Chelsea Hotel,*
> *There was blood on his clothes, they were dirty.*
> *I could see by his face he was not feeling well,*
> *He'd been to one too many parties.*
> *He walked in the lobby a picture of doom,*
> *It was plain to see he'd been a-drinkin'.*
> *I had to follow him up to his room,*
> *To find out what he was thinkin'.*
> *"Train, Train, Train,"*
> *From the outlaw in his brain.*
> *But he's still the same refrain*
>
> *He walked in his room and he fell on the floor,*
> *Hangin' in his hangover.*
> *Now the act from the stage he plays on the street,*
> *Handing out piles of money.*
> *His audience now is the bums that he meets,*
> *Is he a phony or funny?*

A fantasy about the adventure of the bar Che:

> *There was a bar in the Village,*
> *Pirates go along the plank,*
> *Many a robber was seen in there,*
> *After a day at the bank.*
> *And the cops come in for a nightcap,*
> *No one ends up in the jail,*
> *Here everyone is equal.*
> *Che, Che,*
> *Where the revolution is released,*
> *In the belly of the beast . . .*

"Street Actor":

> *Lady can you spare that dog*
> *Maybe you can spare your leash*

> *And if you will*
> *I'll spare mine . . .*

"Give Me a Break":

> *I walked out on Prince Street,*
> *Somebody said that I'm dead,*
> *Thought that he was kiddin'.*
> *Then a rock flew at my head,*
> *Fifteen guys came running at me,*
> *I ran the other way,*
> *Never knew I could run so fast.*
> *Jesus Christ on the cross,*
> *Joan of Arc at the stake,*
> *I made it to Sixth Avenue,*
> *Come on, God, give me a break . . .*

John Train remembering Phil Ochs in "I Was Born Before":

> *I was born by the Rio Grande*
> *Between Texas and Mexico*
> *Sometimes it seems in the dreams of the night*
> *That I've been born before . . .*

Train had written liner notes for the projected album:

> Threw the Pope out of the Vatican onto the streets
> Fired all the owners, attacked Wall Street
> Became the reincarnation of Joey Gallo, Jesus,
> Audie Murphy, Charles Manson, John and Robert
> Kennedy, Che, Appointment with Fidel Castro for
> Armed revolution . . .
> John stands for Kennedy, Butler stands for Yeats
> Train stands for hobos at the missed silver gates.
> They won't understand what I've done
> They've even taken away my gun
> I must be public enemy number one
>
> I was the reincarnation of Cornfield
> The South won the Civil War
> Who can you trust when the Lord is flush
> And Jesus is reaching for his gun
> God is a has-been
> He doesn't have it anymore
> The Holy Ghost is out to lunch
> I've seen his act before

I may not look like much
But I own the world
And I have it all my way
Now I'm an actor on the streets
And I do it for no pay
My father was a camera
My mother was a screen
I'm a child of the movies.

Jerry Rubin finally convinced Phil to have himself committed. Rubin arranged for Phil to check into Gracie Square Hospital.

Phil was petrified of doctors, especially psychiatrists. He was frightened of confinement, of being unable to move. He tried to be totally co-operative when he was admitted. After having a shower and getting a complete physical checkup, he was instructed to report for a group therapy session being held that evening.

He showed up for the meeting wearing a long white hospital gown. He sat down in one of the chairs and waited for the others. Soon the room was filled and they began. He was shocked—the meeting was being conducted in Spanish. Train excused himself to go to the bathroom. He walked out the front door of the hospital, still wearing his gown. He walked all the way to Arthur's house, where he stopped to get some clothes. He would listen to nobody now. He put on a pair of dungarees and left. He fell asleep in the boiler room of the Chelsea Hotel.

He wanted to return to Los Angeles. He asked Sonny to take him to the airport. When they passed Shea Stadium, he insisted Sonny pull into the parking lot. Rubin was there. He wanted to say goodbye. "Phil," Sonny asked, "how are you going to find Jerry in the middle of fifty thousand people?"

"I'll find him."

He found him. Once more Rubin tried to get Phil to commit himself. This time, though, Train was in charge. He'd only come to say farewell.

Weston handled Train easily, without causing a scene. When Train showed up at the door with a huge machete stuck into his belt, Weston simply told him all weapons had to be checked at the front door. Dodge City stuff. Inside, Train behaved. Except for one time.

He'd come to see Van Morrison. He loved Morrison's "Madame George," the song with the longest fade-out in rock-and-roll history (*say goodbye, goodbye, goodbye . . .*). Train sat quietly at a table in the back. Morrison sang every song he knew except "Madame George." Finally, Phil stood up and asked him to sing it. Morrison refused. Phil got so angry he began to knock things over. He went into the men's room and gripped the porcelain sink with both hands. Furiously, he ripped it out of the wall. He wanted to hear that goddamn song.

Once again, Michael got in touch with Phil's friends. He was sick. He needed help. If he were busted, let him stay in jail, for his own good.

Sure enough, Phil was arrested one night for driving without a license, being intoxicated, insulting an officer, and carrying a semi-automatic pistol.

The next morning Phil started calling his friends, asking them, one by one, to bail him out. Nobody would help him. In the meantime, Michael's lawyer talked with the judge, and reported that there was little chance of being able to detain Phil longer than two or three days for observation. When he appeared before the judge the next day, Phil looked perfectly normal, even clean, almost neat. He told the judge he was famous, that he knew Frank Sinatra. The judge was a kindly old white-haired fellow used to having celebrities before him many times. Phil then called upon a character witness who offered to put up bail. It was a fellow from A&M Publishing who was a Phil Ochs fan. Phil had called him after trying to think of someone who would bail him out, someone Michael wouldn't have thought of.

The judge released him, telling him in effect to be a good boy.

Train called Michael and told him he was going to kill him for what he'd done. He then paid a visit to all those who'd refused to bail him out. No one would admit that Michael had given specific instructions not to help. There was no use trying to reason with Phil. Everyone knew he needed little in the way of an excuse to violently attack Michael.

So they lied to him. He knew they were lying and felt betrayed, down the line. One of the few who told him the truth was Lee Housekeeper.

He banged on Housekeeper's front door. Lee opened it and asked him in for a beer. Train stood near the door. He asked Housekeeper if he'd tried to keep him in jail. Housekeeper said yes, absolutely. Train looked Housekeeper straight in the eye. "I want you to know that I'll never talk to you again, but thanks for being honest with me."

It was the last time Housekeeper ever saw or spoke to Phil Ochs.

Train went to Andy's apartment. He knocked on the front door. Andy wouldn't answer. "I know you're in there, Wickham. Now, open this door." Wickham opened it and stood in the way of Train coming in.

"I don't want to see you like this. Don't give me this Train bullshit, because I don't buy it. Not for a second. Don't come back until you know how to behave." He closed the door in Phil's face. Train left the building.

He turned up a few nights later at a private party for Three Dog Night. Michael was there, so was Doug Weston. Both tried to talk to Phil, but he refused to speak with either one of them. He left the party later that night, drunk. It was the last time Michael or Weston ever saw him.

Somehow, Train managed to acquire a couple of trucks. He started emptying out his apartment. He was never coming back to Los Angeles. He went to The Troubadour and asked Marty, one of the bartenders, if he'd drive a truck to New York for him. He told Marty a whole fleet of trucks were going to arrive in New York on a secret mission. Come closer. They were being used for the purpose of smuggling Cuban exiles into the country. He hinted to Marty he was really a CIA agent and was recruiting for the government. Marty had never been to New York and said sure, he'd drive a truck there.

The next day Marty drove the large two-tonner out of L.A. on his way to the Apple.

He ran out of gas somewhere east of Tucson and had to abandon the truck in a garage. Phil never recovered any of his belongings.

He went to Peter and Betsy Asher's house in Beverly Hills to ask for money. He was desperate. He stood there, wrinkled and filthy. Betsy gave him a hundred dollars. He demanded more, but they told him they never kept much cash around the house.

He arrived at Henske's a few days later at seven in the morning, coated with vomit. Henske's husband was on the road, which was fortunate because, instead of ringing the doorbell, Train threw rocks at the windows. He was dressed in the gold suit, his last bit of clothing. "Phil, you can't wear that suit, it's full of vomit, it smells," Henske said after she let him in. She ordered him to take a bath. While he was soaking in the tub, she washed out the suit. When he came out of the bathroom he was wearing Henske's big fluffy pink bathrobe. He asked if he could live at her house. She said no, she was sorry, but her husband wouldn't understand. He proposed marriage to her, and she gently refused. She asked where he'd been.

"I went to see Howard Hughes in Las Vegas." He told her a tale about his trying to see Howard Hughes, and of being stopped at the entrance to the Sands Hotel by Hughes's personal bodyguards. He told her he'd almost made it before they roughed him up and had him arrested. He outsmarted them while he was in prison, though. Hughes came to see him, in a vision, and they talked for a long time. Robert Kennedy also floated down and the three of them just had a great time in jail. Henske studied his face.

"Phil, that really didn't happen."

"I know. It's a metaphor."

Train started making lists:

Shellfish toxin
Fort Dietrich
Apr. 25
All past activities
Cobra venom
Chantilly race track
Baroness Guy de Rothschild

The Dutchess [*sic*] of Bedford
The Duke of D'Orleans [*sic*]
Alexis Lichine
Possible agency use
Concealed in a silver dollar
De Witt Clinton Park
Wollman Skating Rink
Statue of Liberty Boat
New York Cornell Hospital
Roosevelt Island
Ward's Island Park

He actually believed he was a member of the CIA. Some of his friends began to wonder. How had the entire staff of the FREEP been discovered working on the CIA-Patty Hearst story? What was Phil Ochs doing on that beach in Tanzania anyway? Could it be? It was a dismal reflection of the way a lot of his friends saw him. Or failed to see him at all.

Train made plans for putting on "The Greatest Show on Earth for the Greatest City on Earth—Save New York City." It was to star Frank Sinatra, Barbra Streisand, Bob Dylan, Carole King, Neil Diamond, and John Denver. It was to be held at Shea Stadium. Rotating on alternate days were to be Stevie Wonder, Simon and Garfunkel, Ella Fitzgerald, The New York Philharmonic with Leonard Bernstein, The New York City Ballet, Ethel Merman, Bette Midler, Tito Puente, Liza Minnelli, Bob Hope, Bill Cosby, Arthur Rubinstein, Joe Namath, Sammy Davis, Jr., Beverly Sills, Zero Mostel, Herbie Hancock, George Jessel, John Lennon, Woody Allen, Maxine Lewis, John and Bonnie Raitt, Harry Chapin, and Al Green. It was to be televised on CBS, and it was to include twenty minutes from every ethnic group in the city. The event was to last three days. The price of a front-row seat was to be the purchase of a one-thousand-dollar city bond. General admission was to be five dollars.

Train wanted Elliott Mintz's help. He'd interviewed every rock star at one time or another, including John Lennon. Train showed up at Elliott's house with the machete in his belt.

He hadn't eaten in days and devoured whatever was in the refrigerator, mostly Ritz crackers and tuna fish. Then he moved to the tequila. He said he was hiding in Los Angeles because the Mafia in New York was looking for him. They had physically threatened him. That was the reason for the machete. "Phil," Elliott said gently, "the only way you need to defend yourself is with a guitar."

"You think so," Train said, and pulled the blade. He held the knife two inches from Elliott's nose. Mintz looked into Phil's eyes, searching for his friend. Finally, he asked, softly, "Is there something you'd like to hear on the stereo?"

"No," Phil said, withdrawing. "Put on whatever you'd like."

He was starting to come down from Train when he left Los Angeles. He called Alice and told her he was coming to Mill Valley for the weekend, on his way to New York.

It was October. They hadn't spoken in over a year. Alice opened the door and was shocked by the sight of the bloated stranger. He came in and collapsed, exhausted, in a chair. After a drink, he began talking rapidly. "Okay, I have a new name now," he said. "I have no family, they tried to commit me," he continued. "They're all traitors. I hate them all. You and Meegan are the only family I have. Alice, I want you to make a list of all the people that fucked you over during the last couple of years, because I have connections now. I can get them taken care of." She asked him what he meant, and he said he knew people in the Mafia.

Later, he sent Alice out to get some more liquor. Alice took Meegan with her. As they walked to the store, Meegan grabbed Alice's hand and jumped up and down. "Daddy cares about us!"

They went to the flea market. He asked Alice if she had any weapons, any guns, because his guns had been taken away in Los Angeles. She suggested he might be able to get something at the market.

He was carrying a notebook around with him. Inside were a couple of dollars, all the money he had left. A couple of bums walked by and he gave them each a dollar. They were, after all, he told Alice, his comrades.

Phil bought Meegan ten volumes of the Encyclopaedia Britannica. That night they read from it together.

Sunday night, he and Alice made love while Meegan slept in the next room. They were almost like a real family.

The next day he left forever.

XIV

> *The troubadour comes from the country,*
> *Falls by the factory,*
> *Sliding on simple strings.*
> *Armed with his anger,*
> *He sings of the danger,*
> *He senses a stranger,*
> *Is in the wings.*
> *But the fledgling has learned to fly,*
> *All the innocence leaves his eye,*
> *Echoes explode, rolled from the road—*
> *The melody dies.*
>
> Phil Ochs, "The Floods of Florence"

It was November. The city was turning colder. Phil Ochs performed one more time at Folk City. Mrs. Porco had arranged a surprise party for Mike and invited all his friends.

The Rolling Thunder Review had come together. A year and a half after the Chile concert, Dylan had the tour he and Phil had talked about doing.

Dylan showed up the night of Porco's party with a film crew to shoot sequences for what would eventually become part of his film *Renaldo and Clara*.

Phil was drunk early, wandering around, a glass of wine in his hand, a soft smile on his face. At one point, someone said hello to him. Although he recognized the voice, he couldn't remember who it belonged to. It was Wendy Winsted. He was about to ask her how she was, when Loudon Wainwright passed between them. Phil looked again, but she was gone.

Dylan and Baez started the entertainment off by doing a set together. When Dylan came off the stage, Phil took his white hat. Dylan went to Bobby Neuwirth a few minutes later and said, "Hey, we got to get that hat back."

It was four in the morning. Phil was still wearing the white hat when he got on stage to perform. He did a medley of old songs, then segued into "The Blue and the Gray," a Civil War song about two brothers, one from the North, one from the South. Phil sang the song to Dylan. He'd always felt the song described their relationship.

He followed with "Jimmy Brown the Newsboy," and then a moving, hushed "Too Many Martyrs," a song he hadn't sung in years. Everyone in the club was standing. Dylan was on his feet. "I haven't heard those songs for so long . . . this is fantastic . . ." He was still worried about getting his hat back. He instructed David Blue to stand at one side of the stage, Bobby Neuwirth at the other. Whoever was closer to Phil when he came off the stage was to grab the hat.

As Phil was about to sing one more song, he saw Dylan walking out of the room, and thought he was leaving. "No . . . don't go, Bobby . . ." Phil said from the stage.

"I'm not going anywhere, Phil. Just getting a drink."

"Why don't you come up and sing with me?" Dylan said no. So Phil sang one of Dylan's songs. After which he left the stage. On the way, David Blue plucked the hat from Phil's head and returned it to Dylan.

Phil and Dylan met several times after that night to discuss whether or not Phil should come along on the Rolling Thunder tour. They finally agreed it wouldn't be in the best interests of either one. When Dylan came to Madison Square Garden with the Review in December 1975, for the "Benefit for Hurricane Carter," Phil was there. In the fourth row.

He had no money. He would go to Folk City and Mike Porco would give him five or ten dollars. Porco offered Phil gigs, but Phil wouldn't perform any more, it was too painful. "Phil, why

Guitarist and arranger Steve Cropper, John Prine, and Phil at Jose Feliciano's house, Los Angeles, Easter Sunday, 1975, about one month before the "backgammon affair" (*Photo by Lenny Berman*)

The rhythm of revolution (*Courtesy of A&M Records*)

THE WAR IS OVER!

A CELEBRATION
SHEEP MEADOW
CENTRAL PARK
12:30 P.M. MAY 11, 1975

(Courtesy Cora Weiss)

After singing "There but for Fortune" with Baez at the 1975 "War Is Over" rally in Central Park (*Courtesy of the Phil Ochs estate*)

Later that day, with Sonny, Michael, David, and Gertrude (*Courtesy of the Phil Ochs estate*)

John Train with (from left to right) "Tony," Sammy Walker, Francois
(with camera), a reporter from *People* magazine, a friend, and Arthur
Gorson (with arms crossed) (*Julia Fahey*)

The last picture taken of Phil before he died—a few moments after he had performed for Sonny's friends at her home in Far Rockaway (*Sonia Tanzman*)

PHIL OCHS 1940-1976

ROBB

(*Courtesy of Ron Cobb*)

don't you listen to me. Go and get some sleep. You don't look good."

"How am I going to sleep," Phil asked, "if I have no place to go?"

"Are you tired?"

"Yes. Very tired. I want to go to sleep."

Porco made arrangements with one of the local transient hotels for Phil to have a room. He went there to sleep, but there was trouble. He demanded a room with a radio and television. When they refused to give him one, he started to scream uncontrollably, beating his fists against the wall.

He showed up at Jay Levin's apartment early in January. Levin had left Prince Street and moved to a place further uptown. He told Phil he could stay for as long as he wanted, giving him a set of keys and trying his best to leave him alone. Phil watched television all the time. Jay had just bought a new stereo, but Phil never wanted to listen to music.

Finally, on a black-and-white afternoon in January, Phil knocked on Sonny's door in Far Rockaway. She was surprised to see him. "Can I stay for a few days?"

"Of course you can, Phil. Come in."

Sonny was living in the house next to the one they'd all grown up in. He was almost home.

The days rolled into nights, the nights into days. Phil stopped drinking. He played cards with Sonny's two boys—David, fourteen, and Jonathan, eleven. They'd play at the kitchen table for hours.

David was thrilled to have Uncle Phil in the house. He followed him everywhere, became Phil's constant companion. Phil would flip comments over to David, who would lob something appropriate back over the net.

David and Jonathan were into an adolescent competition trip with a lot of back-and-forth bickering. Sometimes their verbal duels became too much for Sonny, who would explode, screaming for them to stop it already. Phil, involved with his hand, would say nothing. Once or twice it got so bad he picked himself up from his chair without saying anything, left the house, walked up and down the block, and finally back inside to continue dealing.

When he'd heard from Michael that John Train was finished, Andy Wickham called Phil. They talked for a long time, each glad to hear the other's voice. Wickham started calling regularly; the calls became an important part of Phil's routine. In March, Wickham arranged to come to New York for a few days. He would stay in the guest room.

It was like the old days. They visited a couple of neighborhood bars, and went to a couple of Mandarin roach palaces. Andy had a Master Charge credit card and told Phil they could do anything they wanted to. At one of the local beer joints they discovered, by talking to the next guy at the bar, that Walter Seeley, one of Wickham's favorite fighters, lived nearby. Phil and Andy decided to try to find the elderly boxer. They hit bar after bar until they found someone who knew where the ex-pugilist lived.

Andy knocked on Seeley's door. His wife answered and invited the two of them in. Before long, Seeley appeared in a silk bathrobe and bedroom slippers. They all had a drink and spent the better part of that night reminiscing about his days in the ring, Seeley recalling the finer moments of his career, when he was in his prime.

When they left the house, Phil was animated. Andy smiled and patted Phil on the back. They took a walk on the Rockaway boardwalk at dawn. Andy asked Phil to come back to Los Angeles with him for a while. Phil told him he would think about it.

Michael called Phil every week to find out how he was doing. Phil complained about having no money. "No problem," Michael said. "All you have to do is go back on the road, Phil. I can set up a tour in a month."

"It's not that easy."

"Yes, it is. Even if the show was mediocre, even if you couldn't sing at all, your fans would still be there. You would still be valid. It's what you stand for that's important."

"It's not that, Michael. I just don't have the confidence any more."

Phil apologized for blowing all the money during the "Che" episode. Michael told him he'd managed to "hide" a thousand dollars from him, for Meegan. "Is that all you hid?" Phil asked, and they both laughed. Michael tried to talk about touring again. He was sure it could work. Phil told him he'd gone too far with Train. He'd alienated his fans along with his friends.

"Who did you alienate? Me? We're brothers. Jerry Rubin? Rubin calls you every week. Sam Hood? He's one of your best friends. Arthur? Arthur's crazy about you. Van Ronk? One telephone call and that's all straightened out. Cobb? Cobb spent your birthday with you. Andy Wickham told me what a great time you guys had in New York."

It was no use. The drawbridge was raised.

David asked Phil to sing. With great discomfort, Phil took Sonny's guitar and played a few songs. As much as he didn't want to hold a guitar in his hands, he couldn't refuse David. The boys sat at his feet as the songs passed through him one more time.

They were at the dinner table. Sonny had the radio tuned to WKTU-FM, "the mellow sound," songs from the sixties. A Phil Ochs song came on. "Outside of a Small Circle of Friends." "They're playing your music on the radio, Phil," Sonny said. Phil, sitting in a rocking chair, just stared ahead, unmoved by the sound of his own voice.

Gertrude knew a psychiatrist in the neighborhood. She asked Phil if he would go to him. He didn't want to, he really didn't, but she pleaded with him. She would pay for it. Finally, he agreed. He got dressed the next day and walked the few blocks to the doctor's office.

When he returned home, Gertrude asked him how it had gone. "Okay." Would he go back and see him again? "Monday, April twelfth, I have an appointment."

"Are you going to keep it?"

"If I'm around."

Sonny bought a couple of tickets to a B. B. King concert at Madison Square Garden. She talked Phil into taking her to it. It was one of the few times he went into Manhattan.

Another day she took him to the movies to see Jack Nicholson, one of his favorite actors, in *One Flew Over the Cuckoo's Nest*. It was the last movie he ever saw.

Saturday night, April 3. Sonny invited some friends over, from the high school where she was teaching, for a party. David asked Phil to sing. They gathered around, and Phil performed "The Highwayman," "The Bells," "There but for Fortune," and "Changes." They clapped for him and patted him on the back, telling him how much they enjoyed his singing. He went upstairs to his bedroom, followed by David, excited about the show. Phil sat on the edge of his bed, David next to him. "Maybe there's hope," Phil said, looking straight ahead.

Monday. Sonny thought he might be coming out of it. Phil wanted to buy a new guitar. She brought him into Manhattan, to Manny's on Forty-seventh Street, and spent hours with him as he went through one guitar after another, then from store to store, before returning to Far Rockaway without having found one that was just right.

Tuesday. Jerry Rubin and Ron Cobb were in New York. They wanted Phil to come into Manhattan for dinner. Ron and Rubin had just returned from Cuba, filled with stories. They were staying at a friend's apartment, just north of Washington Square Park. Rubin was already there when Phil arrived.

During the course of the evening, Phil slipped away from his friends and went to the open window. He climbed out on the ledge, turning his head to say, "Well, this is it, folks." Ron sidled up to the wall, in case he had to grab quickly for Phil, who looked down from the twelfth floor, started to laugh, and came back in.

He said he was still hungry, so they all went to Katz's Deli on Houston Street. Rubin and Phil were kidding around with a couple of cute girls at the next table. After corned beef and pastrami, they all headed for the subway. Ron, Rubin, and Jerry were going to a party in Brooklyn. They asked Phil if he wanted to come along. He shook his head no, he was going back to Rockaway. While standing on the subway platform, Phil turned to Cobb to ask him how he would kill himself. Ron was at a loss for suggestions. Phil asked about the third rail. Ron rejected it. "I'd probably just burn myself severely." Phil agreed. His train pulled into the station. He got on, and as it started to pull away, Phil, through the door windows, pantomimed a rope around his neck, threw his head to one side, crossed his eyes, and stuck his tongue out. It was the last time any of them ever saw him alive.

Wednesday. Wickham called. He'd scheduled a trip to New York for that weekend, but now it would have to be postponed. He had to go to Texas on business. Phil said he understood. Later, Michael called to tell Phil he was coming to New York that Monday, to start making plans for the tour. Phil told him he would see him, "if I'm still alive."

"Don't kill yourself," Michael said to Phil, trying not to sound desperate. "And give up food?"

"Right," Phil said, and laughed.

It was two o'clock in the morning. Sonny heard noise coming from the kitchen. She came downstairs from her bedroom to see what was wrong. She found Phil standing in front of the refrigerator, his arms resting on top, his chin on his wrists. He was staring at the clock radio, inches from his face. "Is anything wrong, Phil?" she asked. He just kept on staring. It seemed to her he was trying to make up his mind about something.

The next day during cards, Phil began to laugh.

Later that afternoon, he went over to see Gertrude. They took a long walk on the beach. Phil was calmer than he'd been in weeks, almost peaceful. As they walked, she took his hand and they started talking about the old days, about Dave Sweazy, the good times with Jim back at Ohio State, the crazy adventures with Alice, the times Fanny had come all the way from Rockaway just to see Phil perform at Carnegie Hall. They talked until evening. Phil brought Gertrude back to her apartment and left. From her window she could see him walk down the block, toward Sonny's.

David discovered the body the next morning. He was horrified. He'd cut school that day to be with Uncle Phil, and had only left the house for a few minutes, to get something at the store. When he returned he couldn't find him. He tried every room in the house. When he came to the bathroom he couldn't get the door opened. When he looked up he saw the garrison buckle wedged at the top.

The body was cremated the next day. Andy Wickham took the ashes to Scotland, where he scattered them from a small turret in the "Queen's Post" of Edinburgh Castle under the supervision of Sergeant Warder McLeod as the Pipe Band of the Queen's Own Highlanders played "The Flowers of the Forest." The deed was done.

The sailor had come to port. For Phil Ochs, the war was finally over.

Epilogue.

SECOND NEWSPAPERMAN

Say, what did you find out about him anyway?

THOMPSON

Not much.

SECOND NEWSPAPERMAN

What have you been doing?

THOMPSON

Playing with a jigsaw puzzle—I talked to a lot of people who knew him.

GIRL

What do they say?

THOMPSON

Well—it's become a very clear picture. He was the most honest man who ever lived, with a streak of crookedness a yard wide. He was a liberal and a reactionary. He was a loving husband—and both his wives left him. He had a gift for friendship such as few men have—and he broke his oldest friend's heart like you'd throw away a cigarette you were through with. Outside of that—

THIRD NEWSPAPERMAN

Okay, okay.

from Scene 116 of *Citizen Kane*

ACKNOWLEDGMENTS

Very simply, I could not have written this book without the co-operation of Phil Ochs's family. I wish to thank Michael Ochs, in particular, for permitting me to delve into the Phil Ochs archives, even though he never asked for editorial approval of the final manuscript.

Sonny, Phil's sister, and Gertrude, Phil's mother, were gracious and open with me as I dragged them through the memories of the bad times as well as the good. *Merci*.

Alice Ochs deserves special thanks for the many hours spent, both on the telephone and in person, endlessly reminiscing about Phil. The contribution of her photos was a gesture of love.

While writing this book I interviewed hundreds of people, and it is impossible to thank them all individually. So I wish to offer one grand collective thank you to them all. In particular, I want to thank Suzie Campbell Harris, David Blue, Ramsey Clark, Stew Albert, Paula Ballen, Joan Baez, Oscar Brand, Peter and Betsy Asher, Tina Date, Eric Jacobsen, Jim Glover, Deni Frand, Bob Gibson, Judy Henske, Larry Marks, Van Dyke Parks, Eve Adelman, Jack Newfield, Jerry Rubin, Larry Sloman, Carol Realini, Nancy Cohen, Jay Levin, Dave Van Ronk, Wendy Winsted, Doug Weston, Dury Parks, Eric Andersen, Julia Fahey, William Kunstler, The Center for Constitutional Rights, Francois De Menil, Paul Krassner, Jerelle Kraus, Michael Thomas, Elliott Mintz, Mike Luckman, Frank MacShane, and Lee Housekeeper.

A special thanks to Sam Hood for the morning brandy and the afternoon memories; to Cora Weiss for the Cuban rum, the dinner, and the slides; to Jean Ray for the evening of champagne and the garage tapes; to Andy Wickham for the lousy Chinese food and the cocktails at the Algonquin; to Ron and Robin Cobb for the cuppa tea and the great pictures.

Thanks also to Harold Leventhal, a man of dignity and vision in a business crowded with the undignified and the blind.

A sigh of gratitude to Lenard Lexier for the measure of sanity when I was at my craziest.

A nod of appreciation to Andy Bamberger, Ozzie Alfonso, Robert Lorick, and the Chairman of the Board, Dennis Klein.

A private love and a public hug to Jane McCutcheon, for doing overtime in limbo.

A bottle of Coke and a pack of Camels for David Herwitz, who did better legwork than Carl Bernstein.

A kiss on the cheek for Miriam, who diverted my sexual advances in 1965 by holding a Phil Ochs album between herself and me—the first time Phil Ochs entered my life.

A slice of *madeleine* for Ernie, my first collaborator.

A special thanks for Marie Brown and Bob Hutchins for their confidence, guidance, and assistance.

There is no way to adequately thank my editor and unindicted co-conspirator, Charlie Priester. Charlie was the first one to agree with me that there was a book to be written about Phil's life. As the months went by, he became more and more involved with the manuscript until, toward the end, he literally moved into my apartment and set up a typewriter in the corner of the living room to help edit the final draft. Through the nights we typed, fixed, added to, took away from, laughed, drank gallons of soda and coffee, argued, pondered, debated, and agreed as the fury of the final push came upon us. Charlie is more than my editor. He is a gentle, happy friend who keeps reminding me that nice guys are a dime a dozen.

And finally there is Arthur Gorson, who searched through the closets of his mind to come up with the facts, who carries the pain of Phil's death in his eyes; who is the kindest of souls; who sits in his office and goes about his business, waiting to have his head turned in the direction of the next major lunacy.

DISCOGRAPHY

All songs written by Phil Ochs unless otherwise noted.

ALBUMS

Broadside Ballads, Vol. I

Folkways Records   BR–301   1963

Appearing on the album are The New World Singers, Pete Seeger, Blind Boy Grunt (Bob Dylan), Peter La Farge, Gil Turner, Happy Traum, M. McGinn, Mark Spoelstra, and Phil Ochs. Phil appears on side one:

THE BALLAD OF WILLIAM WORTHY.

PRODUCER: Folkways

Newport Broadside

VSD–9144   Recorded 1963 at the Newport Folk Festival, released 1964

Appearing on the album are Bob Dylan, Tom Paxton, Sam Hinton, Bob Davenport, The Freedom Singers, Jim Garland, Ed McCurdy, Peter La Farge, Joan Baez, and Phil Ochs. Phil appears on side two:

THE BALLAD OF MEDGAR EVERS, TALKING BIRMINGHAM JAM.

New Folks

Vanguard Stereolab   VSD–79140   1964

A compilation album featuring Eric Andersen, Lisa Kindred, Bob Jones, and Phil Ochs. Phil appears on side two:

WILLIAM MOORE, THERE BUT FOR FORTUNE, TALKING AIRPLANE DISASTER, PAUL CRUMP, WHAT ARE YOU FIGHTING FOR?

The Broadside Singers

Broadside Records   BR–303   1964

Appearing on the album are Eric Andersen, Patrick Sky, Buffy Sainte-Marie, Bob Dylan, and Phil Ochs. Phil sings on most cuts, and solos on side one:

LINKS ON THE CHAIN.

All the News That's Fit to Sing

Elektra Records   EKL–269, EKS–7269   1964

Side One	*Side Two*
ONE MORE PARADE	AUTOMATION SONG
(Ochs/Gibson)	THE BALLAD OF WILLIAM WORTHY
THE THRESHER	KNOCK ON THE DOOR
TALKING VIETNAM	TALKING CUBAN CRISIS
LOU MARSH	BOUND FOR GLORY
THE POWER AND THE GLORY	TOO MANY MARTYRS
CELIA	(Ochs/Gibson)
THE BELLS (Ochs/Poe)	WHAT'S THAT I HEAR

PRODUCER: Jac Holzman
RECORDING DIRECTOR: Paul A. Rothchild
SECOND GUITAR: Danny Kalb

The Newport Folk Festival

Vanguard   VRS–9184, VSD–79184   1964

The evening concerts of July 23–26. Appearing on the album are Pete Seeger, Sleepy John Estes, Buffy Sainte-Marie, Jose Feliciano, The Rodriguez Brothers, Frank Proffitt, Jim Kweskin and The Jug Band, Wes Montgomery, The Weavers, and Phil Ochs. Phil appears on side two:

DRAFT DODGER RAG, THE POWER AND THE GLORY.

I Ain't Marching Anymore

Elektra Records   EKL–287, EKS–7287   1965

Side One	*Side Two*
I AIN'T MARCHING ANYMORE	LINKS ON THE CHAIN
IN THE HEAT OF THE SUMMER	THE HILLS OF WEST VIRGINIA
DRAFT DODGER RAG	THE MAN BEHIND THE GUNS
THAT'S WHAT I WANT TO HEAR	TALKING BIRMINGHAM JAM

THAT WAS THE PRESIDENT
IRON LADY
THE HIGHWAYMAN
   (Ochs/Noyes)

THE BALLAD OF THE CARPENTER
   (MacColl)
DAYS OF DECISION
HERE'S TO THE STATE OF
   MISSISSIPPI

PRODUCER: Jac Holzman
RECORDING DIRECTOR: Paul Rothchild

Folksong '65

   Elektra Records   15th Anniversary Commemorative Album
   S—8 Mono only   1965

   Appearing on the album are Tom Rush, Judy Collins, John Koerner, Dave Day, Tony Glover, Hamilton Camp, Dick Rismini, Tom Paxton, Butterfield Blues Band, Kathy and Carol, Mark Spoelstra, Fred Neil, Bruce Murdoch, and Phil Ochs. Phil appears on side two:

   THE POWER AND THE GLORY.

PRODUCER: Jac Holzman
No longer available.

Phil Ochs in Concert

   Elektra Records   EKL—310, EKS—7310   1966

   Recorded at concerts given by Phil Ochs in Boston and New York in the winter of 1965–66.

Side One
I'M GOING TO SAY IT NOW
BRACERO
RINGING OF REVOLUTION
IS THERE ANYBODY HERE?
CANNONS OF CHRISTIANITY

Side Two
THERE BUT FOR FORTUNE
COPS OF THE WORLD
THE MARINES HAVE LANDED ON THE
   SHORES OF SANTO DOMINGO
CHANGES
LOVE ME, I'M A LIBERAL
WHEN I'M GONE

PRODUCER: Mark Abramson and Jac Holzman

The Folk Box

   Elektra Records   EKL—Box   1966

   A four-record set from the Elektra catalogue. Phil's version of "The Thresher" was included.

PRODUCER: Jac Holzman
No longer available.

Phil Ochs—Pleasures of the Harbor
    A&M   133   1967

Side One   *Side Two*
CROSS MY HEART   THE PARTY
FLOWER LADY   PLEASURES OF THE HARBOR
OUTSIDE OF A SMALL CIRCLE OF   CRUCIFIXION
    FRIENDS
I'VE HAD HER
MIRANDA

PRODUCER: Larry Marks
ARRANGED BY: Ian Freebairn-Smith, Joseph Byrd
PIANO ACCOMPANIMENT: Lincoln Mayorga

A & M Family Portrait
    A&M   SP—19002   1967

    An anthology album highlighting the catalogue of A&M records.
    Phil performed:
    CROSS MY HEART.

Tape from California
    A&M   SP—4138   1968

Side One   *Side Two*
TAPE FROM CALIFORNIA   THE HARDER THEY FALL
WHITE BOOTS MARCHING IN A   WHEN IN ROME
    YELLOW LAND   THE FLOODS OF FLORENCE
HALF A CENTURY HIGH
JOE HILL
THE WAR IS OVER

PRODUCER: Larry Marks
"The War Is Over" ARRANGED BY: Bob Thompson
"The Floods of Florence" ARRANGED BY: Ian Freebairn-Smith
MUSICIANS: Jack Elliott, Van Dyke Parks, Lincoln Mayorga

Rehearsals for Retirement
    A&M   SP—4181*   1968

Side One   *Side Two*
PRETTY SMART ON MY PART   THE SCORPION DEPARTS BUT
THE DOLL HOUSE   NEVER RETURNS

I KILL, THEREFORE I AM
WILLIAM BUTLER YEATS VISITS
    LINCOLN PARK AND ESCAPES
    UNSCATHED
MY LIFE

THE WORLD BEGAN IN EDEN
    BUT ENDED IN LOS ANGELES
DOESN'T LENNY LIVE HERE
    ANYMORE?
ANOTHER AGE
REHEARSALS FOR RETIREMENT

PRODUCER: Larry Marks
PIANO ACCOMPANIMENT: Lincoln Mayorga
GUITAR AND BASS: Bob Rafkin
No longer available.

Phil Ochs' Greatest Hits

A&M   SP—4253*   1970

Side One
ONE-WAY TICKET HOME
JIM DEAN OF INDIANA
MY KINGDOM FOR A CAR
BOY IN OHIO
GAS STATION WOMEN

Side Two
CHORDS OF FAME
TEN CENTS A COUP
BACH, BEETHOVEN, MOZART AND ME
BASKET IN THE POOL
NO MORE SONGS

PRODUCER: Van Dyke Parks
MUSICIANS: Clarence White, Bob Rafkin, Chris Ethridge, Ryland Cooder, James Burton, Gene Parsons, Bobby Bruce, Don Rich, Mike Rubini, Tom Scott, Gary Coleman, Richard Rosmini, Laurindo Almeida, Anne Goodman, Clydie King, Mary Clayton, Sherlie Mathews
No longer available.

Get Off

NAPRA   1973

Released to radio stations only. Anti-drug messages by a number of artists, including Phil Ochs

Broadside Reunion

Folkways   FR—5315, BR—315   1972

An anthology of previous Broadside albums. Phil appears on:

Side One
HUNGER AND COLD

Side Two
CHANGING HANDS

PRODUCER: Agnes Friesen

The Bitter End: The First Ten Years

> RLX—300   Roxbury Records   1974
>
> An anthology of live performances from The Bitter End. Phil appears on side one:
>
> I AIN'T MARCHING ANYMORE.

No longer available.

Gunfight at Carnegie Hall

> A&M   SP—9010**   1975
>
> A live recording of Phil's Carnegie Hall "Gold Suit" concert. Recorded April 3, 1970.

Side One
MONA LISA (Livingston/Evans)
I AIN'T MARCHING ANYMORE
OKIE FROM MUSKOGEE
  (Haggard/Burris)
CHORDS OF FAME
BUDDY HOLLY MEDLEY:
  NOT FADE AWAY
  (Hardin/Petty)
  I'M GONNA LOVE YOU TOO
  (Maudlin/Sullivan/Petty)
  THINK IT OVER
  (Holly/Petty/Allison)
  OH BOY (West/Tilghman/
  Petty)
  EVERYDAY (Petty/Hardin)
  NOT FADE AWAY
  (Hardin/Petty)

Side Two
PLEASURES OF THE HARBOR
TAPE FROM CALIFORNIA
ELVIS PRESLEY MEDLEY:
  MY BABY LEFT ME (Crudup)
  I'M READY (Robichaux)
  HEARTBREAK HOTEL
  (Durden/Presley)
  ALL SHOOK UP (Blackwell/
  Presley)
  ARE YOU LONESOME TONIGHT?
  (Turk/Handman)
  MY BABY LEFT ME—encore
  A FOOL SUCH AS I (Trader)

PRODUCER: Phil Ochs
BAND MEMBERS: Bob Rafkin, Lincoln Mayorga, Kenny Kaufman, Kevin Kelly

Available only as an import, from Gem Imports.

Song for Patty

> Folkways   BR—5310   1975
>
> Sammy Walker's Folkways album. Phil appeared on side two, singing harmony on BOUND FOR GLORY (Ochs), along with Sis Cunningham.

PRODUCER: Phil Ochs

Phil Ochs: Songs for Broadside
   Folkways   FD—5320   1976

   An unauthorized "memorial" album. Recording quality is extremely poor.

Side One
PLEASURES OF THE HARBOR
THAT'S WHAT I WANT TO HEAR
I'M GONNA SAY IT NOW
CHANGES
ON HER HAND A GOLDEN RING
DAYS OF DECISION
THE MARINES HAVE LANDED ON
   THE SHORES OF SANTO
   DOMINGO

Side Two
UNITED FRUIT
CRUCIFIXION
OUTSIDE OF A SMALL CIRCLE
   OF FRIENDS
WHAT ARE YOU FIGHTING FOR?
RINGING OF REVOLUTION

PRODUCER: Paul Kaplan and Gordon Friesen

Phil Ochs: Chords of Fame
   A&M   SP—4599   1976

   A two-record memorial album released by A&M, with the co-operation of Elektra Records.

Side One
I AIN'T MARCHING ANYMORE
ONE MORE PARADE
DRAFT DODGER RAG
HERE'S TO THE STATE OF
   RICHARD NIXON
THE BELLS
BOUND FOR GLORY
TOO MANY MARTYRS
THERE BUT FOR FORTUNE

Side Two
I'M GOING TO SAY IT NOW
THE MARINES HAVE LANDED ON
   THE SHORES OF SANTO
   DOMINGO
CHANGES
IS THERE ANYBODY HERE?
LOVE ME, I'M A LIBERAL
WHEN I'M GONE

Side Three
OUTSIDE OF A SMALL CIRCLE
   OF FRIENDS
PLEASURES OF THE HARBOR
TAPE FROM CALIFORNIA
CHORDS OF FAME
CRUCIFIXION

Side Four
THE WAR IS OVER
JIM DEAN OF INDIANA
THE POWER AND THE GLORY
FLOWER LADY
NO MORE SONGS

The album was compiled by Michael Ochs. The following cuts were different from the way they appeared on previous albums:

"I Ain't Marching Anymore"—Electric version produced by Paul Rothchild

"Here's to the State of Richard Nixon"—Produced by Arthur
    Gorson and Phil Ochs
"Pleasures of the Harbor"—As it appeared on the "Gunfight"
    album
"Tape from California"—As it appeared on the "Gunfight"
    album
"The Power and the Glory"—Produced by Arthur Gorson and
    Phil Ochs
"Crucifixion"—Acoustic, produced by Michael Ochs

Interviews with Phil Ochs
    Folkways   FH–532   1976
PRODUCER: Paul Kaplan

SINGLES

I AIN'T MARCHING ANYMORE / THAT WAS THE PRESIDENT.   1966

Elektra; Harmony Music Ltd. EKSN. Initial release in England.
Subsequent release as a paper record in *Sing Out*—1966.

CROSS MY HEART / FLOWER LADY   1967

A&M 881. PRODUCER: Larry Marks

OUTSIDE OF A SMALL CIRCLE OF FRIENDS / MIRANDA   1967

A&M 891. PRODUCER: Larry Marks
Also released in an edited two-sided version for radio stations.

THE WAR IS OVER / THE HARDER THEY FALL 1968

A&M 932. PRODUCER: Larry Marks

KANSAS CITY BOMBER / GAS STATION WOMEN   1973

A&M 1376. PRODUCER: Ochs Brothers, Lee Housekeeper ("Kan-
sas City Bomber"), Van Dyke Parks ("Gas Station Women")
"Kansas City Bomber" was recorded in Australia and re-mixed in
Hollywood.

BWATUE / NIKO MCHUMBA NGOMBE   1973
> A&M. Released in Africa only. Recorded in Kenya.
> Recorded by Phil Ochs and the Pan-African Ngembo Rumba Band.
> Bwatue was recorded in Lingala.
> Niko Mchumba Ngombe was recorded in Swahili.

THE POWER AND THE GLORY / HERE'S TO THE STATE OF RICHARD NIXON   1974
> A&M 1509. PRODUCER: Gorson/Ochs

INDEX

ABOUT THE AUTHOR

Marc Eliot was born in the Bronx in 1946. He graduated from Manhattan's High School of Performing Arts, received a B.A. degree from the City University of New York at City College, an M.F.A. degree from Columbia University's School of the Arts Writing Division, and studied film for two years at the doctoral level, also at Columbia University. He has taught film and English courses at Marymount Manhattan College and Columbia. His writing has appeared in numerous publications. Marc Eliot and Phil Ochs were friends for many years, and spent long hours arguing about movies, music, politics, women, and food. At present Mr. Eliot is at work on a novel and a book about television.

ABOUT THE AUTHOR

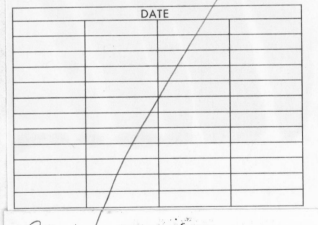

COPY 1

B
OCHS

Eliot, Marc

Death of a rebel

$4.95